Parenting to a Degree

Parenting to a Degree

HOW FAMILY MATTERS FOR COLLEGE WOMEN'S SUCCESS

Laura T. Hamilton

THE UNIVERSITY OF CHICAGO PRESS

Chicago and London

Laura T. Hamilton is associate professor of sociology at the University of California, Merced. She is coauthor of *Paying for the Party: How College Maintains Inequality*.

The University of Chicago Press, Chicago 60637
The University of Chicago Press, Ltd., London
© 2016 by The University of Chicago
All rights reserved. Published 2016.
Printed in the United States of America

25 24 23 22 21 20 19 18 17 16   1 2 3 4 5

ISBN-13: 978-0-226-18336-7 (cloth)
ISBN-13: 978-0-226-18367-1 (e-book)
DOI: 10.7208/chicago/9780226183671.001.0001

Library of Congress Cataloging-in-Publication Data

Names: Hamilton, Laura T. (Laura Teresa), author.
Title: Parenting to a degree: how family matters for college women's success / Laura T. Hamilton.
Description: Chicago; London : University of Chicago Press, 2016. | © 2016 | Includes bibliographical references and index.
Identifiers: LCCN 2015039580 | ISBN 9780226183367 (cloth: alkaline paper) | ISBN 9780226183671 (e-book)
Subjects: LCSH: College student parents—Research. | Women college Students—Research. | Academic achievement. | Parenting.
Classification: LCC LC1568 .H36 2016 | DDC 378.1/98—dc23 LC record available at http://lccn.loc.gov/2015039580

♾ This paper meets the requirements of ANSI/NISO Z39.48-1992 (Permanence of Paper).

To the families who made this book possible

Contents

Introduction 1

1 *Five Visions of College* 21

PART I: **PARENTING APPROACHES**

2 *Helicopters* 47

3 *Paramedics* 76

4 *Bystanders* 98

PART II: **PARENTING CONSEQUENCES**

5 *Funding Fun* 119

6 *Predictability or Possibility* 140

7 *Failed by the University* 162

8 *College Outsourced* 187

METHODOLOGICAL APPENDIX: STUDYING PARENTING 210

APPENDIX A: PARENTS AND DAUGHTERS 217

ACKNOWLEDGMENTS 219

NOTES 225

REFERENCES 239

INDEX 255

Introduction

I t was move-in day at Midwest University.[1] A line of standstill traffic
stretched a mile past a cluster of dormitories. Observing the vehicular chaos, I thanked my friend for the ride and went in on foot.
Police were telling frustrated parents who parked illegally to move
their vehicles. Dumpsters were overflowing with boxes no one had
bothered to break down. I nearly collided with a father carting cases
of weight-loss shakes for a slender woman, who was overdressed for
moving in a ruffle skirt and tall heels.

Inside, I was acutely aware of my status as a researcher. In reality, I
was nearly invisible. Mothers buzzed around me in navigator mode—
locating food, classes, laundry, and mail. They drew maps and traced
out paths on brochures. A mother was on her cell phone asking about
the shuttle schedule so her daughter would know exactly when and
where to catch it. A few worried about how difficult it was to lock the
doors, as this posed a possible safety issue. One was fighting with her
daughter over who would turn the key and kept trying to grab the
doorknob with an exasperated let-me-do-it gesture.

Several mothers quizzed their daughters about social connections:
"That was your neighbor, wasn't it?" Daughter, with sarcasm: "That
would be why I said hi." They were also doing their own networking:
mothers jointly fussed over the arrangement of the rooms, sizing
each other up in the process. Decorating was a high-stakes activity.
Groups of mothers and daughters made rounds to see—and judge—
others' interior designs. As one observer scoffed, "Some people did
too much. An air purifier? Come on."

Fathers were bearers of goods. A cluster of three could be spotted sitting on the wraparound couch near the dolly return, exhausted after a day of manual labor. Another remarked, with relief: "We got a lot of stuff in that room. I didn't think it would all fit!" Some were dispatched as emissaries for needed goods. Ethernet cords and a difficult-to-locate bed-bunking tool were in high demand. One father, who was told to canvass multiple stores, apologized profusely to his daughter for not procuring a pink rope light.

These loud and loaded-down parents took up a lot of space. They were hard to ignore. But they were not the *only* parents of college students on the floor I was studying. Some did a perfunctory delivery, stopping only long enough to get their daughters settled. They skipped parent orientations and receptions because they "really didn't like that sort of thing" or to honor their daughters' burgeoning independence. Others never made the drop-off. They could not afford time off work or did not realize that help was needed. Their daughters were in no danger of overflowing their rooms. These women quietly schlepped their minimal possessions up the stairs and shut their doors, muting the lively commotion just outside.

Move-in day is a defining moment for many families, marking the achievement of a parenting milestone. As Mitchell Stevens explains in *Creating a Class: College Admissions and the Education of Elites*, college shapes the decisions that parents make about what jobs to accept, neighborhoods to live in, K–12 schools their children should attend, and extracurricular activities to encourage.[2] In preparation, hundreds of dollars a month are tucked away from paychecks, mortgages are overdrawn, and retirements drained. Some parents seek SAT prep and college choice consultants for their children and rewrite college essays.[3] They push for their favorite schools, and children make a case for their own. Numbers are crunched. Decisions are made, and disappointments are weathered. Families stock up, pack up, and make the drive. Emotional drop-offs may ensue, and houses become empty nests. And then the swarms of parents abate.

But what happens next? I wrote in my field notes that day: "No wonder there are pamphlets [placed everywhere] teaching kids how to eat, make friendships, and handle alcohol. Once their parents leave, someone has to step in." What I came to realize was that, in many ways, some parents never left. Although most did not have an embodied presence on the dormitory floor, socially, emotionally, and logistically it was as if they were there all along. "The world's longest umbilical cord," the cell phone, made it easy for these parents to hover over their children's college experiences.[4]

The media refers to these parents as helicopters, and they are among the most reviled figures of twenty-first-century parenting.[5] As the *Washington Post* puts it, "They are needy, anxious and sometimes plain pesky—and schools at every level are trying to find ways to deal with them. . . . Parents—specifically parents of today's 'millennial generation,' [as] many educators are discovering, can't let their kids go."[6] They are described as "stunt[ing] student development and test[ing] the patience of college officials."[7] Educators worry about "how their school climates are affected by intrusive parents trying to set their own agendas."[8] We are told to "blame parents for Millennials acting entitled. . . . Helicopter parents have [coddled] trophy kids who end up boomerang kids [back at home]."[9] Most recently, the narrative has centered heavily on the intensely parented and overstressed students at elite colleges and universities, raising the alarm about helicopter parenting.[10]

But is it true? Do involved college parents damage their children and burden universities? What does active parenting look like outside of the Ivies, for students in less-pressured residential college contexts? In *Parenting to a Degree: How Family Matters for College Women's Success*, I argue that many parents of college students face a terrible paradox. Especially at mid-tier public institutions like Midwest U, educational and professional success almost *requires* moderate to extensive financial, emotional, and logistical parental support through college and the transition to the labor force. If parents can manage it, the right kind of help provides students with a distinct advantage—

one that is hard to deny. Contrary to popular opinion, universities also recognize the value of invested parents: many institutions seek to recruit, rather than evade, parents to whom they can outsource a wide array of tasks and responsibilities. By ensuring student success, these parents also contribute to institutional standing.

Yet this arrangement often comes at a cost. Heavy parental involvement during college drains parents' monetary and psychological reserves. It tends to create greater dependence among youth than parents originally imagined. Thirty or even forty years of intensive parenting may be necessary to ensure children's success. Often it is hard to know what the best investments are and how much money and effort to devote to them. Concerns over *how* to parent are warranted, as not all forms of involvement are equally effective. Parental efforts to support college students can even backfire, taking some parents by surprise.

Perhaps the greatest price, however, is the potential for increased inequality. Students with involved parents often outperform and outmaneuver those whose parents take a less active role. Typically, involved parents are affluent, highly educated, and have the ability to meet high financial and interactional demands. The intent to help is not enough. Often the efforts of parents with more limited means fail when not backed by class-based resources. *Parenting to a Degree* explores the consequences of building the expectation of parental labor and funds into a college degree, when not all parents can offer the same degree of assistance.

Invasion of the Helicopters

Individualistic attacks on helicopter parents as bad, harmful, or just plain annoying miss an important point. They did not emerge out of thin air. Nor are helicopters a product of some new age psychosis. Instead, these parents are responding to real structural, economic, and social conditions that have been building for decades.

The problem is partly numeric: youth have entered into higher education at unprecedented rates, with no real increase in spots at the top of the prestige hierarchy.[11] As a result, there is an oversupply of qualified candidates for selective four-year residential schools and graduate programs, leading to increasingly competitive admissions.[12] We reached the apex of this trend in 2010–2011; however, estimates suggest that twenty-one states (primarily in the South and West) will continue to see growth in the numbers of youth graduating from high school, resulting in further capacity pressures for colleges and universities.[13]

Income inequality has also increased.[14] Current generations of young adults can no longer count on replicating, much less surpassing, parental social class. Millennials have seen the housing and education benefits available to many of their parents drastically curtailed.[15] The college wage-premium—the difference in earnings between those with and without a college degree—has risen sharply, as has the difference between less and more desirable jobs (i.e., stable, well-paying, flexible positions, with more autonomy over work production).[16] High rates of unemployment and reduced job security make it hard to start careers, obtain financial security, and form families.[17] While not new, these circumstances are particularly acute on the heels of the Great Recession.[18]

We have entered a "college for all" era, characterized by belief in the power of college to provide security for all youth, in the face of great structural barriers.[19] Yet the cost of a college education has risen precipitously. For the past fifteen years, tuition has steadily increased at four-year public institutions, peaking in 2011–2012 with an 8.5 percent annual increase.[20] Many states have reduced the number of affordable in-state seats in favor of costly out-of-state and international seats, making it harder for many families to rely on their state systems.[21]

A greater array of options also makes navigating the postsecondary system more challenging than in the past. Types of schools, available college majors, and extracurricular activities have diversified over the past fifty years.[22] Not all choices are good, particularly for less-privileged students. The potential for academic and social missteps is larger than before and may take greater savvy and know-how to avoid.

These conditions suggest the need for greater parental assistance to young adults—not less—but they contrast with negative public opinion of helicopters. Parents of college students may feel torn. What are they to do?

It is reasonable to turn to social science for answers; after all, there is a rich literature on how parents influence the educational experiences of younger youth. K–12 scholarship consistently finds parental investments (in the form of educational aspirations, interactions, money, social ties, and cultural knowledge) to be significant predictors of educational success.[23] More is generally seen as better: the more involved and invested parents are, the more academic success their younger children enjoy.[24]

Parenting research, however, often stops at the college gates. Young adulthood, the period between adolescence and adulthood, has been dubbed an "age of independence." During this time, college students are thought to be mostly autonomous actors and parents are perceived as distant funders.[25] Parental funding is understood to be important for college students' rates of attendance and completion, but virtually all other details of parent-child interactions are neglected.[26] While scholars often track the frequency of parent-child conversations or assistance with schoolwork for K–12 students, we know little about forms of parental support specific to college.[27]

The erasure of parents is ironic. They create, support, guide, and enable the model "young adults" (traditional-aged students, who are not employed full-time, married, or parents themselves) that four-year residential institutions presume. No story of young adulthood—or, more accurately, its most celebrated form—is complete without parents. And no story of parenthood is complete without understanding how college parenting affects middle-aged adults, who carry dependents far longer than in the past.

The Family-University Relationship

The relationship between families and the university, once mediated by a generous state, has changed considerably over the past seventy-five to one hundred years. Slowly after WWI and rapidly after WWII, the state offered universities the resources to help families battle economic depression, poverty, and marginalization on the basis of race, class, gender, and religion.[28] This collaboration fundamentally reshaped the life course. Federal and state support facilitated an expansion of higher education, underwriting an extended period of self-development for a broader population.[29] Young adulthood became a recognizable, if varied, life stage.[30] Families, the labor market, and mating processes organized around this reality.[31]

Cooperation between the state and the university began to sour between the 1960s and 1980s, and worsened into the twenty-first century. The government significantly cut its sponsorship of academic research and shifted financial aid from grants to loans, making student debt the primary financier of higher education.[32] Legislation beneficial to for-profit institutions siphoned funds from the public system, and state and local appropriations for public universities decreased significantly—causing them to function more like their private counterparts.[33] Universities entered a period of heavy and expensive administrative growth.[34] Without the supportive buffer of the state, families would eventually absorb these costs.

Parallel changes were occurring in student-university relations. *In loco parentis* (Latin for "in the place of a parent") began to dissolve in the 1960s—as did gendered restrictions and free-speech limitations on student life.[35] It was replaced by the 1974 federal Family Education Rights and Privacy Act (or FERPA), which granted students control over personal records—and kept their parents at arm's length.[36] Universities claimed "no duty" to protect students, beyond upholding their privacy, and took a bystander stance on student safety issues—including alcohol abuse, hazing, and sexual assault.[37] Parents were outsiders but could not assume that universities prioritized students' interests.

Today a market model is taking root in higher education.[38] Colleges and universities, in concert with their home states, often set prices according to market demand and what they believe families will pay.[39] Students and their parents are positioned as consumers, who—with variable information and purchasing power—hope to select the best "product."[40] Rather than a collective social good to be supported by an invested society, college is frequently viewed as a high-stakes, high-cost personal amenity.[41] Parents are to secure the opportunity for "individuals [to] act out their private dramas of personal fulfillment and ambition."[42]

Colleges—now in the role of service providers—face new, intense accountability pressures.[43] As state governments seek to justify every dollar spent on the post-secondary system, scholars are for the first time quantifying what students learn in college.[44] Universities are not shielded from litigation, unfavorable press, or claims that they are not creating safe and equitable environments for their students.[45] Parents, staggering under the weight of college costs, want to assess their purchase in the same way they might stock market investments. What returns will they see for their money? To aid them in this task, the federal government has developed a post-secondary institution comparison tool for consumers.[46]

So how do universities today produce quantifiable outcomes with fewer resources? They rely, in part, on parents—particularly those with money, time, and connections—to meet basic needs. Among those needs, solvency is the most pressing issue for a number of institutions. Net tuition now accounts for 47 percent of all *public* higher education revenue, so schools necessarily prefer applicants who do not require financial aid.[47] Public institutions particularly value out-of-state families who pay top dollar.[48] However, paying parents typically bring more than funds: they often engage in university promotion; conduct admissions interviews; interface with donating alumni; assist with their students' emotional, cognitive, and physical needs;

and help place graduates in valuable internships and jobs.[49] Competition to attract them is stiff.

Given this context, helicopter parenting makes good sense. Administrators' complaints about parental "meddling" are now tempered with interest in a "partnership relationship" with parents.[50] As colleges recruit parents into the labor of producing successful students and workers, helicopter parents are incorporated into the form and function of post-secondary institutions. The problem is, of course, that very few parents can play this role. Many send their children to college expecting mostly to receive the necessary support from universities, as they do not have much to give.

The Study

At the heart of *Parenting to a Degree* are fifty-nine interviews with mothers and fathers, representing forty-one families from a wide range of social class backgrounds.[51] Their daughters started college in 2004 and lived on the same dormitory floor at Midwest University, a large, mid-tier state flagship. A third of all first-year students at MU resided in this housing neighborhood, known for its "party dorms," where socially oriented students clustered. Many women (even their parents) actively sought out party dorms. Others, who might have been better off in alternative housing options, had no idea what they were getting into.

Parental interviews were collected at a critical juncture—four years after the start of college and around graduation.[52] During this time, mothers and fathers reflected on their parenting approaches. Many of these conversations were filled with regret and frustration. Most of the interviews were conducted in-person, in parents' homes, workplaces, and communities. At the time, I was visibly pregnant with my first child. Parents were eager to impart their hard-earned wisdom to a young scholar who was soon to join their ranks. They fed me home-cooked meals, offered transportation, and worried about my health just as many did for their own daughters.

Parents' candidness with me, and their willingness to be interviewed, was partly a result of my relationships with their children. I met these young women at the start of their college careers. My co-director on the college women study, Elizabeth A. Armstrong, a team of researchers, and I occupied a room on their dormitory floor in order to conduct a yearlong ethnography. I soon became the primary ethnographer and did most of the yearly interviews with the women. Interviews would continue after college for a total of five waves.

Of the fifty-three women who lived on the dormitory floor, forty-eight were interviewed at least once, with the majority completing at least four interviews. Roughly 85 percent of the women in the interview sample (and 77 percent of the ethnographic sample) are included in the parent study.[53] With the two studies combined, I have a parent-child data set of unprecedented depth and richness, offering a glimpse into parenting on the precipice of adulthood.[54]

Midwest U parents are not typical Americans raising typical young adults. While two-thirds of recent high school graduates go on to some form of higher education, only a select group attends four-year residential schools—often with the assistance of their parents.[55] During the 2010–2011 academic year, just 30 percent and 12 percent of first-year college students enrolled in four-year public or four-year private institutions, respectively.[56] Thus, this is not a comprehensive book about parenting youth through the late teens to early twenties. Nor is it a generic account of post-secondary parenting, if such a thing could exist.

The institutional setting is also important.[57] The organization of social and academic life at MU exerts a draw on parents and students who are interested in, or at least not repelled by, a vibrant social life. Parenting approaches that work poorly at MU may work better at a well-endowed private institution or, alternatively, a regional campus—and vice versa. Putting college parenting in an institutional as well as a historical context offers a deeper understanding of why and how it matters, and where barriers to student success often lie.

Parents from a variety of social positions send their children to MU, from jet-setting CEOs seeking to purchase "fun," to regional elites with deep MU ties, to the less-privileged who have great hopes for the state flagship. Some plucky, motivated, and ambitious youth manage to attend without any parental support. Midwest U typically does not appeal to the rich with academic superstar children, for whom an elite public school is a "safety" option. Nor does it seek to compete with open-access regional universities that serve low-income families in the state at high rates. Most four-year college-seeking families, however, give a school like MU a thorough look. In fact, nearly half of all students attending a four-year college or university land at a "moderately selective" public school like this one.[58]

It is not incidental that this book is about parents and their *daughters*. Today the majority of college students are women. They enroll in and complete college at higher rates than men and earn higher grades while they are there.[59] Women's strides in higher education over the past fifty years have been facilitated by changes in gender attitudes, access to birth control, delays in age at first marriage, and a reduction in sexist institutional policies.[60] However, you can still go to a school like MU to receive a (postponed) MRS, or "Mrs." degree.[61] While some parents hope to raise engineers, others seek to raise homemakers who are married to engineers.

MU's small minority population, combined with de facto racial segregation on campus, meant that all women on the floor I studied self-identified as white, as did their parents.[62] The lack of racial diversity is a limitation of this study—as is the focus on heterosexual students and parents.[63] The homogeneity of my sample had one benefit, however: it allowed me to zero in on variation along the lines of social class. I interviewed everyone from a CFO of a Fortune 500 company to a waitress at a roadside diner.

I argue that social class goes hand in hand with beliefs about gender to shape how parents approach the college years.[64] Parents draw on "commonsense" understandings about college, young adulthood, and women's roles in society that are inflected by their class position. These understandings guide parents' practices. Below I review what we currently know about classed and gendered parenting and high-light central contributions of this book.

Classed Parenting

In *Unequal Childhoods: Class, Race, and Family Life*, Annette Lareau argues that parenting styles are classed.[65] "Middle-class" parents of elementary-aged children (many of whom are more accurately upper-middle class) strive for "concerted cultivation"—marked by management of children's everyday activities and educational intervention. In contrast, working-class and poor parents exemplify the "accomplishment of natural growth." They provide for children's basic needs, but leave education up to the schools. Concerted cultivation translates to an educational advantage for affluent youth, placing them in line with institutional standards for success. Less affluent youth lack parent advocates and are less comfortable in school.

Ten years later, Lareau followed up with ten families in her original study.[66] She found that the early class differences in parenting styles she observed were long-lasting—even affecting the transition to college. Middle-class parents had the knowledge and resources necessary to help their children enroll in four-year institutions. But only one working-class or poor student made it to a similar school, and most of the others were forced to move into adulthood quickly. These findings underscore the importance of parental support for college attendance.[67]

Lareau's work was groundbreaking. She was one of the first to show *how* cultural and social reproduction occurred in the context of family life, building on scholarship from the late 1970s and 1980s.[68] Around the time her book was published, the extent to which class mattered for parent-child relations was contested: some thought class played little to no role in how parents raised their children.[69] This book owes a theoretical debt to Lareau, as I show that college is now a parenting project, cut—in broad strokes—by class distinctions.

It is necessary, however, to move beyond the juxtaposition of two large, and arguably heterogeneous, class groups.[70] Lareau's model cannot be used to understand variation in parenting *among* the affluent or less affluent. It does not account for approaches that are neither concerted cultivation nor natural growth. Parents who do not fit the mold are either invisible or unexplainable oddities. Her framework may be less useful in trying to understand the role that parents might play in helping their children accomplish unexpected upward mobility or in failing to reproduce class standing. At times, it feels very deterministic: middle-class kids get middle-class lives, while the working class and poor remain disadvantaged.

In recent years popular self-help books suggest a more variegated parenting landscape, particularly among the college-educated. *Battle Hymn of the Tiger Mother* discusses what might be thought of as concerted cultivation on steroids.[71] *Bringing up Bébé* advances a more relaxed, independence-based model of concerted cultivation.[72] *Free-Range Kids* embraces backlash against intensive parenting among the middle classes.[73] These books do not describe the same type of parenting approach.

Previous scholarship may miss such variation by selecting parents who fit into clean, unambiguous class locations.[74] In contrast, parents in this book are included only for their tie to a child on the dormitory floor. Their class histories—marked by cross-class marriage, financial emergencies, divorce and death, and rapid upward mobility—reflect the "messiness" of social class in the United States.[75] This complexity translates into a broad array of parenting approaches.

It may also be the case that there are simply more culturally acceptable ways to parent young adults than children. Young adulthood is an unsettled period of the life course, in that it is not yet universal or normalized.[76] Parents are not required to provide a particular standard of care for youth who are no longer minors; neither are they legally, nor often even socially, held responsible for their older children's actions. Consensus on the definition of "good" parenting for eighteen- to twenty-two-year-olds is harder to reach.[77]

Gendered Parenting

Recently, Susan Patton, known as the infamous "Princeton mom," urged college women to find a husband on campus or risk "an unwanted life of spinsterhood with cats." She did not offer the same advice to her two Princetonian sons. (About the youngest, she remarked: "The universe of women he can marry is limitless.")[78] Her advice, enshrined in *Marry Smart: Advice for Finding THE ONE*, nudges women toward traditionally feminine selves, (relatively) earlier marriage to high-earning men, and motherhood.[79]

The case of the Princeton mom offers a reminder that parenting is not gender neutral.[80] Families are one of the central vehicles through which youth become classed, gendered, raced, and (hetero)sexualized adults—and these lessons are not independent. This book considers ways in which class and gender systems intertwine, creating distinct cultural models for how women should pursue economic security. The work/family configurations that parents imagine for their daughters often reflect their family's multiple forms of privilege or disadvantage.[81]

For example, among the upper class, women's roles as wives, mothers, and helpmates have been facilitated by the ability to live comfortably on a single salary—a benefit historically not available to poor, working-class, and non-white women.[82] This model presumes a future match between a traditionally gendered homemaker and her breadwinner husband, in a heterosexual marriage.[83] Gender is thought to be complementary, with women's skills and interests in the domestic sphere and men's in the public sphere.

In contrast, upper-middle-class professionals often foster non-traditional femininity, preparing their daughters for a competitive workplace.[84] The goal is to create women who are men's equals (or superiors), at least in terms of income and occupational status. Many of these parents will see their daughters consolidate class privilege by eventually pairing with equally credentialed mates (as suggested by educational homogamy).[85] But this possibility varies with race: college-educated black women often find more limited marital options.[86]

Finally, women from less-privileged families may be encouraged to pursue pragmatic, pink-collar vocations, as they offer familiar avenues to women's economic stability.[87] These women do not count on men's financial support—although finding a solid earner is a plus. Less-privileged women tend not to reap the same marital benefits from college attendance as affluent women, as they are less likely to form social connections with college-attending men.[88] Therefore, improving or solidifying economic standing via a romantic partnership may not be a viable option.

Parents typically, but not always, guide their daughters to invest in the kind of femininity that matches their social class.[89] For example, some highly affluent parents bank on women's feminine charm, personality, and appearance, hoping these traits will eventually land their daughters wealthy husbands. Working professionals are more likely to see the development of academic skills and credentials as key to their daughters' success in both labor and marital markets. Both approaches involve intensive parental labor; however, the difference lies in *what* parents choose to cultivate.

Gender also structures dynamics between mothers and fathers. The notion that parenting should be "child-centered, expert-guided, emotionally absorbing, labor-intensive, and financially expensive" is relatively new—and often unequal in practice: the most intensive approaches rely on the sweat and tears of women, even when the message that mothers seek to impart to their daughters is gender equality.[90] The phrase "intensive mothering" describes the sheer amount of time, money, and energy that many mothers pour into their children.[91] *Parenting to a Degree* documents the extension of this work into the young adult years. Active, high-quality parenting, however, does not need to take on these dynamics.

Parenting Approaches and How They Matter

In my previous book, *Paying for the Party: How College Maintains Inequality*, coauthored with Elizabeth A. Armstrong, we detail the role that universities play in producing unequal class trajectories. Parents remain, for the most part, in the background of the story. Here, they move to the forefront.

My goal is not to account for all possible varieties of college parenting, as this is an impossible feat for research from just one university. Instead, I situate the minutiae of parent-child relationships—from the accounts of mothers, fathers, and daughters—in the context of MU, the entire post-secondary system, and the larger history of higher education in the United States. I use my deep knowledge of a particular group of parents and students to flesh out the role that parents play in processes of class reproduction and mobility at the post-secondary level.[92] Below I offer an account of the resulting theoretical model, visually illustrated in Figure I.1.

Parental social class and gender beliefs combine to form distinct cultural visions of what college is and should be for young women.[93] These interlinked understandings of the primary purpose of college, women's paths to economic security, and appropriate levels of dependence for young adults have their roots in particular class positions. They crystallize when a model of college works (or is thought to work) for women in a given class group to achieve reproduction or mobility. Some visions of college require significant levels of parental financial resources and are thus not imaginable for less-privileged families. However, cultural understandings of college are not entirely *determined* by current class status. That is to say, some parents adopt visions that are a poor match for their class resources.

Visions of the ideal college experience motivate parents to raise, fund, and interact with their college-attending daughters in patterned ways. I refer to this set of practices as parenting approaches. Parenting approaches may not be calculated and deliberate plans of action. Instead, parents are often steered by emotion, instinct, and habit. They do what is intuitive, given their class background and current lifestyle—which frequently (but not always) mesh. Parenting approaches do not have to make logical sense or work the way

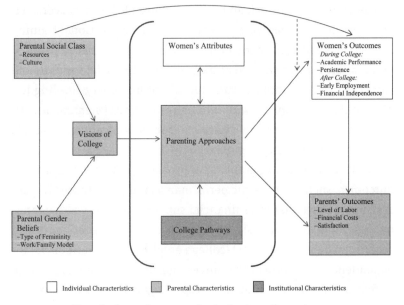

FIGURE I.1. The role of parenting approaches in shaping college outcomes.

parents assume that they should. They may even lead to decidedly irrational ends.[94]

Many parents are sensitive to who their daughters are—just as women's capacities and personalities are deeply molded by their parents. Parents often know, for example, if their daughters are more prone to partying than studying. A few, however, are tone-deaf or actively resistant to their children's interests, abilities, or work ethic.

Parents may also respond to the way a university is organized. Most institutions offer three main organizational pathways, built to accommodate different types of families. At MU the robust party pathway offers socially oriented students a lively party scene and less rigorous academic programming. Parents who want this for their daughters will find themselves shelling out seemingly endless amounts of cash for clothes and alcohol. The competitive professional pathway offers the academically engaged selective programming and extracurricular options needed to move into professional careers; parental help is needed to stay on track and avoid the lure of the party scene. Finally, the mobility pathway, designed to provide vocational training for all who want it, is nearly non-existent at MU. In theory, it would build tailored academic and social guidance, financial support, and career counseling into the function of the university, leveling the playing field for families with limited resources.[95] *Parenting to a Degree* demonstrates just how difficult it is for less advantaged parents to ensure their daughters' mobility at MU.

What influence do parenting approaches have on educational outcomes, such as academic performance and persistence? In general, approaches that offer financial support and detailed guidance help students tremendously. Parents can also play a beneficial role in securing women's early post-college employment and financial independence. They provide resources and assistance that are central to finding jobs after graduation—especially when it is necessary to compensate for poor academic performance. At every stage, money, educational know-how, and valuable social connections can increase the odds of success.

However, it is not just *what* parents have but *how* they use it that matters. Some affluent parents intentionally hold back resources and involvement. Others give freely but make their daughters agree to an accountability contract to ensure judicious use of funds. Less-privileged families may manage to pull together strategic financial investments and step up involvement. Some parents encourage their daughters to develop normative femininity at the cost of human capital. What I found in this research is that the details matter. When scholars model the role of parents by proxy—looking only at parental income, education, and occupation—we miss the mechanisms (i.e., the underlying beliefs and practices) that explain important variation in student outcomes within larger class groups.

While often overlooked, the ripple effects of college parenting on parents themselves are also central to this book. College parenting requires significant labor, and it has long-term financial consequences.

Parents vary in how satisfied they are with the result. Though it may seem obvious to some—or come as a surprise for others—the most effective approaches demand the most of parents. However, there are ways to reduce financial and emotional costs and divide the work in a more egalitarian fashion.

Organization of the Book

Chapter 1 details the five visions of college that underlie the parenting approaches at the center of *Parenting to a Degree*. These visions are rooted in social class but can spread past their origin or combine class elements. I highlight a vision not held by parents in my study and discuss the tight link between college visions and parenting approaches. Finally, I address potential disagreements between mothers and fathers.

The remainder of the book is divided into two major sections. Part I, encompassing chapters 2 through 4, provides portraits of the parenting approaches common at Midwest U. Approaches are grouped around their level of involvement and funding, moving from two types of highly intensive helicopters, to the strategically involved paramedics, and finally to bystanders, who are sometimes supportive but unable to offer guidance.

In part II, I assess parenting consequences. Chapters 5 through 7 group parenting styles around parental satisfaction (or dissatisfaction) with what their daughters got out of college. Parents' evaluations are often connected to the financial costs they endure, as well as the level of labor required. I discuss women's academic records, persistence, initial post-college employment, and financial independence.

In the end, I describe the benefits enjoyed by students with involved and well-resourced parents—those who are a part of the new family-university partnership, through which many crucial tasks are outsourced to parents. This partnership is a product of the privatization of higher education and is likely to deepen existing class, as well as racial, inequities. I emphasize the gendered costs to both women and men, and highlight the problems associated with institutionalizing extended dependence on parents. I end with several policy solutions, invoking the market, status-based processes, and the state.

ONE   # Five Visions of College

W hat is the ideal college experience? How much is social and how much is academic? Parents do not all agree. I found five different visions of college that reflect what parents accept as logical labor and marital market strategies for their daughters. These often taken-for-granted assumptions tend to develop among families with similar financial, social, and cultural resources. College is, in part, about producing the right "kind" of woman (or man) for a particular social class.[1] At the same time, mismatches and creative combinations can occur, as not all parents adopt visions of college that fit their current class position.

Below, I detail the categories that I use to describe parents' class locations. The chapter then turns to the five visions of college and their class roots. I describe one vision not represented in my sample. There may be more. I also highlight the strong connection between parents' visions of college and their approaches, identifying a few exceptions. The chapter ends with a discussion of intra-couple disagreement about parenting practices—as well as the rare conflict over visions of college.

Social Class Categories

Upper class, upper-middle class, middle class, lower-middle class, and working class are common class categories in the United States. They take into account experiences with the labor market, which are central to how many social scientists define class.[2] These categories also refer to the cultural components of class—lifestyles, types of consumption, and tastes that create patterned and familiar ways of being among those who share a class location.[3]

I placed families into class categories primarily on the basis of current parental education, occupation, and economic resources. These three measures, in various combinations, are frequently used in research to capture class status.[4] Table 1.1 identifies the characteristics typical of each group, as well as the number and percentage of families in each group.

- *Upper-class families* (15%) were marked by fathers' positions as chief executive or chief financial officers. Most mothers were homemakers. Both parents were at least college educated. These families earned well over the threshold for the 1 percent in the United States (around $525,000 for a household as of 2013). In their communities, they were at the top of both economic and prestige hierarchies. On the East Coast, this required greater wealth and status than in the Midwest. Personal jets, frequent international vacations, and a great distance from necessity characterized upper-class lifestyles.
- *Upper-middle-class families* (41%) included at least one, often two, parents who worked in well-compensated professional fields requiring advanced degrees (e.g., doctors, accountants, administrators, and professors). Money in these families was plentiful but finite. Out-of-state tuition was possible—although, for those who were tenuously upper-middle class, it could exert a strain on family resources.[5] When I use the terms affluent or privileged, I am referring to upper- or upper-middle-class families.
- *Middle-class families* (12%) typically included two college-educated parents. Fathers' jobs were often in middle management (e.g., a tractor company distributor and food factory supervisor) and not as secure of those of the upper-middle class. Mothers were often teachers or in retail management. Middle-class families could be at the top of the class ladder in their in-state towns, but compared to more privileged families at MU, they were closer to the bottom. For

Table 1.1. Typical Characteristics of Class Groups

Class	Mother Education	Father Education	Mother Occupation	Father Occupation	Income Category	Residency	Family Structure	N
Upper	College degree	≥ College degree	Homemaker	CEO/CFO	> $525,000	Out-of-state	Intact	6 (15%)
Upper-middle	≥ College degree	≥ College degree	Professional	Professional	$125,000–$525,000	Mixed	Mostly intact	17 (41%)
Middle	College degree	College degree	Teacher, Management	Middle mgmt.	$80,000–$125,000	In-state	Mostly intact	5 (12%)
Lower-middle	≤ Some college	Some college	Secretarial or sales positions	Sales mgmt.	$40,000–$80,000	In-state	Mixed	7 (17%)
Working	≤ Some college	≤ Some college	Low-paying service work	Manual labor	< $40,000	In-state	Mixed	6 (15%)
								41 (100%)

this reason, I view the middle class, along with the lower-middle and working classes, as (relatively) less privileged.

- *Lower-middle-class families* (17%) often included parents with some college experience, but both parents did not hold four-year degrees. Fathers were typically in sales management, although a few held better-paying manual positions (e.g., firefighting). Mothers were usually in pink-collar secretarial jobs. Divorce or parental death were common in this category, as well as among the working class, and contributed to a sense of economic constraint.
- *Working-class families* (15%) were characterized by poor economic security. Mothers generally worked low-paying service jobs (e.g., waitressing or retail) and fathers did seasonal manual labor (e.g., highway construction and farming). Work was not consistent. These families had little exposure to higher education, and many were from rural areas. The flagship state university was far outside their realm of experience.

The Ideal College Experience

In my study, five visions of the ideal college experience are represented. These visions incorporate understandings of the primary purpose of the college years, women's future work and family configurations, and expected levels of dependence on parents. Typically, parents shared beliefs with those in their class groups, given similarities in their everyday lives, worldviews, and resources. However, class culture sometimes spread to nearby class groups, and some parents combined disparate elements from their complex class histories into a hybridized view of college.

1. *The Career-Building Experience*

Seven sets of parents saw college as the career-building years in which life opportunities are forged. As Anna explained, "[College is] a fresh opportunity to become anything you want to be. The whole world is your oyster. Education is just the most . . . I'm gonna cry now.

I really see education as a marvel. . . . It's such a wonderful enriching pathway to accomplish your dreams." These parents wanted to offer their children the chance to demonstrate worth and justify positions in the upper-middle class, via schooling.[6] This vision of college is closest to what many scholars tend to think of higher education as providing—specialized knowledge, skills, and credentials that allow youth to achieve professional security and economic success.

Anna's language suggests that anyone can achieve through higher education. Yet the career-building process is reliant on the intergenerational transmission of class-based resources. Most parents offering this experience had a rich legacy of family post-secondary investment that they passed on to their daughters. As Anna described:

> My father was a teacher and then a professor. I'm an educator and now I'm an educational administrator in a school district. In terms of their value system . . . [t]hat's our priority. In my own personal life, anytime I've had a challenge with a career or just been stuck, education has just been the pathway for me to deal with things positively.

Not surprisingly, Anna was convinced that hard work in college would secure her daughter's future economic security.

Parents with professional degrees in engineering, medicine, accounting, educational administration, and other specialized fields had an understanding of how to move within the educational system and how to use it for advancement, as well as a belief in its power. The lucrative nature of their careers offered access to money that could smooth the way. Indeed, there was no economic investment that these parents would rather be making.

Women's academic and career success was a norm in these families and modeled in everyday life. As Andrea noted in reference to my career path, "You're going to have your PhD, so what kind of bar does that set for your kids? Where does it end? You set the bar. . . . They're going to watch you teach. They're going to watch you research. I think it's just kind of the way it is." Their households offered a version of peer marriage (at least in the realm of work), with two well-educated, high-earning individuals paired together. As Keith would joke, "Andrea is a PhD. I'm . . . the least educated [adult] in the family with my MBA!" They expected the same type of partnership for their daughters, as it consolidated the privileges earned by two professionals into one household.[7]

Only two families focused on the career-building experience were located outside the upper-middle class. Brenda's upper-class parents had grown up in the upper-middle class and still maintained these sensibilities. Roger prominently displayed the logo of a moderately ranked southern flagship university, where he received the title of certified professional accountant, on the glass divide of his multi-suite office directly overlooking Central Park. Mary's middle-class parents had come to value higher education through experience teaching at primary and secondary levels. They shared an enthusiasm for schooling and a commitment to helping their daughter achieve her law school dreams.

Parents who adopted this logic were not responding to their daughters' stellar academic records. Most had average students—or else they would have encouraged women to select more prestigious schools. As Steven described of his daughter, "Erica happens to be a very social person. . . . She seems to travel with a kind of crowd that's just a little . . . more socially active." Anna worried about how Erica would do in college because "in high school she just was not all that motivated." Yet they still sent her out of state to MU for the competitive Business School, believing in her potential.

2. The Social Experience

Rhonda's view of college could not be further from Anna's. As she candidly remarked, "College is the time of your life. I know that you're not supposed to say that to your kids, but I do. [Laura: Really? How come?] Because you don't want them to think that once it's over, then it's not going to be that much fun. College *is* the time of your life. And I think right after college is too, before you're thirty. I want her to have a good time."

Ten sets of parents, including Rhonda, saw college as an enjoyable social experience and opened their pocketbooks to finance it. The creation of a protected space before the onslaught of adult responsibilities echoes the historical development of childhood, and later adolescence, as years of fun and freedom that parents owe their cherished youth.[8] These parents believed that partying was a central college project—not something that they should, begrudgingly, expect their daughters to do behind their backs. As Walt wistfully noted:

> I look back and say it was the best time of my life. . . . I'm sure Natasha will look back with fond memories, and that's not just because she got a degree. . . . More because of the friendship and the fun time and the experience and the growth she had. I drank a lot so I just figured that was gonna go on. I felt that's just part of it.

When asked whether or not he thought his daughter partied, Tom said matter-of-factly, "That's what it's for. That's what going to school is for." Connie similarly commented, "Pot smoking is something that definitely Abby's been doing for a long time. I completely understand. Everybody explores and does that kind of thing."

Parents' investment in partying was premised on a series of assumptions about how university life is organized. Rick explained, "My own concern was that Nicole get a true experience in college, and that means she goes to parties . . . but more importantly that she's safe. At the university, we're able to build a structure around these kids because you know they're going to party. . . . They can live within a safety zone." His concerns were heightened in other settings that he viewed as less protective—spring break, for instance.[9]

These parents often handpicked Midwest U specifically for the social experience that it offered. As Alexis described:

We looked at other places [and] applied to a bunch of schools. Hannah is big into the rah-rah scene. She's very social. She loves sports. . . . I could never picture her going to a small school. . . . She likes to be involved in . . . everything. So we saw a college advisor [outside of her high school]. . . . [The advisor] said, "I have a great school—what about Midwest U? It's a [major sports conference]. Hannah wanted to go for photography, so it's got a great photography program." I'm like, "Oh my God, Hannah's gonna end up going to MU!" When we left there I came home crying. Because everything about MU was absolutely perfect for Hannah.

Alexis highlights many of the features that appealed to these parents: big-time college sports, lively campuses, an array of not particularly difficult majors, and many ways to belong (e.g., Greek houses and social clubs).

It is possible that parents were accurately reading their children's strengths. They may have adopted this vision, in part, because it fit their daughters. For example, Rhonda described her stereotypical "sorority girl" daughter in this way: "If you say 'party,' Tara says where. . . . She is extremely social." I agreed. Tara was focused on having fun. She also displayed low academic motivation. However, a few of their daughters were decidedly non-social and disinterested in mainstream college life. As Cathy told me, Natasha was "very shy. . . . I think that paralyzed her socially a bit."

With few exceptions, parents could have nudged their daughters toward a more academic experience but chose not to. Frank explained, "Listen, I would've loved all of [my children] to have been engineers or doctors. But I think . . . focusing in on . . . the college experience [is important]. If she was going to Harvard, maybe it'd be a different view, but she's not a Harvard kid." While Hannah did not have a stellar record, it was solid—mostly A's and some B's from a well-ranked out-of-state high school. She could have been a good student at a moderately selective university like MU. However, Frank was a CFO for a Fortune 500 company. He and his wife, Alexis, were from generations of wealth. Virtually all of Hannah's cousins and family members qualified for admission to more prestigious colleges. When Hannah did not, Frank decided that a social experience made sense.

Frank understood—even if only intuitively—that fun could be functional. Indeed, for the sons of wealthy elites in the nineteenth and early twentieth centuries, it facilitated the building of social networks and the cultivation of social skills and cultural tastes necessary for future success in business or politics.[10] Later, women were incorporated on campus as future wives and mothers, a position reflected in the domestic nature of women's social clubs and majors.[11] Privileged parents often sent their daughters to college primarily to find a husband.[12] This was colloquially known as the "Mrs." degree, or MRS.

At the start of the twenty-first century, Hannah's parents hoped she would eventually marry a man who was a proven success. (As Hannah remarked of her father, "He always says to me, 'Marry rich, marry rich.'") For women, the social experience could hone the traits—charm, fashion sense, attractiveness, and rich network ties— that parents believed would lead to the ideal marriage. The notion that a woman's future should be secured through a mate's earnings and credentials reflects a gender complementary vision of gender relations, whereby a male breadwinner is paired with a female homemaker.[13] This path to economic security is most common among wealthy, white, heterosexual women.[14]

Today the social experience is widely accepted. The Greek party scene, immortalized in the 1978 film *Animal House*, has been replicated ad nauseam in youth media. MTV made college spring-break parties famous by filming hordes of scantily clad, drunken coeds dancing on beaches around the world. Demand for the perfect party school is reflected in the development and dissemination of numerous ranking systems. Alcohol industries, fashion brands, media conglomerates, local bars and restaurants, and universities benefit from college partying and use it in their marketing campaigns.

Many parents saw the social experience as essential to college. Some felt compelled to provide it, despite more limited means. For example, Barb was a widow, living off of savings. She opted to send Mara to MU instead of an affordable in-state school.

> I didn't wanna deny Mara. Believe me, I got a lot of pressure from my family not to send her to MU. Because it cost so much. But I felt like . . . those four years are like magic, and they can dictate the way the rest of your life goes. . . . . It's not like I have the money, really, to do this. I just decided that I would make it work.

This decision made little financial sense, although it was difficult for Barb to see that at the outset. It would drain the families' resources, forcing Mara's little sister to pay her own way at a local school. This family's story reflects the diffusion of the social experience from the upper class, to tenuously upper-middle class, even middle-class parents.

3. The Mobility Experience

At different historical periods, disadvantaged groups have used higher education to improve the living conditions of future generations and combat discrimination based on race, class, gender, and religion.[15] Most accounts have focused on students seeking mobility, potentially on their own.[16] In some cases, however, mobility is a family project. It may even be a parental project, when children do not display their own drive and determination.

Parents seeking the mobility experience believed in the power of education to provide economic security for their daughters, beyond what they had experienced in their own lives. Robert argued that college would dramatically improve his daughter's chances on the job market. He explained:

> Those that are giving out the jobs, they're looking for a reason to pick one over the other. It's pretty concrete when you say, "We picked him because he has a bachelor's degree." End of story. . . . We've told Stacey that every year of college you have increases your

salary by at least ten grand a year. Four years of college could in-crease your salary by about forty grand.

Robert did not distinguish between an academic or social experience. He believed in the general promise of a college education. The degree itself was, in his mind, the ticket to a better future.

Six sets of parents, including Robert, shared this view. Middle-class parents recognized the difficulty of reproducing their own class po-sition, much less advancing further, without a college education. Lower-middle-class parents were stalled in their careers because they lacked the right educational credentials. As Janice explained, "The fact that I don't have a degree has stopped me twice from getting a job that I wanted. I'll be fifty-seven years old [soon], and it still has haunted me a couple times in the last ten years." She spoke from a place of missed opportunities and vowed not to let her children ex-perience the same frustrations.

College was not a taken-for-granted educational step, but one that these parents had to pursue enthusiastically, intentionally, and along-side their children. As Eileen proudly put it, "We're very into both kids getting a degree." Most parents had not received such support growing up. Janice explained, "I did not go to college, and it was never talked about in my home." They responded by making college a fam-ily priority. As Janice continued, "When the kids were . . . very young we talked about it on a regular basis. . . . I wouldn't say exactly there wasn't a choice, but it was something that was going to happen." The single best way to guarantee enrollment, parents realized, was to offer financial support. They were not going to leave to chance something this important.

Mobility-seeking parents were economically pragmatic, empha-sizing the need for women to be self-sufficient.[17] A solid earner to partner with was ideal, but they viewed financial reliance on men as unrealistic. As Robert explained to his daughter, "There's only two ways that you make it in the world. You either have to earn your money or have somebody give you your money. Well, I don't think

anybody's gonna give us any, so that leaves the earning part." They
assumed college would provide vocational training. Teaching and
nursing offered the most direct and typical paths for women in their
communities to achieve economic security.[18]

These parents had trust in MU that ran deep, often built through
generations of family ties to the surrounding area. As Robert described of Stacey's college choice process:

> I have family that lives around Fairview so I was familiar with the
> area. There's a rich culture and history there. I love the campus
> with the hills and stone. My mother's twin brother [worked] down
> there . . . his whole life. Retired from there. I have several cousins,
> aunts, uncles that live in that area. A cousin teaches in [a nearby
> rural town]. My mother was born and raised down just outside of
> Fairview. So we had always been MU-oriented. . . . We always liked
> the campus and all the activities. We thought it was all in all a better
> value [than other in-state schools].

It was reasonable to assume that MU would be a safe bet for mobility;
after all, it was the most prestigious public university in the state.
Parents who shared this vision were ready to wager everything on
the flagship.

4. The Adult Experience

Not all parents can offer their offspring a young adult life stage.
While some can afford to protect and fund their children beyond high
school, others cannot.[19] It may be implausible for parents who are
struggling to support themselves and younger children. They may,
instead, expect older children to become entirely self-sufficient before or during college.

To understand how beliefs about the transition to adulthood vary
with social class, Frank Furstenberg and collaborators developed a
module for the 2002 General Social Survey, administered to a nationally representative sample of Americans. They found that adults who

did not attend college and were in the bottom third of the income ladder had a much earlier expected timetable for adult transitions—such as leaving home, finishing schooling, holding a full-time job, and entering into marriage or parenthood.[20]

In my sample, six sets of parents treated college as the start or extension of the adult years. They looked at me quizzically when I asked about growing up. As Diane corrected, "Amanda's an adult already." These families were the most disadvantaged in the sample; five hailed from the working class and one the lower-middle class. Physical, emotional, and financial barriers made them unavailable as parents. Their daughters were, in some ways, anomalies. Attending a moderately selective four-year school like Midwest U with very little parental help is a challenging prospect. Most students in this position instead opt for lower-priced, lower-status alternatives—or no college at all.[21]

Parents who understood college as an adult experience did not assume attendance was inevitable or even desirable. For instance, Luann had mixed feelings about college:

> I am not totally convinced that as soon as you graduate from high school you [should] go to college. I have known people that [did]. . . . They either end up quitting or they are in college for eight or nine years. . . . So I didn't press her to go to college. . . . Megan just left saying, "I am going to college. I am going to go to MU." And I said, "Well, that is great." That is just basically how it was. We have no qualms with her going to college or not going to college.

Luann knew that Megan was "very mature and very reasonable thinking and applies herself to situations," so it was not necessarily a surprise that Megan would want to attend college. But Luann did not see this as a parent's choice.

For Luann, the returns of college were quite uncertain. It could cost a lot, take a long time, and potentially be for nothing if a student dropped out. Certainly, as Megan would confirm, the paths through higher education experienced by youth in her community validated her mother's views. If they went, many attended community or for-profit schools for years but did not finish. It was not surprising that Luann played no part in getting Megan to MU. Her disenchantment with higher education is echoed in research on working-class adults, who often come to distrust colleges and universities.[22]

Parents like Luann needed their daughters to be financially self-reliant as soon as possible. They favored the military or going to work full-time as substitutes for college. As my field notes report: "Amy's dad wanted her to go in military. We talked about that for a while, and how much better for her it was that she decided to come to MU." When I asked Heather, "Would [your father] rather that you just have gotten a job right out of high school?" she remarked, "He definitely would have." Early marriage was also viewed positively, especially if it improved economic circumstances.

Once college started, however, these sorts of decisions were out of parents' hands. Parents seeking an adult experience believed their job was done. As Luann put it, "Whatever Megan has made her mind to do, if that is what she wants to do, then that is what she should do. I am never going to try to talk her out of it." In fact, by intervening, parents felt they would only undermine their daughters' abilities to function as adults.

5. The Hybridized Experience

Parents' views of college are not just shaped by their current class standing; they carry their complex class histories with them.[23] The material, social, and cultural conditions under which people live often change over the life course. Shifts in financial resources, educational attainment, or occupational status can place individuals in contact with disparate class cultures. They may respond by creating new class culture that does not neatly reflect either origins or destinations.[24]

Twelve sets of parents, from a range of class positions, fused diverse beliefs about the purpose of women's college years into a hybridized ideal. They saw the value in moving more rapidly into adulthood, like many working-class parents. But they also internalized the necessity of a supported young adult life stage, like wealthier parents. Parents typically arrived at this blended logic in one of two ways: They experienced extreme upward mobility over the course of their lives; or they accrued experience with higher education, pulling them slightly away from the working class, without an accompanying shift in class resources.

The hybridized experience emphasized personal development, and not just in compartmentalized arenas of life. As Theresa explained, "You [want them to have] mind, body, and spirit[ual] kinds of growth in every way, shape, and form." Most parents' holistic ideals were pragmatic. They told me that their daughters needed to be capable of paying bills, cooking a meal, being alone, navigating a new city, carrying on intelligent conversation, and performing at their jobs. Among the parents I studied, this was the *only* vision of college that touched on college as offering broader life enrichment—not just instrumental career or social network development.

For these parents, autonomy was the most important trait that youth could develop in college. As Kenny put it, "College should be a time of independence. I think they need to learn to take care of some things on their own. [For example,] Monica was three and a half hours away when she had a car problem. I wanted my daughter to know enough to be able to call a garage, call a tow truck. She shouldn't have to depend on Dad to do those things. . . . I wanted my daughter to be that independent." An emphasis on women's autonomy ruled out a gender complementary model of gender relations, in which women's dependence on men is central. Independent women did not rely on future spouses—or their parents—for comfort, completion, or security. They were self-reliant and confident in their own capabilities.

Encouraging independence necessitated allowing small to moderate mistakes to happen, uninterrupted. As Theresa emphasized, "You don't wish bad things away, because they learn a lot from them. . . . No helicopter stuff [allowed]." At the same time, a safety net was important. She continued, "People would say 'Oh, they're off on their own.' No, they aren't. College is when you are [on] alert." Parents sharing a hybridized vision of college thus wanted youth to practice being on their own—but offered emergency support to catch them when they (inevitably) fell. In melding cultural elements from across the class spectrum, these parents had arrived at a unique vision of the college experience.

Who Is Not Represented?

Midwestern U is a typical "multiversity" in that it is many different things to many different people.[25] Perhaps more than any other type of post-secondary institution, it draws parents with a wide array of views toward college. However, there is at least one vision that I did not see from my vantage point at MU.

It might be called the cultivation of excellence experience, geared toward the realization of a particular talent or potential. It is most common among those with an elite academic pedigree, although not necessarily great wealth.[26] As recently described in the *New York Times*:

> By the time a child rounds the corner into high school and certainly before he sets up an account with the Common App[lication for colleges] . . . he needs to have a passion that is deep, easy to artic- ulate, well documented and makes him stand out from the crowd. This passion, which he will either stumble upon or be led to by the caring adults in his life, must be pursued at the highest level [that] his time and talent, and his parent's finances, will allow. It is un- derstood that this will offer him fulfillment and afford him and his family bragging rights that a mere dabbler would never earn.[27]

This vision is driven, in part, by parents' desperation to secure a spot for their children in prestigious colleges and universities. Increas- ingly, these institutions are looking for investment in a unique "passion"—an avant-garde multimedia artist, Olympic-quality swimmer, or oboe genius to fill a specific niche for the incoming class.[28] Parents comply, but they expect colleges to further hone this excellence. There are not many world-famous neurosurgeons, Nobel Prize winners, or poets laureate. But most people who succeed at this level come through college.

Parents (and schools) may fall back on a benign self-actualization narrative to justify these extreme beliefs, pulling on pieces of the liberal arts mission.[29] Thus, there may be elements of the cultivation of excellence that point to the societal good, such as developing capacities to help solve local, national, and global issues. Youth are expected to demonstrate a constellation of characteristics that often hang together: creativity, work ethic, competence, strong analytical reasoning, and deep social skills—hallmarks of a complete education. They need to sympathize with and understand the plight of the marginalized to be good leaders. Yet it is not okay to self-actualize in obscurity as a missionary. Or to pursue a love of music as a starving street musician in Amsterdam.

Parents who seek to cultivate excellence tend not to send their children to schools like MU. If they do, a party dorm is an unacceptable housing option. This group is likely to ensconce their daughters in living learning communities or alternative housing units for liberal, feminist, queer, vegan, and intellectual students. Honors Colleges are often good academic options, as they usually offer small classes with a select group of students. Thus, when these parents opt for MU, it is only with the knowledge that their children will be heavily sheltered and receive special attention that might be lost in a more competitive setting.

Translating Visions into Practices

The visions of college that parents articulated corresponded with particular parenting practices during college—what I refer to as parenting approaches. Without following parents over time, it is difficult to determine the exact nature of this link. Did beliefs about the ideal college experience cause parents to act in distinct ways, or did they explain their actions with the cultural understandings available to them? There is evidence to suggest that visions of college were *both* motivators and sense-making tools.[30]

It was easiest to see parents using culture to justify their actions. The timing of my parent interviews, at or near the end of their daughters' college careers, led me to get retrospective accounts of college years one through four. Parents were, by necessity, acting then explaining. For example, occasionally two different groups did the *same* thing (e.g., ask their daughters to join sororities), but in justifying this to me, they pulled on divergent cultural frameworks. It was hard not to see this as an after-the-fact search for meaning.

At the same time, however, I saw how the seemingly same decisions evolved differently over time, as parents applied divergent frameworks. Some parents, for instance, pushed back against normative femininity in sorority life while others embraced it. These two groups appeared to be guided by (or, at the very least, reacting to) very distinct beliefs, although I could not directly observe this process.

After interviewing the women in year five, I found the strongest case for a causal link between beliefs and practices. I compared parents' earlier predictions of their own actions for the post-college period against women's reports of what their parents actually did after college. In several cases, parents told me they were going to do something drastic, such as cut off funding, for reasons that were not entirely financial. Later I would find out that they actually acted in ways that were consistent with their earlier visions of college. It seemed hard for parents to change course. In fact, their visions were sometimes so deeply internalized that I doubted parents were entirely aware of the assumptions that guided them.[31]

With the ongoing dialogue between beliefs and practices, there was a high level of consistency between them. Table 1.2 details the visions of college linked to the five parenting approaches highlighted in this book. Parenting approaches can be subdivided into three key

Table 1.2. The Five Visions of College

Vision of College	Parenting Approach	Gender Relations	Funding Level	Parental Involvement	Social Class	Number of Families	Chapters
Career-building	Professional helicopter	Encourage peer marriage	High	High	≥ MC	6	2, 6
Social	Pink helicopter	Embrace complementarity	High	High	≥ MC	9	2, 5
Hybridized	Paramedic	Reject complementarity	Moderate	Strategic	UC–WC	12	3, 6
Mobility	Supportive bystander	Support pragmatic model	Medium-high	Low	MC, LMC	6	4, 7
Adult	Total bystander	Support pragmatic model	Low	Low	LMC, WC	6	4, 7

Notes: UC = upper class; UMC = upper-middle class; MC = middle class; LMC = lower-middle class, WC = working class.
Two families are not included in this table or in chapters 2–7.

practices, which are bundled together in distinct ways: parents encourage their daughters to expect particular work/family configurations, offer a certain amount of funds (in particular ways), and display a distinct level of involvement. In my study, parents who shared a given vision typically raised, funded, and interacted with their daughters consistently.

Parents who valued a career-building experience were financially supportive, highly involved *professional helicopters*, who encouraged the eventual formation of peer marriages. The social experience was promoted by high-funding, intensely involved *pink helicopters*. They nudged women toward gender complementary work/family arrangements. *Paramedics* followed the hybridized experience, funding at moderate levels, intervening strategically, and eschewing gender complementarity. *Supportive bystanders* espoused the mobility experience. They funded at moderate to high levels, displayed low levels of active involvement, and held a pragmatic vision of women's economic security. Finally, *total bystanders* believed in the adult experience. Their low levels of funding and logistical support pushed women to develop a pragmatic work/family orientation.

There were a few exceptions. Two families shared beliefs about the ideal college experience with others in my sample but did not act on them in similar ways. Janet, Linda's mother, supported a career-building experience, and Barb, Mara's mother, a social experience. Yet they did not become intensively involved, like their professional and pink helicopter counterparts. Why not?

In Janet's case, this was due to a cross-class marriage. Linda's father "grew up in New England and went to Ivy League schools and skied in the Alps," while Janet attended MU with limited parental assistance. Janet was the primary parent but had little contact with Linda: "[We will talk] fairly often for a while, and then it will be months." Janet's new class position led her to assume that her daughter would become a well-paid professional; however, given her own college experience, she did not see the need to help Linda get there.

Unlike Janet, most parents who send their children to MU for career development know the perils of a robust party pathway. The Greek party scene can derail students. Less rigorous majors, such as interior design or event planning, are readily available—but many do not lead to jobs requiring a degree.[32] Parents generally recognize that dialing down their efforts is risky, particularly in this institutional context.

Barb's case is also unique. She unexpectedly found herself a widow unable to share parenting or work duties. Barb would have assisted Mara in crafting the perfect social experience, if she had the time, energy, or money to do so. Because MU is designed to offer precisely this experience, the situation was not as precarious. However, the school attracts students from diverse class backgrounds. Those from affluent families may not rub shoulders with other wealthy, well-connected students displaying the "right" kind of interactional styles and cultural tastes. Most parents seeking a social experience want to ensure that that their daughters eat, sleep, and play with youth from elite backgrounds.

Because Linda's and Mara's parents are outliers in my sample, I do not discuss them in chapters 2 through 7, and they are not included in table 1.2. Their cases suggest the existence of parents who are happy to fund at high levels to acquire particular experiences but expect institutions to do much of the work of crafting students into members of the upper classes. Presumably, most of these parents send their children to elite private institutions that may be better equipped to do so. Yet if we believe recent media coverage, many elite schools are just as—if not more—overrun with involved parents.[33] Privileged parents may not be willing to risk class reproduction. This is why they often place their children at more prestigious institutions in the first place.

Did Mothers and Fathers Ever Disagree?

Mothers and fathers generally developed consistent visions of college. Years of raising children together and, in most cases, sharing a similar class background facilitated this process. It was more typical for parents to disagree about specific parenting practices. For example, those committed to career development might not agree on exactly how often they should call their daughters or how much money they should send on a monthly basis. These differences, in most cases, were not visible to daughters, as parents tried to present a unified front.

Conflict over parental involvement was the most common. Fathers often claimed that their wives were doing too much; it was never the other way around. Walt explained, "My opinion is [that Cathy] can be a little controlling, which if I was a kid, would drive me nuts. . . . She tends to worry a lot more than I do. Then the worry spurs action on her part, where I'm kind of going, 'Eh, they'll be fine. They're kids. I know they're gonna figure it out.'" As I discuss in chapter 2, most fathers responded to mothers' push for intensive parenting by simply allowing their wives to do most, if not all, of the parenting work. It was unclear if fathers genuinely believed a less interventionist approach was ideal or if it proved convenient for them, or both.

Parents did not always agree on how much to fund, especially in cases of cross-class marriage.[34] Thus, Janet—who, as noted above, married a much wealthier man—was uncomfortable with her husband's desire to pay for everything:

> I'm not sure that you have as much ownership in the education. . . . It gives you a false sense of what the world is like, and how many people have that kind of experience? Hardly anybody. I have some problems with that kind of a privileged experience because of what it does to your worldview. How I counter it is I take them on a mission trip somewhere . . . so that they can see not everybody has the same opportunities.

Janet's accommodating response was typical. When financial resources were not restricted, the bigger spender won out. It was hard to construct an argument for holding back funds if they were available.

In contrast, when financial means were limited, one parent might want to give more, but the more frugal parent had economic constraint on his or her side.

It was uncommon for parents to diverge dramatically in visions of the ideal college experience. Nicole's parents were one of the rare cases. They chose to interview together, despite my gentle requests otherwise.[35] However, the dynamic proved fascinating. Rick clearly believed in the virtues of college fun. Marian was not so convinced.

> *Rick:* The reality is they're going to drink anyway.
>
> *Marian:* That's where we differ because to me it was very black-and-white. It's illegal. There are consequences. You're not supposed to do it.
>
> *Rick:* Keep in mind, there were different levels of her partying. Certainly, when she was in the dorm, she partied, but I don't think she was a major partier. When she got into the sorority, where it was more socially accepted to drink like a fish . . . she definitely became much more of a drinker.
>
> *Marian:* In her second year . . . [I] had thought, well, I don't know if by then maybe the frat parties already got old?
>
> *Rick:* Do frat parties ever get old? No [*chuckles*].

Nicole would get a social experience. Marian was not going to block it, and it would have been hard to—given that Rick had already offered his backing.

I could see no obvious signs of conflict in Rick and Marian's marriage. However, in openly acrimonious relationships, parents were more likely to put their children at the center of clashes over beliefs and practices. Such cleavages were more frequent in divorced families, although they were a feature of ongoing conflict rather than divorce itself.[36] For example, while Carrie suffered as a result of her divorced parents' disagreements (see chapter 4), I suspected that had they remained married, the situation would have been more intense and unmanageable. An amicable divorce could even bring formerly warring parents' views closer together, as was the case for Morgan's parents (see chapter 3).

The process of divorce shaped college parenting in other ways. The need to finance two households reduced monetary resources available for young adults.[37] Single parents typically lacked the necessary time and energy for intensive parenting. Particularly in the short term, upheaval and change could limit parents' abilities to be actively involved in their older children's lives.[38] These sorts of disruptions often reduced parents' overall investments and were more likely to occur among families with limited means.

Part I of the book immediately follows this chapter. It moves into the five parenting approaches, briefly highlighted above. These sets of patterned practices were distinctive and—as I detail in part II—had real consequences for the lives and well-being of mothers, fathers, and daughters. Chapters 2 through 4 map parenting approaches on a continuum from the most involved and expensive to the least. I begin with the divergent approaches of two types of highly interventionist helicopter families.

PART I

Parenting Approaches

TWO

Helicopters

A few days after she dropped Taylor off at college, Andrea got a phone call from her daughter. The wounds in Taylor's mouth from a recent wisdom tooth surgery had gone septic. Andrea dropped everything and "drove up there immediately. I left [my university in a neighboring state], and by the time I got there Taylor's eye had disappeared." Andrea quickly located an oral surgeon in town. Afterward, she booked a room at the university hotel and put Taylor to bed. The next morning, "Taylor was so freaked out about missing her class. I just said, 'I'll go to your classes'—which was kind of fun for me as a professor to sit in somebody else's classes and see what people actually do. I took her notes and she got better."

Around the same time, another parent was responding to a very different type of emergency. The first practice of Cindy's daughter's poms team (a form of cheerleading) was to occur at a local Christian church. The family was Jewish. When Naomi told her team "'I'm not going to church,' . . . they looked at her like what do you mean?" Naomi went to practice but "hysterically" called her mother to come and get her. Still in town, Cindy marched into the church and left with Naomi. Later she wrote a scathing letter. The head of the sports department called her back with an apology of sorts. Eventually the poms coach was fired. However, the whole incident had "put a bad taste in [Naomi's] mouth, and I knew she was not going to go back [on the team]. And we sent her to an out-of-state college primarily for this."

Over a third of the families that I studied included helicopter parents—although mothers did virtually all of the actual work. These parents were defined by their hovering and their readiness with supplies, assistance, and guidance. A constant stream of cell and Internet communications alerted them to potential challenges, missteps, or emergencies. Mothers were in perpetual action, even across state lines, and did not assume that their children, or Midwest University staff and administrators, could manage difficult situations without their interventions.

It is tempting to view all helicopters as engaging in a similar form of parenting. After all, they carefully orchestrated their daughters' social and academic experiences and did not hesitate to intervene in educational institutions. Their interventions were costly, requiring time, considerable financial resources, social savvy, comfort with authority figures, and cultural knowledge of higher education. These parents were at least middle class, college educated, and—with one exception—married.

However, there was a split among helicopters. Six families operated like Taylor's. Her parents sought a career-building experience. Andrea's involvement was about developing Taylor's human capital—the skills, credentials, and knowledge base that often lead to career success and economic security. Ensuring Taylor's success, in the face of romantic and social distractions, involved constant surveillance and necessitated pushing back against normative femininity. I refer to these parents as *professional helicopters*, referring to their own career status, the precision with which most parented, and their goals for their daughters.

In contrast, Cindy represented nine sets of parents who prioritized a social experience and hoped to facilitate the "best years" of their daughters' lives. Poms were what Cindy thought college should be about: fun, school spirit building, and reinforcement of the traits she saw as Naomi's strengths—her sociability, style, and appearance. I refer to parents like Naomi's as *pink helicopters*, due to the traditionally gendered bent of their cultivation. They invested in their daughter's social activities, consumption, and sorority status, hoping to increase the likelihood of marriage to a wealthy man.

Table 2.1. Characteristics of Helicopter Approaches

Approach	Professional Helicopter	Pink Helicopter
Division of Labor	Inegalitarian: A mother's job	Inegalitarian: A mother's job
Interventions	Academic, social, and romantic	Social; only intervene in academics to prevent drop out
Early Career Development	Steer toward profession offering an ideal fit; utilize professional connections for internships and information	Facilitate internships in the big city (mostly in media-based industries)
Guiding Gender Model	Encourage later partnership to equally credentialed mate	Encourage gender complementarity; emphasis on normative femininity
Funding	A social contract: A parental duty to pay, child expected to perform	Paying is parental duty, with no limits
Ideal Resources	Knowledge of higher education, money, time, and social connections to other professionals	Extreme affluence, time, industry connections, and detailed understanding of the college social world
Families and Class	N = 6	N = 9
	UC: Gayle and Roger (Brenda)	UC: Connie and Logan (Abby); Alexis and Frank (Hannah)
	UMC: Carol and Nate (Alicia); Denise (Bailey); Anna and Steven (Erica); Andrea and Keith (Taylor)	UMC: Rachel and Matt (Julie); Cindy and Ed (Naomi); Cathy and Walt (Natasha); Marian and Rick (Nicole); Rhonda (Tara)[d]; Allison and Tom (Sydney)
	MC: Alice and Jim (Mary)	MC: Lacey and Arnold (Blair)

Notes: UC = upper class; UMC = upper-middle class; MC = middle class.
[d] = parents divorced or other parent deceased.

Andrea and Cindy did not share the same parenting approach. Not only class but gender mattered deeply, as it shaped the college experiences they sought for their daughters, the types of femininity they valued, and the futures for which they planned. The greatest commonalities between the two approaches were how much work and funding they required and who was expected to do the labor. Below I look at the burden that helicopter mothers shared, before examining differences in what they hoped to cultivate.

"Mom's Job"

Intensive parenting is a relatively new and deeply gendered phenomenon.[1] Mothers, but not fathers, are asked to give it their all. It
is a brutal competition: "Intensive mothering is the ultimate female
Olympics. . . . The competition isn't just over who's a good mother—
it's over who's the best. We compete with each other; we compete
with ourselves. The best mothers always put their kid's needs before
their own, period. . . . For the best mothers, their kids are the center of the universe."[2] The process continues well beyond high school
graduation.

Mothers were the primary pilots during the college years. In pink
helicopter families, they were mostly homemakers, assigned the task
of caring for their children. But in professional helicopter families,
having more time or earning less than their husbands did not explain women's involvement. Andrea, for instance, was a professor at
a well-ranked liberal arts college, while her husband, Keith, was a
certified professional accountant. They were both highly successful
and prepared to assist their children in developing careers; however,
only Andrea took on this extra burden—much like *The Second Shift*
famously described by Arlie Hochschild.[3]

Erica's parents exemplify the gendered division of labor typical in
all of the helicopter families that I studied. As her father, Steven, explained, he left parenting almost entirely up to his wife, Anna:

> I personally have a really laissez-faire relationship as a parent. I
> love my kids deeply and I care for them. But I'm not the kind of per-
> son that does hands-on. . . . My wife is much more active with them
> and more hands-on, talking to them on the phone all the time and
> checking up on them. She's more of a helicopter parent than I am.

Although his wife was employed as an educational administrator,
Steven went on to claim that he was simply too busy to hover: "I also
have a business where I have nineteen employees, so I have a lot of

stuff going on. I don't really have the time to devote to micromanaging how my kids spend their lives."

The fact that Steven's schedule was prioritized over Anna's became apparent in attempting to schedule the interviews. Erica only offered Anna's contact information. At the end of the interview, Anna asked if I wanted to interview her husband.

Anna: Great. Are you gonna want to talk to Steven?

Laura: I would love to. Is that something . . . ?

Anna: I don't know that he can talk for an hour and a half. That's what he said.

Laura: Okay. We can do a much shorter interview.

Anna: I don't think he's ever talked for an hour and a half unless it's about politics. Then he will talk for hours!

Laura: We could do forty-five minutes to an hour.

Anna: Oh, that would be great. . . . I would think some evening would be better for him. Let me look at my calendar. Just a minute. [*Long pause*] I have to look at two calendars.

Laura: [*Laughs*] Yours and his?

Anna: You know what I'm thinking? I know I have a meeting on Tuesday the fifteenth. So how about that? . . . Could you do six-thirty?

Laura: Okay.

Anna: Send me that e-mail confirming, and then I'll talk to him when he comes home from tennis.

The task of scheduling *both* parental interviews was often assigned to mothers. In this case, Anna had already talked with Steven, assessed his interest, likely informed him that he needed to do this, realized that he was only so knowledgeable about his children (as opposed to politics), negotiated the interview length with me, and located an ideal spot in his schedule during a time that she was not going to be home. I was even instructed to send the reminder to her.

Like other men married to helicopters, Steven made assumptions about the knowledge domains of fathers versus mothers. When I asked him what type of issues his daughters would call him about, he noted, "Anything that has to do with fixing anything. Or problems they have with the car. I don't get the crazy calls where they're having trouble with . . . their friends or relationships. They have assigned that to their mother, and we're okay with that." He explained that his wife possessed special talents that made this arrangement work well. "She speaks to their emotional needs. . . . I don't know how much help I would actually be because I'm pretty clueless with all that stuff myself." By claiming incompetence, Steven exempted himself from sharing the burden.

When asked if it was possible to "over-parent" a college student, many fathers revealed that if it was up to them, they might have preferred a less intensive parenting style for their children. Steven explained, "There have been times when I think [my wife] should . . . She's been a little bit of a buttinsky. She's been that way as long as I've known her. By and large I think the kids kind of appreciate that. They like that somebody's really concerned about every move they make. And I don't really care because it's not me doing it." Most husbands of helicopter wives arrived at this same conclusion.

Had I not interviewed fathers, I may not have realized how much of the work that I discuss in this chapter was deemed "Mom's job." Helicopter mothers tended not to complain about doing it mostly alone. They were sometimes annoyed at the depth of their children's needs. They got tired. More often they were frustrated or angry when their children, university staff, or daughter's boyfriends and friends got in the way of their well-orchestrated plans. They did not, however, call out their husbands for their limited role in parenting their college-aged daughters. They may have remained silent, in part, after internalizing the notion that the parenting Olympics are an individual, not a team, sport.[4]

Cultivating Success

Six professional helicopter families prioritized the academic and career-building aspects of the college years—a task for which most were well suited to assist, given their own career successes. They helped their daughters to get on—and stay on—MU's exclusive professional pathway. One of the first challenges they faced was identifying their children's academic strengths, a process that started before college.

Professional helicopters conducted a realistic inventory of their daughters' academic capabilities. They believed in their children but were not inclined to set them up for failure. Gayle, for example, got a crash course in architecture before encouraging Brenda to pursue her budding interests. She explained, "When we looked at all the colleges, we looked at all the architecture departments. As we looked at people's portfolios, we're going, this is probably not happening." Architecture was unlikely to work out for Brenda due to her limited math skills. Frank assessments of daughters' abilities enabled these families to avoid costly career detours.

The diversity of academic options at a school like Midwest U posed a potential risk for professional helicopters. They did not want their daughters to select a major that did not offer a clear career payoff. Socially oriented students flocked toward fields like communications, fashion, tourism, recreation studies, and fitness. At MU, there were also a number of "business-lite" majors, such as arts management, outside of the nationally ranked Business School. Many of these majors are linked to low-paying media- or entertainment-based jobs. Some lead to fields not requiring a college degree, such as event planning. Nor do they offer direct avenues into graduate school. Such majors were a key piece of the party pathway at MU.[5] It was easy to get shuttled in this direction, even for students who arrived with other career plans.

Professional helicopters pushed back. As Andrea told me, "Some of her friends were going to be . . . communication majors. We said, 'Taylor, you can write and you can comprehend. . . . You can take those skills and do something else with them.'" Instead, she nudged her daughter toward biology, in preparation for the dental career in which Taylor had expressed interest. Similarly, Roger explained, "I felt [telecommunications] was a useless degree. . . . Because what do you do with telecom? That's the problem. . . . I was happy when she came up with the nursing idea. . . . It fit my criteria. You're not wasting your time. You're still taking anatomy, which will translate as a science. That's good." Notably, it was his wife, Gayle, who did the reconnaissance work, sending her daughter newspaper clippings about the demand for nurses and their average salaries.

Professional helicopters tapped their social networks when they did not have personal information about particular fields. Thus, as Anna described:

> We have friends who are very successful in marketing. Erica . . . called them, and they counseled her and said, "It's okay to go into marketing. You can be very successful there, and there's lots of different directions you can go." [Laura: Did she do that on her own accord?] No, [it] was me urging her to do it. . . . But once she did it, it was a fabulous experience. . . . That really taught Erica how to write a note and say thank you for taking the time. Which she transferred to all her job interviews.

Anna had been leery of marketing, aware of its reputation as a business-lite major, even though Erica was going through Midwest U's highly ranked Business School. Her friend assured Anna that Erica could get a good marketing job and provided Erica with new contacts—the kind of social ties that would lead to internships and, later, employment. Anna used this as a learning opportunity to teach Erica practical skills that would be useful in navigating the job market.

Career planning was a long-term game. Professional helicopters prepared for graduate school well in advance. Taylor's parents, for example, sat down with her at the start of college and looked at dental school applications to see what she would need to get accepted into a top dental program. As Keith described:

Andrea is a professor so she knows what everybody is looking for. She has interviewed people for scholarships and she . . . [knew] that the service component is a big thing. They're looking for a certain kind of person. The academics tell you a part of it, but then they are looking for people to be good spokespeople for their schools when they get out. [Knowing this] gives you a big leg up.

This "leg up" required inside knowledge of graduate school and the ability to research what specific programs entailed. Taylor did not receive this information from MU, despite being on a pre-dental track from the start. Her parents also arranged a shadowing opportunity that helped build her résumé and gave Taylor the opportunity to ascertain if dentistry was for her.

Professional helicopters fostered dialogue around academic progress. As Nate noted, "Alicia always talked to us about the grades and stuff. There was always open communication if she was doing well or not well in a class." Through such conversations, parents could carefully track their children's progress. They were able to step in and provide assistance before it was too late. As Andrea described, she would

have Taylor call us before a test [and] after the test. If she was struggling, we would say, "Go get tutoring." I told her I paid . . . $20 an hour to have somebody tutor me through doctorate-level statistics. It made all of the difference in the world. These MU tutors are charging $15 an hour. I [say], "Taylor, pay them $20 an hour. Go get the help that you need to get through these classes."

It was less likely that their daughters would make problematic missteps, or that these missteps would go unnoticed and become compounded, when someone was watching.

Successful helicopering, however, required a daughter's cooperation. For instance, Carol often felt that Alicia ignored her academic advice. She warned against a more advanced math class early in college, fearing it would pull down Alicia's GPA, but, as she recounted:

> Alicia didn't listen to me, which was a mistake, because she took that Finite Mathematics class her first semester, and that sunk her ship. [Laura: And you had told her not to?] I begged her not to. The law professor at one of the orientation sessions said, "Honestly, wait until your sophomore year." It's a weed-out class. . . . She was being stubborn.[6]

This grade would bar Alicia from admission to the competitive Business School, as her mother had feared. Carol also suggested that Alicia take advantage of study abroad. Yet she "couldn't entice Alicia for anything. . . . Her sister went to Australia for student teaching. . . . And it was a great experience, but Alicia wasn't even remotely interested."

These parents were aware of the risks posed by the party scene. Andrea, a professor, explained, "It's horrible, and I watch it at [my similarly ranked college]. I watch these kids and these science majors. We get the fallout when they don't get the good grade in organic [chemistry]. . . . It's grueling and it's hard when all of your friends are out partying . . . and you've got to study . . . but it's the choice you've got to make." Gayle rejoiced when Brenda got placed in a room near the resident assistant. She noted, "When Brenda first moved in, she was next to the RA, which she didn't like. I'm like, 'Yes!' [*Laughs*] I said, 'This won't be the party room, that's good.'"

At the same time, professional helicopters recognized the value of extracurricular activities. Gayle emphasized, "You've gotta get into something. You've got to join some clubs. . . . You can't just go to class. You have to do a little bit more than that." Four mothers even suggested sororities. As Andrea explained:

> I pushed Taylor to join a sorority because I thought MU was so big and it's a place for you to connect. . . . A lot of things happened

through the Greek system at MU. . . . After watching [my oldest daughter in the alternative dorm] with all of these people that didn't want to do anything mainstream, I thought, well . . . maybe this will provide those outlets.

Andrea hoped the sorority would offer Taylor a rapid path to social integration on campus.[7]

When the social scene also introduced derailing temptations, parents helped their daughters balance competing demands. During a difficult week, Taylor reported that she

had a long talk with my mom today. I wrote it down. Homecoming week is this week, and my roommate plans everything. . . . She's all pressured. She's planning all these activities with one of the frats. . . . I planned to study all week, and then I could celebrate. But then my roommate is like, "Why doesn't anybody come out?" My mom was like, "Just try to stay out of her room as best you can during the day."

This advice, which Taylor took so seriously that she wrote it down, gave her the confidence to focus on her studies and a plan of how to do so, without avoiding the festivities altogether.

Professional helicopters provided a veritable guidebook for safe partying that went beyond the "don't drink and drive" cautions offered by others. As Gayle discussed:

My last message to all three [of my children before they went to college was], "Promise me you won't [funnel] because you can die!"[8] I talk to them about it all the time. . . . "You put your drink down, absolutely don't pick it back up. . . ."[9] The only time they went on spring break, senior year of college, I said, "Please, just be so careful. . . . Always have someone with you. Never walk alone." . . . You just hope that they think about it in the back of their mind. When something starts to happen, maybe they'll think, "Mom said not to do that."

Women heard the messages their mothers gave them. Many repeated this advice to their peers within my earshot. Those who had exposure to this advice took fewer risks and were less likely to find themselves in dangerous circumstances. Colleges often find it difficult to offer this type of precautionary advice to students because it reads as victim blaming. Only those students with savvy, college-educated mothers may come equipped to deal with the risks of the party scene.

An intense surveillance system also helped parents monitor their daughters' social activities. Andrea had the contact information for all of Taylor's roommates and their parents programmed into her phone. She would call Taylor's roommates to ask them to care for Taylor when her daughter called home drunk. These parents intentionally incorporated themselves into peer networks. Thus, Denise would invite Bailey's friends over for small parties, even though it was a few hours' drive to her house, with the intent of getting to know them.

Many also instituted a checking-in system. As Denise reported, "Bailey's twenty-two. [I said,] 'I know you're going to go out. . . . You have to call me when you wake up the next day.'" If children did not make the required call, parents acted immediately. One morning after a night of partying, Taylor was not answering her phone. Despite being out of state, Andrea "was on my way. I was driving up to Fairview in a panic, and I had campus security coming."

Cultivating Fun

Pink helicopters believed that a social college experience required just as much oversight and involvement as a career-building experience. They understood that both fun and valuable connections flowed from participation in college social life. Roommate selection and sorority admission were thus immediate concerns.

Affluent out-of-state partiers flocked to the dormitory I studied because it boasted a strong social reputation. Despite the fact that this residence hall was far from undergraduate classes and had few amenities and uninspiring food, pink helicopters supported this decision.

Sometimes they even did the online and word-of-mouth research to figure out the "best" (i.e., most social) place to live. If their daughters were not placed in the correct dormitories, they called and complained until the situation was remedied. For example, Cindy "took care of it" when Naomi was initially placed in a less social dormitory. The threat of walking with tuition dollars was often effective.

Parents also took action when roommate assignments appeared to block social success. Alexis believed this was why her daughter initially struggled to make friends: "Hannah went from this unbelievable crew of friends . . . like forty to fifty kids. They called Hannah 'the Mayor' [because she was so well connected]. Then she goes to MU . . . and she knows no one and she doesn't have any friends and her roommate stinks." When I asked what was wrong with Hannah's roommate, she noted, "Alyssa didn't ever want to go out with Hannah, meet people. Because you chummy up with your roommate, you go out, you mingle. [Alyssa] was a total homebody. . . . She didn't want to do anything. She was a total trip. That made it really hard."

The two women did not connect because they lived in different worlds and had different interests. Alyssa was from a working-class family and could not afford to party. She was not the "right" sort of tie to pull Hannah into the dominant social scene. Her parents decided to act. "After the Christmas break, we told her: Change your roommate [or] change your room. . . . She changed her roommate."

Rachel got embroiled with the residence hall staff when Julie was unhappy about her roommate, a woman who came out as a lesbian. For someone from a conservative religious background, this was a difficult roommate assignment. Rachel recounted:

I fought with them all the time. I called the director . . . of the dorm area. She kept saying, "We can't move Julie because it's a bias. It's a prejudice, and this girl has every right to be in the dorm as Julie does. . . ." I'm thinking, "Oh, come on." Julie said when she went into her office, there was rainbow stuff all over. . . . I don't know if she, herself, was [a lesbian], and then felt bad about it. But I kept calling, saying, "You've got to get her out of here. You've got to be able to do something." [They said,] "Well, we'll get to it." I was really getting impatient.

Rachel was impervious to the residence hall director's explanation that her daughter's discomfort with homosexuality was an unacceptable reason to move. She only relented when Julie's roommate independently decided to transfer to a more supportive living situation and a spot for Julie's high school friend opened up.

Most pink helicopters expected their daughters to join sororities. As Rachel told me, "I was in a sorority, and we always talked about sorority, sorority, sorority. So I just assumed that Julie would be in a sorority. I never questioned that she wouldn't be." When her daughter missed the deadline to enroll in rush that first year, her mother flipped. She asked her, "You have goals, right?"—revealing the extent to which this was to be a priority.

These parents did everything in their power to make sorority admission happen. However, as Cathy described of her futile efforts:

Natasha probably could've gotten in. She said it cost too much, and she didn't want to do it. She read the book about pledging and she was scared to death. [Laura: Oh, that book *Pledged*?] Yeah. She was afraid they were gonna strip her down and make fun of her and [make her] go through hazing. . . . I had letters. I had a biography for her. I mailed them to sororities. I had everything in order for her, but she wouldn't do it. [Laura: Did you ever address her concerns about the stuff they talked about in that book?] I said, "Natasha, they aren't gonna do that." But I didn't really know. . . . I thought some things might go on. I said, "You need to do this to make new friends."

Cathy would only become more frustrated when her top-choice sorority called to invite her daughter to lunch and Natasha refused.

The preparation of letters claiming legacy status gave women an advantage in sorority recruitment. Several pink helicopter mothers secured these, combing their family and friends for potential connections. Rhonda "tried to get a rec [for Tara], but I really only knew people that were Jewish, and so I didn't have recommendation for anything but the [two Jewish sorority houses]." She deemed these houses lower status and instead tried to help Tara game the system in other ways.[10] "I found out you get points when you visit [sorority houses] before Rush." Armed with this information, she encouraged her daughter to accompany another floormate, who regularly ate with her older sister, to meals in a top sorority house. Rhonda was pleased with the result. "[Top sorority] was her number one pick. She got in. She had no trouble."

Pink helicopters also took care of mundane aspects of life that might have distracted their daughters from socializing. They made medical and dental appointments, provided morning wake-up calls, did laundry, brought or shipped special items from home, kept track of school supplies, and helped to decorate rooms. Rachel even prearranged for a new carpet, cut to size, to fit over the university floor so that Julie might be more comfortable. Social emergencies required immediate action. As Alexis reported of a last-minute need for a formal dress, "Hannah calls me in the morning [and says,] 'I can't find anything.' . . . It was a Thursday [two days before the formal] . . . and it was like three-thirty. . . . I said, 'Hannah, I'll overnight them to you.'"

The heavy involvement of pink helicopters was compartmentalized: that is, they were relatively unconcerned with how their children were doing in the classroom. When I asked Walt whether he talked to his daughter about her classes and major selection, he responded, "Not a lot. Umm, she just . . . Natasha wasn't, like . . . Uh, you know, we probably didn't, we probably didn't have a lot of dialogue about that. . . . Umm, and so she, she had no notion, I think, [of] what she wanted to do."

Naomi's parents did not find out her major until the end of college. Her father, Ed, noted, "Actually, Cindy and I didn't even know . . . until [graduation] day. We saw it was kinesiology. She'd never told us that. We looked in the program and we saw it. We had no idea." Still, this was still not quite right. Kinesiology was the department housing Naomi's sports communication major. This lack of information was remarkable given that Naomi and her mother, Cindy, spoke "every day," sometimes more than once.

It would take a serious academic issue to push pink helicopters into action. If women were failing a class, threatening their ability to stay at MU, mothers got involved. As Marian told me, "Nicole was like, 'I'm going to fail my math class,' so I made her go through tutoring. I said, 'You have to go because we're not going to lose this money out of pocket.'" Similarly, Rachel explained:

> The only time I got mad at Julie, in grades, was this blasted math class she had. She got a D. . . . That was freshman year, and then again sophomore year she retook it and ended up with another D again, and had to retake it a third time. . . . Being a parent, I said, "Do you know how much money this one class cost us? Nine credit hours at MU."

Concerns about money were ironic, given just how heavily pink helicopters funded their daughters' social lives, as detailed below.

Pink helicopters were active in one area of early career development: they secured internships for their daughters in big cities, predominately with media-based companies. For wealthy entrepreneurs, this was not too challenging. As Connie remarked, "Abby's fortunate to have a nice-looking résumé right now [because] . . . she's worked for some of my husband's businesses."

Other parents drew on their social networks to advantage their children. Alexis reported, "One of [Hannah's father's] really good friends in the city knows the owner of [a major media studio]. . . . They interviewed her and she got the [internship], and then she got it again the next year." Cindy saw no way around this sort of parental intervention, "I hate to say it but that's how you get [internships]. . . . If it's a ten-point plan, you get eight points by somebody you know, and then you have to be a raving idiot not to get it then. That's the only way to get them."

These positions often involved scut work, although better and more powerful connections came with more substantive tasks. They were typically unpaid, but pink helicopters were happy to financially support their daughters as they completed internships. Internships accomplished a record of "prior experience" for women's résumés— something less affluent or less connected families could not afford to provide. Most importantly for pink helicopters, positions in major metropolitan centers allowed women to grow comfortable in the cities where they would reside after college.

Cookie-Baking Mom vs. Career Woman

Helicopters' focus on cultivating success or cultivating fun was, in large part, informed by beliefs about women's place in labor and marital markets. Pink helicopters encouraged their daughters to eventually become cookie-baking moms, while professional helicopters worked hard to develop them into successful career women.

Rhonda offered the most unfiltered commentary on pink helicopters' support of gender complementarity. Rhonda saw the fact that she herself had to have a career as a failure and did not want this for her daughter—regardless of Tara's own interests:

> I don't want Tara to be a career woman. I'm sorry. A lot of people do. I don't. I have this one girlfriend whose daughter is going to be a doctor, and she's so excited. I wouldn't want Tara to be a doctor. No way. . . . I don't think it's necessary to be a doctor, a female doctor. . . . If you're a female doctor, how are you going to . . . be with your kids? And she's not the doctor type. She's too social. I wouldn't even care [for her] to ever be a lawyer. [Although] she wanted to be a lawyer, maybe.

Rhonda did desire a professional career for a son-in-law, though:

Rhonda: I would love her to meet someone like that. I told her to go to the law library, but she said you can't do that.

Laura: You want her to go to meet somebody there?

Rhonda: Yeah. I thought you could meet some law students. But you can't go to the law library, she said.

Laura: If you're not a law student?

Rhonda: Yeah.

Finding a successful mate was central to Rhonda's plan for Tara. "I want Tara to get married and have kids. . . . She'd like to have three kids, and I'd like her to have three kids. She wants to be a cookie-baking mom."

Most pink helicopters were not as explicit as Rhonda. However, they all believed their daughters would eventually be dependent on husbands for economic support, rather than relying on their own earning power. For instance, Cindy remarked, "Ideally, I would like Naomi to get married because I do not think . . . she's a great provider for herself. . . . I think she has to marry a millionaire." They did not assume their daughters were capable of financial self-sufficiency outside of marriage.

This assumption colored parents' interactions with their daughters and what they chose to emphasize as ideal work/family arrangements. Thus, Alexis told us that Frank urged Hannah to "just go for the money!" when selecting a marital partner. Natasha informed me that

> [my mother, Cathy] is constantly telling me I need to find someone. She told me that she'll start praying for a man. . . . [Laura, sarcastically: That's nice.] She says dark hair, cologne, and Catholic. Those are her requirements. And he should also have a PhD of some sort. The PhD equals wealth for her.

A year later Cathy confirmed her daughter's report by telling me, "[Natasha is] very talented. She loves to cook. She'll make a beautiful home, and she will have dinner ready. She will have that every night, and I hope he will appreciate that."

What these parents referred to is a postponed MRS, or "Mrs." degree, as discussed in chapter 1. They hoped their daughters would locate potential candidates during college, perhaps by hanging around the law library, but no one in this group advocated marrying during school or even right after graduation. Rhonda advised Tara to wait for a proven pool of candidates before committing to her current boyfriend, whose career path was uncertain:

> Her grandmother's told her, [and] we've all told her, we think she could do better. . . . I think she needs to go out and meet other people and give them a chance—particularly guys out of college. I think a working guy is different than a college guy that's drinking and smoking pot all the time. [They have] more direction in life.

The time to marry was well after college, when Tara would hopefully be networked with elite, successful men.

Given belief in gender-specialized marriage, cultivating traditionally feminine traits made sense for pink helicopter families. It started early. As Rhonda described:

> I loved dressing her, like dressing a doll. And she was very small, because she was on Ritalin, and it kept her kind of tiny. I used to buy . . . all this pretty appliquéd stuff and tights, and she had the hair bows to match every outfit. She just always looked so cute. People used to say, "Oh, I wish I could have her hand-me-downs." She just learned. And she's got her own sense of style. She does her own thing now.

The process was often intergenerational. Rhonda noted, "[Tara]'s got a real hip grandma. [She] dresses like Tara wants to dress, with the Dior and all the designer stuff. That kind of made Tara the way she is." For this family, the emphasis was on appearance—that is, looking "cute" and being "tiny"—as well as labels and material goods.

Most pink helicopter mothers spent a lifetime refining femininity with their daughters. They often felt it necessary to protect their investments by policing women's bodies. Several mothers commented on their daughter's shape or weight. As Cindy told me, "I know Naomi's chubby now. She tells me to prepare myself when I see her tomorrow because I'm going to have a heart attack." (I saw Naomi not long after this. She was far from what I would define as "chubby.") Many interceded in apparel choice. Alexis sent Hannah bags of designer clothes. She chided her, "Go shopping! . . . Are you crazy? . . . You deserve it. What is wrong with you? Are you a child?"—implying it was immature not to attend to one's looks through consumption.

In direct contrast, professional helicopters were adamantly opposed to a Mrs. degree, postponed or not. Although far from alone, Andrea was the most vocal. "At Midwest U—it's probably the same thing at any school in the Midwest—I sense a percentage of the girls are there, still in 2008, to find a man. It drives me crazy. Maybe it would have been on the coast too. Maybe it's just everywhere." These parents prioritized women's credentials, training, and knowledge, and found the gendered messages transmitted to students on MU's party pathway to be affronting.[11]

Andrea, for example, would come to dislike the sorority system because of how much it exposed Taylor to normative femininity:

> [The sorority has] outgrown its usefulness. . . . There's a ditziness that was pervasive in terms of what's important. They're . . . going to decorate for Christmas and decorate for this and decorate for that. . . . It's like you've got to be kidding me. [Even the] moms [are asking] how are we going to decorate the living room? [Laura: Their moms?] Yes. It's like who cares. I have a hard time—not that I want it to be a mess or whatever—but it's college. It's not really why they're there, to decorate.

Andrea countered this with what she referred to as the "I am woman, hear me roar" mantra. She informed Taylor that she was a strong, independent thinker and that it was "okay to outgrow" her sorority friends.

One of the central challenges professional helicopters faced was making sure their daughters did not downgrade career ambitions for a romantic partner. Thus, Andrea was on the alert when Taylor started dating a man with a large trust fund:

> He spends a lot of money frivolously to buy friends and buy acceptance. . . . All of these other girls [were] saying, "Wow, Taylor!" [Laura: The girls were thinking this was some amazing catch?] Right. Her worst semester was last fall when she was doing all of that fighting with Owen. I just said, "Taylor, you can only keep this all together for so long. You can't take organic lab and physics and biochem and be fighting with Owen twenty hours a week. Something's got to give and it was your grades." I think if Taylor hadn't given up on Owen, she wouldn't be going to dental school.

Convincing Taylor that Owen was not the right match required considerable work. Brenda's parents would encounter a similar situation and, over the course of several years, gently nudge her away from a religiously conservative man from a "wealthy family . . . [who] would buy her exorbitant presents." As Roger noted, "[We] did not want her to be bought."

These parents urged their daughters to place their own professional development ahead of that of their partners. As Gayle discussed:

> It's funny, our oldest daughter is dating this really nice guy. But he's been working now, wants to get his MBA, and she's working on her PhD. He's thinking about going somewhere, and she said, "If you have to go away [I can't] . . .'cause my parents raised me not to plan

my life around a guy." [*Laughs*] I was very happy to hear that. In other words, she's going to stay there to do her PhD and . . . [Laura: He's gonna have to make some accommodations.] Right.

Preserving space for self-development meant keeping marriage—to anyone—on the distant horizon. As Anna put it, "Right now Erica's career is of great importance to her, so she wants to launch that. . . . They really get married later now, you know? Thirty-plus wouldn't shock me. . . . None of [my daughters] are close to getting married right now. Or even thinking about it, to tell you the truth. . . . We've been more focused on the careers."

The goal was not for daughters to avoid marriage. In fact, several professional helicopters clearly had a "too late" age of marriage, just as they had a "too early." They simply wanted women to wait and develop a career before marrying, so as to avoid putting it in jeopardy. Eventually, marrying a similarly high-earning partner was necessary to maximize economic security. As Denise succinctly noted, this partnership "should be fifty-fifty"—with both partners offering relatively equal financial contributions. To get there, however, women had to first devote full attention to their own careers.

Footing the Bill

Both types of helicopters expected college to be expensive. Funding it was a taken-for-granted parental duty. As Marian commented, "It's our responsibility to pay for education. . . . It's a kid's responsibility . . . to go [to college]." Similarly, Anna described, "We're not millionaires, but . . . we felt it was our obligation as a parent to pay for our children's undergraduate education." Tom remarked, "I always expected that part of what you do as a parent [is] provide for the kid's education."

Putting the financial needs of college-aged children first was considered a baseline qualification for being a good parent. As Walt explained:

We're no saints [for paying]. We have a good lifestyle . . . but I don't belong to a country club. The car I have is older than the car my kids have. . . . Heck, I could've bought a second house, and I could've bought a boat, and I could've had no money to spend on them for college. . . . Whatever I have, I'm gonna spend it on my kids.

When I asked about parents with limited means, he indicated that "if you're not able to [pay the whole cost] . . . the debt should be somehow shared. Get a PLUS loan . . . or the parent makes a promise that, even though the loans are all in the name of the kid, they'll pay what they can once [their child] graduate[s]." Walt could not fathom what might compel other parents to not provide at least some financial support.

Helicopters shielded their children from the financial backstage of college. They paid their children's bills directly, put money into their accounts when they ran low, and provided their daughters with a steady supply of credit. Lacey described:

I guess Blair doesn't have a lot of responsibility, because we still pay all her bills. Even though we put money in her checking account . . . I just don't know that she is that good about checking it. Last year she had so much trouble with her checking account. I said, "You just can't write checks if there's no money in your account." And she said, "I only write checks for things I really need."

Daughters rarely made their own transactions or even had to think about the fact that funds were finite and needed to be managed. Their parents protected them from this worry. As Anna noted, "She doesn't have any idea how irritating the financial part was. [*Laughs*] That's our responsibility. That's not to put on Erica, who's a total wild spender."

It was hardest, however, for pink helicopters to set spending limits. Costly designer clothing, restaurant bills, bar tabs, spring break travel, and study abroad (or, as Cindy called it, "the party abroad") seemed justifiable if they enhanced the college experience parents desired for their children. Every cost was potentially legitimate. These parents readily admitted they were "spoiling" their children but felt that this was to be expected. As Alex remarked, "Everybody wants the best for their kids. And if they have the means to do more for them, not just physically but economically, I don't see why you wouldn't do it. Of course, what you're doing is you're spoiling them."

At the high end, women spent $600 to $700 a month for discretionary purchases (in 2004–2008). This was on top of tuition and fees, room and board, books and supplies, computers and other electronics, travel between school and home, automobile and medical insurance, cell phone bills, summer internship expenses, sorority fees, spring break costs, family vacations, and holiday gifts. As Rhonda admitted, "I give Tara $350 [for] a month's allowance. . . . And then I get a credit card bill for $350. So in essence, she's spending $700 a month."

One month Naomi reported her typical (parent-paid costs) as follows: $150 for one pair of designer jeans and $40 for a "cute top" to accompany it; a $200 bar tab (it would have been more, but men picked up many of her drinks); $100 for five meals at restaurants not covered by the meal plan; $100 for appearance-related items: one haircut and eye shadow plus lipstick from Smashbox—her favorite makeup company; $20 for a fifth of Absolut vodka, necessary to "pre-party" (i.e., get buzzed before heading out for the night); and $40 in taxis to get home from bars and fraternities. The total damage? $650.

Several pink helicopters described having to pick up additional hours of work, take on new jobs, and dip further into their savings than they had initially planned. For example, Allison had to go back to work. She explained:

> I get the bill from the checking account, and I see where all the debit cards are spent. [Laura: Connelly's Sports Bar perhaps?] R: Yes. [Laura: Ryan's?] Yes. You know the list. What's Sydney doing there I wonder? [Laura, jokingly: They do serve some food along with beer.] [Sigh] For the extras we just kind of rolled our eyes and

said okay. I guess we're too easygoing, but you only do this once. Luckily, I work part-time. That was kind of why I was working. [Laura: To help cover . . . ?] Yes, the extras.

The "extras" associated with college life could cost parents a great deal of money.

Because professional helicopters did not see fun as part of what they owed their children, they were less likely to cover every possible cost. As Alicia's father stated, "We don't give them anything for buying sorority clothing and for going out for dinners. . . . It probably cost them $200 or $300 a month . . . of their own spending money [from summer jobs] to do whatever they wanted to do." These parents determined some expenses to be excessive. Brenda's parents (who were interviewed together) told me:

> *Roger:* A lot of her friends wouldn't be caught dead in Kohl's [a lower-cost department store] because that's what their parents have instilled in them. Brenda doesn't have that problem.
> *Gayle:* No. She's not brand-oriented.
> *Roger:* Not at all.
> *Gayle:* The only thing she will spend money on are blue jeans. And then that's her money 'cause I am not paying those prices.
> *Roger:* She wouldn't have got it at home 'cause we're not brand-conscious.

Brenda did not have the "expensive tastes" that Cindy and other pink helicopters ascribed to their daughters, in part because these were not cultivated.

Instead, professional helicopters tended to freely spend money on their children when they believed learning and acculturation were in store. Erica's parents, for instance, were thrilled to offer her "an opportunity to go junior year abroad for a semester—you should really do that." They were not willing to fund less rigorous programs that did not require their daughter to adjust to a foreign culture. Thus,

Erica ended up in a small city in Spain, where she was forced to speak Spanish and had less access to American party culture. This was not Naomi's "party abroad."

For these parents, academics always superseded the importance of earning money through paid labor, even in the summer. As Keith explained:

> We encouraged Taylor to [take summer courses] to give her some relief from her regular course load. . . . [We asked] what's the stuff that's going to make her more successful in the long-term? I don't think it was working during the summer, [instead] doing the academic stuff that would help make her successful in her classes and [help her] to get into dental school.

The trade-off was clear: time spent in paid employment was seen as time spent away from career development.

Unlike their pink counterparts, professional helicopters tied financial support to academic performance. They provisioned money in ways that held their daughters to specific standards. As Anna explained, "Erica has a pretty measly [scholarship] of $500 a semester. That's nothing. [But] we said if you ever lose that, you're out of there. You're completely on your own. We're not gonna have you go to MU and get below a 3.0." Nate referenced a car insurance discount. He told Alicia, "You get a 10 percent discount if you get a B average. She knew she wanted to get at least a B average so that that could occur."

Professional helicopters did not care about the financial aspect of the arrangement. What mattered most was signifying the baseline performance standards they expected in return for their financial support. It was an accountability contract. Parents laid out the conditions under which they had a financial responsibility to their children. If the contract was broken, they were no longer obligated to pay. Denise explained, "I think you can [pay], if you have the means to, and I think you have to set guidelines. Our guidelines were four years, get your grades [a 3.0 minimum]. If they started slipping or not going to classes or not getting their grades, then we would have said, 'No, either get a student loan or you're on your own.'"

Middle-Class Helicopters

Concerted cultivation is often described as a broadly middle-class phenomenon, in contrast to parenting in working-class and poor families.[12] However, among the families I studied, middle-class resources were not enough to ensure that parents could effectively execute a helicopter approach.

Mary's parents offer an example. They both graduated from Midwest U. Alice was a special education teacher who recently decided to go back to school for her PhD, and Jim was a traveling salesman for a farm equipment company. They were financially comfortable enough to pay in-state tuition for two children—although not much more. Mary's pictures and awards were displayed prominently in her parents' home, a beautiful rural 1850s farmhouse, and she had a close relationship with them. It was reasonable to assume that Mary's parents had baseline resources to be professional helicopters, and they certainly tried.

The first clue that they would struggle came in selecting a college. Mary did not start out at MU because she was insistent on being somewhere warm, near the Atlantic Ocean. Her parents were overwhelmed. As Jim described, "We didn't know anything about those universities there. . . . The only connection I could think of was a cousin's boy who went to Florida or Florida State. And that was remote, so we really didn't know anything about it." They soon realized they missed key features of the southern institution they selected.

> *Jim:* One thing about [the college] that I don't think any of us [realized] . . . the big majority of the people who are living in the residence halls are there on sports scholarships. Everybody else drives in [from nearby luxury communities].

Alice: Those are some of the wealthiest communities in the world. So when you see fashion things that say Paris, New York, [city name], that's where she was. It wasn't the same type of . . . kids that she had always been around, and they were very wealthy. They go to clubs. . . . It was just a totally different lifestyle.

It is unlikely these features would have escaped other professional helicopters' attention, since they had a broader, more cosmopolitan knowledge of the higher education system. Few would have even considered this expensive, yet poorly ranked school.

The mistake necessitated a fix. Mid-year, when they realized how unhappy Mary was, they "swooped in. . . . My brother gave us tickets. . . . He had some vouchers so we could fly down. We rented a vehicle and loaded up her stuff." Before she left, Alice called MU and secured a spot for Mary, who agreed to go mainly because there seemed to be no other option—not because it was an ideal fit for her.

While at MU, Mary's parents needed her to work. As Alice noted, "Mary's been a lifeguard. She's been an RA [resident assistant]. She's worked at the offices [on campus]. She worked at the [local bookstore]. She worked out at a Chick-fil-A. She even subbed in school. [When] she's been home for breaks, the high school would call her. . . . It will give her . . . spending money. [Jim: She got what, four W-2s this spring?]"

Alice and Jim also seemed unaware of Mary's academic limitations. They encouraged her to think big and pursue a psychology PhD *and* a JD degree. This plan would be difficult for anyone, and it seemed to be beyond Mary's reach. Despite her hard work, she would struggle. They also pushed her to attend a law conference designed for practicing lawyers, not undergraduates interested in law.

Jim: It was all lawyers. . . . I think she's having a good experience down there, though. She said, "I'm getting introduced to all these people that are supposed to be the hotshots in my area." I said, "Are you taking notes?" She said, "Yeah, I'm getting to learn who these people are." I said, "You need to know that."

Alice: Make connections.

Jim: [Learn] who the movers and shakers are.

I did not know for sure, but I imagined that the "connections" Mary was supposedly forming were unlikely to translate into anything.

Being a middle-class pink helicopter was no easier. Lacey had enjoyed her daughter's social success in the local working-class high school, where Blair was selected as homecoming queen. She wanted Blair to replicate this at MU; however, the family had lost their relative class advantage. Lacey did not anticipate the wealth in the sorority system, where she came to feel that Blair was "living with a hundred spoiled rich girls who get whatever they want." It was hard to keep up financially. As Arnold complained:

> She's out of control. . . . We've got her checking account set up where if she writes a check and there's not enough money in the account it comes out of our account. In a period from November through December it took $1,000 out of our account, and this is basically spending money. . . . This is her going out to the mall.

Blair's parents scrambled to cover their own costs that month.

Mary's and Blair's parents were actively involved in their daughters' lives. A few students and parents even identified Lacey as the classic example of a helicopter mom. Yet their interventions were often missteps, or they failed to help with the same ease, because they lacked some of the same assets. As I discuss in the latter half of the book, it took immense amounts of family resources to successfully navigate children through a school like Midwest U. Even small disparities could translate into serious disadvantages.

THREE

Paramedics

L *ydia's parents lived out of state in a wealthy Midwest community, in* a large and welcoming brick house with a beautifully mani- cured lawn. Alan was a certified professional accountant; Sally was back in college obtaining a second degree in music after a long career in nursing. They ushered me into a formal parlor past a gleaming grand piano. Having come from a nearby suburb where I interviewed Taylor's highly educated and involved parents, I was expecting an- other set of professional helicopters. I was deeply surprised.

Lydia's parents would help me make sense of those who were neither on the highly involved nor uninvolved ends of the parent- ing spectrum. As Alan explained, "When they leave the nest to go to college, it's a transition of cutting strings every week. . . . As a par- ent you're still sticking your fingers in there, making certain they're settling in and everything is going right. . . . They don't need a lot of you . . . but they also know that you're there if they need you." I won- dered if Sally was simply the helicopter in this family, explaining how Alan could maintain such a non-interventionist style; however, she had a similar view: "This is a time where they need to get away, but not. They need some space, but not. It's sort of like short leash, long leash, give them a little more. . . . It's them learning how to flap their wings and start going."

I refer to twelve sets of parents, including Lydia's, as paramedics. Their hybridized vision of college emphasized independence, but under relatively low-risk conditions—essentially a trial run at adult- hood with a safety net. Paramedics sowed the seeds for their daugh-

Table 3.1. Characteristics of the Paramedic Approach

Approach	Paramedic
Division of Labor	Egalitarian: Shared between mothers and fathers
Interventions	Only in event of emergency; otherwise hands-off
Early Career Development	*Prior* to college; provide advice in college when asked
Guiding Gender Model	Reject gender complementarity; dependent on current class position
Funding	Youth financial responsibility valued; privileged parents hold back, and less privileged do what they can. All invest strategically
Ideal Resources	Moderate financial resources and exposure to higher education for rescues; continuity in parenting and independent or motivated youth are necessary
Families and Class	N = 12
	UC: Debby and Bob (Brooke); Sally and Alan (Lydia)
	UMC: Darci and Russ (Brianna); Molly and Vern (Lisa)[d]; Trudy (Madison); Renee and Peter (Morgan)[d]; Sherry (Sophie); Theresa (Tracy)
	LMC: Tami and Charlie (Alana)[d]; Betsy (Michelle)[d]; Don (Valerie)
	WC: Tina and Kenny (Monica)

Notes: UC = upper class; UMC = upper-middle class; LMC = lower-middle class; WC = working class.
[d] = parents divorced or other parent deceased.

ters' career and marital trajectories *before* college. During college they offered strategic financial, emotional, and logistical support, but did not take on routine responsibilities or prevent minor mistakes. However, if disaster struck, they jumped into action to minimize the damage.

Paramedics hailed from across the class ladder—from upper class to working class. Extreme class mobility landed some families in this group. They reined in involvement and held back resources, bucking the trend of extended intensive parenting among their peers. Less privileged paramedics had more exposure to higher education than others in their communities. They diverged from the tendency to offer bare-bones support during young adulthood. The result was a parenting approach that blended typically affluent and less affluent parenting styles. Paramedics rejected a gender complementary model of work/family relations and modeled this in their own relational dynamics: fathers were involved, and the division of parenting labor was much more egalitarian.

Building Independence

College move-in day was more difficult for helicopters than paramedics. Paramedics were not among the tearful parents anxious about leaving their children on their own. They treated college as a normal and healthy next step toward autonomy. As Renee explained to me, "It was a happy occasion. . . . I thought at Morgan's stage of life she was doing exactly what she should be doing. Of course, I missed her, but I was happy for her to be there." She was critical of Morgan's roommate's mother, Cathy, a pink helicopter who "sat in the dark crying" and "would not leave the room. . . . It was upsetting the girls." Renee scoffed, "It's not like they're going away to war! Morgan [and Natasha are] going to college just like [they] should."

Paramedics took a holistic view of independence. They were as invested in good relational skills as they were in English prose, and algebraic knowledge as they were in budgeting. Personal competence demanded edification in many different arenas, all of which paramedics deemed important. The "evolution" of the self, as Theresa put it, was not about narrowly instrumental career goals—nor was it solely about social competency. Rather, it was the ability to function as a well-rounded being, separate from one's parents.

These parents employed several techniques to foster autonomy. They let their daughters determine how often they interacted. As Kenny told me, "[Parents] can initiate too much contact. There [is the] expectation that you can call any time you want and get your student. I'm not convinced that cell phones are a great thing. . . . They need to learn to take care of some things on their own." Vern echoed this sentiment: "You gotta let them be their own people with their own set of circumstances and personalities. You're there when they need you. . . . You give them advice, most of the time hopefully solicited. Don't be a helicopter parent. Don't hover over your kids." While helicopters spoke to their children at least once a day, paramedics could go days or weeks without doing so.

When requests for advice came, paramedics involved their children in finding a solution.[1] Charlie suggested that parents should: "Try to restrain yourself as much as you can. . . . Sit down and talk to them logically about what they're doing and try to get them to think. . . . If you can do that, that's all the parenting you need to do, and these kids will figure out the rest." Alan noted, "I would try to have as much of the discussion come from her." When Morgan called for help, her mother would say to her, "You make good decisions, what do you think?"

Children were encouraged to make their own choices on a variety of issues, both social and academic. Thus, while Alan held anti-Greek sentiments, he did not attempt to interfere with Lydia's desire to become a sorority member: "I wouldn't have encouraged her to do it, but . . . I thought it was her decision. It's her life. . . . If I knew there absolutely was going to be some harm, then I would try to make them aware of it, so at least they can make an intelligent decision." When Tracy brought up the possibility of Greek life, Theresa "th[rew] out the questions and the reasons why . . . [and] the reasons why not." These details were not intended to make the decision for Tracy, but rather to inform her. Ultimately, "it was something that Tracy had to personalize and figure out on her end. . . . You trust their gut and instinct."

Paramedics assumed their daughters could manage the risks of the party scene. As Peter explained, "I didn't lie awake at night agonizing if they were out. I looked at both of my kids as being pretty responsible—not that they weren't doing stuff that I probably didn't need to know about—but I was pretty comfortable that they would make their choices." Likewise, Debby told me, "It was beyond my direct control so I just advocated. I never worried. I would just [say the] usual things. Don't drive drunk. Don't drive with someone else drunk. I knew they had good heads on their shoulders." Assuming their children were capable provided relief from the worries that hounded many helicopter parents.

Academically, paramedics were comfortable taking a backseat. Molly indicated the importance of allowing youth to select their courses. As she noted:

> I remember when [my oldest] started at MU. The day we went for orientation and signed up for classes, [the advisors] wouldn't let the parents go up. There were some parents that were just like, [*gasp*] "I can't believe we can't go!" I'm thinking . . . these kids are college students. . . . It's good that the parents are out of the way.

Parents expected their daughters to drive these important decisions. Thus, when Tracy studied abroad, it was on her initiative and not suggested by her parents. In fact, Theresa told the complaining older siblings, "Well, you guys didn't ask!"

These parents did not anxiously monitor academic performance. When I asked Alan if he "stayed on top of Lydia's grades," he responded, "No, in fact, I don't know that she ever gave us access to the online grading system. . . . We would ask periodically, 'How are you doing in the class?' I feel as a parent that I'm totally not in control. She is the one that has to control that."

Nor did paramedics veto career choices. For example, Kenny only insisted that Monica and her brother try to attend college. Beyond that it was up to them:

> I always told them I don't care what they choose to do. In the closest bigger town to us, there's a foundry. It's dirty, nasty, awful, hard work. But it has helped raise a lot of families in our community. I always said to my kids, if you choose to do that kind of work, I will support you 100 percent. But I want you to be able to choose, and without an education you can't choose.

Similarly, Alan wanted Lydia to have full information but left the decision up to her:

> I hoped that they would find their own path and not do something because Dad did it or because Dad [said to]. . . . If she'd have come to me and said music, I [would have] encouraged her. I would be frank with them about what the outcome would be, in terms of what their income-earning opportunities would be. At the same time, I'd tell them, "Don't make your decision based on what you will earn, because if you don't like what you're doing, you'll feel like a slave to your job."

It seemed likely that Alan would support his daughter's career path—as long as he believed that she had given the issue full consideration.

Even the dreaded "problem" boyfriend—a source of consternation for paramedic and professional helicopter parents alike—was handled diplomatically. Trudy bit her tongue when Madison dated a guy who "wasn't very motivated." As she explained, "I know that the more you push or turn against somebody, the more [they push back]. . . . [My husband and I] felt like we had to give Madison enough space, and this really is a learning experience. I was just hoping she would not stay with him forever."

After several non-confrontational responses, I gave a worst-case scenario. I asked Debby what if her daughter got engaged to the much disliked hometown boyfriend? What would she do then? Her response was telling:

> I think I would just be honest. Be aware that if you want to move up high in your career that it could be threatening to him. And he's probably going to be happy working at a low-level job and living in a little bungalow. If that's what you want, fine. But don't think he's going to get an MBA and make all this money. I think [it is better to]

giv[e] her the real picture as opposed to hitting her over the head with 'Oh, what a creep, don't be crazy and marry him.' Look at the realistic picture. Don't glamorize it.

Although it would pain her, Debby still refused to strong-arm her daughter.

Early Gender Influences

Paramedics gave their daughters the advice, support, and confidence to push back against traditional notions of femininity. However, they did the majority of this work in the years preceding college and hoped that it would bear fruit later.

If their daughters showed aptitude, they encouraged early academic interest in gender-atypical fields. For example, Alan could be hands-off during college in part because he had spotted Lydia's mathematical talent early on and suggested the high school accounting class that got her hooked. As Sally explained, they told Lydia, "There are no limits. If you think you can do it, you can. Alan, being in the field, could give them some real, legitimate information about women in accounting. He could say there's no reason you can't be a partner. There's a lot of women." Lydia was directly admitted to the competitive Business School accounting program. In this way, her career path was decided before she even arrived.

Paramedics also worked hard to downplay the significance of early romantic relationships in their daughters' lives. As Molly described, "Particularly the girls, since they were young teenagers, I talked to them about the need for being well-grounded and taking care of themselves in all kinds of ways. . . . [Do] not to look for somebody else to fill you up. Be a whole person." Theresa told her daughters, "I don't think that you need to have a boyfriend to make your world fulfilled. Don't rule out what [other] friendships and relationships can do." She would always ask, "Are you changing to accommodate them?" as a gauge of whether or not the relationship was a healthy one.

They emphasized the importance of economic independence. As Betsy explained, "I told Michelle for a long time that you have to be able to support yourself and not be too dependent on anybody supporting you. So whatever field of work she chooses, make a livelihood, make sure that if something ever happens to your significant other that you can support yourself, and that you're not depending on anybody else." Paramedics across the class spectrum shared similar advice during adolescence.

By college, paramedics appeared to be cheering on a refusal of gender complementarity that was, in fact, internalized through prior parenting. As Brooke's father commented:

> *Bob:* [My daughters] are not . . . the mean girl, sorority girl stereotype—the ones that are too blond and too pretty and too made up. . . . I respect that. They're willing to stand alone and go work and make a living. They're not just here to get a degree in. . . . What's the joke about?
> *Laura:* The MRS degree?
> *Bob:* The Mrs. degree. Yeah. . . . She doesn't strike me as the type of person that's gonna be happy staying home and raising kids.

He denied having any influence. Yet it was clear to me that her parents had modeled this. Before Brooke was born, Bob left his career to support Debby's. She ran a highly successful business throughout much of Brooke's childhood and did not engage in intensive parenting. Brooke grew up in a household where women's potential for financial and career success was normalized and the work of child-rearing was shared.[2]

While affluent paramedics swore they would not aggressively block any marriages (as Theresa put it, "It's definitely too big of a decision to impose"), they clearly preferred a model of women's economic security consistent with that of professional helicopters. Later marriage to an equal was ideal, as Debby's earlier commentary about the unambitious boyfriend suggests. They mostly imparted this preference structure to their daughters in the early years.

Less-privileged paramedics hoped for a similar future. Kenny "always pictured Monica marrying somebody who was a Mr. GQ businessman, upwardly mobile, maybe a politician" after college was over. However, many less-privileged parents had, themselves, been married between the years of eighteen and twenty-one, and they lived in communities where this was common. Monica's parents would thus come around to her decision to marry her hometown boyfriend when she was only twenty years old and never gave her the hard reality speech that Debby might have. This boyfriend was not an elite businessman, but he did bring in a salary that, combined with Monica's, allowed her to become financially independent from her family sooner than she might have otherwise.

"Skin in the Game"

Paramedics across the class spectrum framed college as a joint financial proposition. As Peter, who spent his adulthood in the upper-middle class, described, "I'm not a proponent of the free ride. I think that it's good for kids to have some skin in the game." Similarly, Kenny, who lived his whole life in the working class, argued, "The ideal would be that students finance part of their education or work to pay their own way through part of their college, knowing that their parents can back them up if needed. In other words, *it's not an entitlement; it's a protection* . . . . If I get in a spot, Mom and Dad are there to help me out" (emphasis added).

The difference in language use among paramedics and helicopters was striking. Paramedics did not see funding higher education as a parental duty. Instead, handing some financial responsibility to young adults was viewed positively: it was integral to the learning experience and kept students grounded. Alan explained:

The more affluent view of the world is what I was concerned with, that everybody has lots of money and they can do lots of things. Lydia maybe got some education [on that]. . . . [In college] I got around some people who were a lot wealthier than my parents were, and they found it a lot easier to do things. . . . But because my dad was on a farm, I couldn't get any money to borrow. You learn the world is not fair.

He suggested the importance of seeing outside the "affluent view of the world," in which young adults have everything they desire.

Paramedics also viewed paid employment as intrinsically valuable, not as a barrier to career development. As Kenny elaborated:

I think [work] helps keep them balanced. It helps keep them fo-cused. . . . There are a lot of people critical of that kind of thinking, but some of those same people will have their kids involved in ev-ery club and every after-school activity. . . . In my mind working teaches responsibility; it teaches interaction with your coworkers, your peers, your bosses. The fact is, unless you are independently wealthy . . . you're going to have to get a job.

Despite his more affluent class position, Peter agreed, "Work brings a tone; it gives you a sense of perspective. You have to balance, and you have to make trade-offs. . . . It starts to teach you little lessons that prepare you for the real game because it doesn't get easier." All para-medics' daughters worked during the summer, and most between five and twenty hours a week during the school year—regardless of class background.

For privileged parents, a paramedic approach meant intentionally holding back funds. Although they were multimillionaires, Brooke's parents' resented their older son's expectations of a free ride. Debby explained, "When our son was going to college, he was looking at all these very expensive schools and then taking it for granted that we would pay for college anywhere. I think we were a little bit . . . our son's sense of entitlement we found kind of galling." They asked their son to pay part of his tuition. As a result, he joined ROTC (Reserve Officers' Training Corps), which would cover costs in exchange for five years of service. His parents did not back down, although "we felt really a little bit guilty because if he gets killed in the war or whatever, he's done this for financial reasons. But in the end . . . I think he understood it, and I'm thinking he appreciates it."

Although privileged paramedics could have afforded all college expenses, some quite easily, they asked their children to cover personal costs, broadly defined. Alan refused to pay sorority fees, which ran into the thousands every semester. He noted, "I told them that if they did it, they would have to pay for all the fees associated with it because that, in my view, was a form of entertainment." Similarly, Trudy explained:

> Madison had to really stick to an allowance and survive. I think she appreciates it a lot more, and she decides what's important enough to spend it on . . . because she knows she can't call home and keep asking for more. . . . When she wanted to go on spring break, [my husband and I] were like, "Great. Now you know what you have to save for that to happen." And she did. She [also] took loans out for Barcelona [study abroad].

Privileged parents did step up financial infusions during key moments. For instance, in her junior year Brooke received a prestigious, but unpaid, internship in Washington, DC. Her parents made it possible for her to go and focus on the job:

> DC is really expensive . . . so [my parents] are like, "We can help you." Even living in a dingy dorm at George Washington, I was paying $250 a week. . . . Then they gave me spending money. . . . People obviously have to have enough money to be able to live in DC and work for free. . . . And pretty much all DC internships are unpaid. . . . There was one girl who . . . worked at a bar at night, so she came into [her internship] a mess. She was, like . . . the worst intern. Like, they'll never hire an intern again for that position because she was so bad.

This was a calculated investment. It would improve Brooke's résumé and ultimately position her to be comfortably self-sufficient sooner than she might have been otherwise.

Less-privileged paramedics also offered strategic financial support, even in the face of layoffs and crushing personal debt. Monica's working-class parents paid all of her direct living expenses during her time at Midwest University, as these were costs for which it was harder to get loans. Kenny noted, "We paid for her books and of course we gave her spending money. We provided a car; we provided all of her fuel, anything except her tuition and room and board—the things you can finance through college loans. . . . We didn't want . . . at the end of four years [for her to come] out owing $100,000." Charlie would fund Alana's housing costs starting her second year. She had trouble locating an affordable apartment, raising the danger of her having to leave school. His assistance made it possible for her to stay.

Hybridization of Class Culture

How could class-based processes possibly explain similarities in parenting approaches between Brooke's upper-class parents, who retired in their fifties after selling a multimillion-dollar business, and Monica's working-class parents, who lived off a small-town pastor's salary? Why did Lydia's paramedic parents not act more like Taylor's professional helicopter parents, despite the fact that both families were quite affluent?

For many American families, classic dimensions of social class do not neatly align, particularly over time and across generations. These disjunctures make it difficult to identify parenting approaches that define all privileged or less-privileged parents. It is important to understand how shifting access to social, cultural, and financial resources, as well as changing exposure to classed lifestyles and environments, shape parenting.

Brooke's family history—which shares similarities to Lydia's, Morgan's, Tracy's, and Brianna's—offers insight into why well-resourced parents might elect to pull back on involvement and financial support. Bob, Brooke's father, had decidedly working-class roots. His wife, Debby, reported, "Bob grew up in [a working-class, in-state city] in a family of seven. They were pretty poor. The kids were all piled into a station wagon [*laughs*]." Although she had a more privileged childhood than Bob, Debby also experienced significant class mobility over the course of her life.

Bob had aspirations to attend college. He and his siblings were the first in his family to do so. As he noted, "My parents . . . just didn't have the time and attention to [help]. They never even brought me to Fairview [the town around MU]. I didn't even know that MU was a better school than [regional school]." During college he "worked at stores and drove trucks on weekends. I worked in heavy industrial kinds of jobs in the summers. . . . I was paying for it myself." The college years were hard on Bob.

Bob and Debby got married in their early twenties. He was a probation officer and she was a nurse. They had a son relatively quickly. As I noted earlier, Debby started a successful business in health care, and Bob left his job to help her. During this time they had their last two children, both girls. Their class status changed suddenly; however, Debby felt their values and the people with whom they were comfortable did not.

> The girls grew up with a much higher level of living and expectation. . . . We lived in some really nice houses. . . . [Other] kids [would say], "Oh, you must be rich!" Yet you are kinda what you are, so even though we started having more money and more things, we still felt more comfortable with people that were more regular. Bob and I are kind of . . . creeped out by the whole social climby [thing]. . . . It was hard for us because, you start having more money, you start living in a nicer house, then people who have lower income are kind of intimidated that you live in that house, and yet you don't want to be with the people in that [type of] neighborhood.

What she describes may be a common response to rapid mobility—not fitting in culturally or socially with those you leave behind or those you are, ostensibly, joining.[3]

Access to the financial resources that would categorize Bob and Debby as upper class did not erase the effects of their more humble origins. As Debby remarked, "I think it's different when you're born to money. When you work hard and make it, you feel very fortunate, but you don't lose that sense of . . . we might be poor one day." They carried experiences and understandings more frequently held by those with limited resources with them into adulthood.[4] How they parented was both a reflection of where they came from and who they are now.

This was particularly apparent for Bob, who struggled with the fact that he had the wealth to provide his children with anything they could possibly want or need. He pushed against the privileges of his current class position by calling on the past:

> My grandfather had to go to work in the coal mines at thirteen. His parents died. People are capable of a lot more than the American middle class and upper-middle class really encourages in terms of self-reliance. . . . The whole idea is that you're preparing them to fare well. Not survive, but to do better than survival. Part of that faring well is to be able to make independent decisions and have some lonely nights and deal with some of their own emotional issues and financial issues.

It was hard for Bob to shed the belief that struggle and self-reliance would ultimately benefit his children. As Peter would describe of his own journey from working class to upper-middle class, "It kind of puts a value system in you."

Divorce could also change available family resources and, relatedly, beliefs about parental support. For example, Renee had many of the early markings of a professional helicopter. Everything changed when she and Peter divorced. She was still nominally upper-middle class, based on the alimony and support she received from Peter, but upending her life also changed her views on what they, as parents, owed Morgan.

> Morgan went from living in a nice, big, two-story house in [an affluent suburb to] . . . a 1,400-square-foot vinyl-sided house that's less than half that size. . . . I [told her] everything is not a Norman Rockwell picture. . . . Our [old] next-door neighbors have five kids, a big family. They all did overseas studies, and [the parents covered] their kids' education. I thought that's a fairy tale. Society . . . makes you feel like if your family's not this perfect little picture, then something's wrong with you.

In this case, divorce brought the couple's individual styles of parenting closer together. Renee's parenting approach would now align more closely with Peter's, ensuring that Morgan experienced paramedic parents.

Less-privileged parents often became more active than many of their peers due to experiences with higher education. Valerie's and Monica's fathers both had associate degrees. Alana's father was a graduate of MU who landed in the lower-middle class due to legal troubles and sustained periods of unemployment. Michelle's family profile looked quite similar, minus the legal issues. As a group, paramedics were the most educated parents in the lower-middle and working classes, which provided exposure to upper-middle-class norms about the life course and the value of college.

Among the less-privileged, college-educated individuals are likely the first to adopt a belief in the necessity of a protected young adult space.[5] Charlie, for example, explained, "I knew she needed to [go to college]. I knew that she wasn't done growing up. . . . I could see sparks of the person that she would become, but I knew that she needed more time. So I was as interested in the maturation process as I was in the education." He clearly absorbed the message that youth require "more time" and at least some parental assistance for optimal growth.

College also provided parents with skills and resources that they could marshal to solve significant problems. Valerie's parents had three similarly aged children (including a set of twins) to put through college. In Valerie's last years of high school, Don was laid off twice. The possibility that Valerie would accrue crushing debt to attend college kept her parents up at night. Her otherwise hands-off parents stepped into action. Don explained, "Valerie happened to get a scholarship, and my wife found that on the MU site. I found a scholarship on another school's website. . . . Before you know it, your school fees are cut in half. So we did all that. We did all the research on that." Impressed by their ingenuity, I asked, "How did you know to do that?" He responded, "It's not broadcast; it really isn't. You really have to do some digging. I'm in sales, and a lot of my job is lot of investigation. We use Google and things like that on the Internet. When you start focusing in on it, you find more and more avenues."

Parents who did not attend college themselves were not aware that such scholarships existed. Don knew to look. He also had specific knowledge about how to conduct Internet research, gained through his previous work, which led him to opportunities other seekers might have missed. Valerie's stellar academic record certainly played a role. But students like her often fell through the cracks at MU. Her parents' efforts helped to keep her out of substantial debt and gave her access to campus services geared toward assisting disadvantaged students. This was an example of a pre-college paramedic rescue.

Red Flags and Rescues

Paramedic parents, regardless of class background, were okay with missteps. As Alan remarked, "Make some of those mistakes . . . and she'll make some. I made some. That's part of growing up. . . . If they really want to do something, they'll figure out how to get it done. There will be stress in it. That's just life." They viewed this as a necessary part of the learning process. Vern explained, "They'll look back and they'll say, 'Boy, I learned from that and I shouldn't do that again.'"

However, paramedics were not uninvolved or disengaged. As Kenny clarified, "We tried with both of our kids to . . . give them some tools to learn with and guidelines to live by, and then let them experience some things without hovering over them. Yet, at the same time, we didn't just throw them out to the wolves without letting them know that we're there." The paramedic style was marked by this careful give-and-take. Parents intentionally gave their daughters room to grow and—ideally, before college—the tools, knowledge, and skills to do it, but they did not pull the safety net.

Paramedics were on alert for problems. As Theresa described, "You have a heightened awareness and your antennas up. If she's always been this way and all of a sudden isn't, then that would be a red flag." One red flag—or even several—did not necessarily warrant action. However, as Bob noted, rescues were necessary "if they screw up or get into legal trouble or have medical issues. Something outside of the norm." Rescues could range from a well-paced nudge to more intensive financial, emotional, and logistical support.

Every student needs occasional rescuing. Alana, for instance, made no friends her first year, leading her to consider leaving school. Charlie realized that her isolation was a consequential problem, and one that she was not taking steps to solve on her own. He began "prodding her just to go out and do different things. . . . She became involved in this outdoor adventure club down there. . . . She has developed into quite the little outdoorswoman." Alana would later define this as a turning point in her college experience.

A year after her initial wilderness forays, Alana broke her back in a diving accident. Her parents rushed to Fairview, set up a network of people in town to help her (as Alana did not want to return home), and kept a close eye from afar. After Charlie saw the effect the painkillers had on her mental abilities, he devised a plan. "I was worried after that back accident because I could see that she was still doped up. . . . I knew I had to do something to try to motivate her so I offered her $800 if she got all A's. The little rat did it! She came over to my house and pulled up the computer grades and said, 'Dad pay up' [*Charlie and Laura laughing*]." This tactic, while costly, was highly effective.

Charlie was not normally this involved. In fact, one reason Alana struggled to make friends her first year was the fact that she lived in a single room. Her parents had suggested there were benefits to living in a double. But Alana insisted. As Charlie noted, "She admitted to me later she thought it was a mistake. But . . . let's face it, she probably learned something." He was not unhappy that Alana made some bad decisions, but was there when she could not handle things on her own.

Not a "Typical" Father

As Charlie's story suggests, paramedic fathers were far more involved with their daughters than fathers in helicopter households. Bob, for instance, placed a high priority on time with his children—pushing against traditional family roles in which men are distant breadwinners and women are nurturing homemakers:

> I hugged them a lot and picked them up and carried them on my shoulders . . . and pushed them on the sled and taught them how to ride a bike, how to drive. . . . I went to field trips with them, and I spent evenings and weekends with them. . . . I think in traditional households the father doesn't spend a lot of time with any of his kids. Certainly, not his daughters. But that's old stereotypical behavior.

Vern also did not see himself as "typical": "I [am] much more connected to my kids than a typical father. I'm more of an emotional person and have feelings probably beyond what a normal father does. . . . If they needed somebody to talk to or a shoulder to cry on or . . . somebody to laugh with, they came to me. And that's great. They should have both [parents available]."

Daughters of paramedics were as likely to seek contact with fathers as mothers. Trudy explained about her two children, "They're both really close to [my husband] too. He's always been hands-on from the day they were born. . . . He's unusual in that regard. He's more involved than most dads." Similarly, Tami described, "Alana is sometimes able to open up more with Charlie than she is with me. He always seems to find out a lot more information than I do. . . . But it does not hurt my feelings. I am just glad to hear it from somebody."

Interviews with paramedic fathers were rich and emotional. These men had given great thought to their parenting approach and saw parenting as a primary role in their lives. In fact, one of the most poignant moments in the study came when talking with Alan:

> Alan: I was writing Lydia a letter for graduation this morning. It makes me teary-eyed to think about it. [Long pause, eyes welling up with tears.]
> Laura: That you're going to give her when she graduates?
> Alan: Let me get it together.
> Laura: I get so many tears. [Pause for Alan while he collects himself.]
> Alan: I forget what the question was.
> Laura: Not to get you crying again, but do you remember what it was you wrote, or where you were going with that?
> Alan: [Voice still emotional] The only thing I can guess is that my train of thought was . . . I suspect a child never fully appreciates, at this age in their life, how much their parents care for them.

When I told Alan that I got many tears during parental interviews, this was true. Numerous mothers required tissues. What I did not mention is that fathers, as a rule, did not cry.

There were a few explanations for paramedic father involvement. One related to early childhood experiences in working-class families. As Bob explained, "Because there were seven kids in my family and I'm the third, I was very comfortable with babies. My mom used to say, 'Here, hold your little sister.' I even changed diapers. . . . I was probably more comfortable around babies than Debby was. . . . I picked

[Brooke] up more. She has pictures [to prove it]." Alan noted that he "had a sister who was eight years younger than me, so I had a baby around me. I had changed diapers when I was very young, so that wasn't [challenging for me]."

A second explanation has to do with the dynamic between mothers and fathers. Paramedic parents shared a belief that measured involvement is desirable, and the consensus created room for both mothers and fathers to be relatively active. In contrast, men married to helicopter wives often disagreed with this approach but were unable to make a convincing argument for a paramedic style. Under these conditions, for men to be truly egalitarian, they would have needed to set aside their reservations about over-parenting and hover alongside their wives. Fathers who were unwilling to do this ceded much control over parenting responsibilities. They may have reacted to women's intensive parenting by dialing down their own efforts.

Continuity and an "Independent Streak"

Paramedic parenting often went smoothly. In a few families, however, this approach did not work well, and parental fixes were misguided or far from sufficient. What distinguished functional from less functional paramedic parent-child relationships?

Continuity mattered. As Debby explained of their earlier parenting style:

> Because [our kids] had to be independent, they became independent. Unlike most kids whose mothers [say], "Time to get up for school," our kids woke us up. They brought us coffee in the morning. . . . We weren't home when they got home from school. We say we did so good by being so bad. . . . They had to do it because we were running this business and we were preoccupied.

Debby's use of the word "bad" suggests awareness that they were working against the model of intensive parenting common among privileged families. Yet a number of highly educated, affluent parents took a decidedly less interventionist approach through childhood and adolescence, making paramedic parenting during college an obvious choice.

In contrast, when parents drastically shifted parenting styles, it could be rocky. As suggested earlier, this was not unusual in divorce. In several cases, mothers pulled back their helicoptering in response. Fathers could seize the chance to become more involved. As Vern remarked, "Lisa and I have grown very close together. . . . It's been incredible." However, the transition phase was awkward, especially if parents were not communicating. For instance, Molly told me she did not help Lisa move to college and set up her room, but Vern also stated, "I'm sure that her mom went down and was there to set her dormitory up. . . . I wasn't involved." Neither found out that the other did not help, and no one was there for Lisa on that day.

Children's own personalities were also consequential. Morgan and Sophie were two of the most passive women on the floor. While these women had other strengths, they did not possess the "get up and go" or "independent streak" that other paramedic parents saw in their daughters. At least on Sophie's parents' part, it was not for lack of trying to cultivate initiative. As Sherry recounted:

Sophie was always the type that wanted to do something, but . . . she had to be pushed to prove to herself that she could. Like she wanted swimming lessons, and [then] . . . she kept arguing with the instructor all the reasons why she shouldn't get in the water. She was probably three years old. . . . I finally said to him, "Push her in." You have to almost force her. He did, and she proved to herself that she could swim.

By college, however, Sophie still needed to be pushed. Sherry noted that on drop-off day, "It was really hard on her. . . . I remember pulling away on the shuttle that morning and seeing her on the curb just hysterical." Sophie would continue to "call and say, 'What are the dogs doing? I want to hear their voices.' Or . . . 'You haven't called me today,'" leaving Sherry to remind Sophie that "'I teach school. I tutor every day. I have stuff going on. You forget.'"

Sherry's choice to take a less involved approach was not punctuated by necessity, as it was for parents discussed in the next chapter. She knew it ran counter to Sophie's natural tendencies. But Sherry was not a helicopter parent, despite Sophie's inability to move out into the world on her own. This was a case of a poor fit between a parenting approach and the needs of a particular child. The mismatch would create problems for Sophie down the road.

FOUR

Bystanders

Robert was on the sidelines of Stacey's life at college. This was an unfortunate consequence of his limited college experience and his occupation. As Robert explained:

> If we were doctors, we'd lead them down the doctor path. If we were attorneys, we'd maybe lead 'em down that path and know all the ins and outs about it, but we're not. I'm a firefighter and I told [them], "You really don't wanna be a firefighter. I've done this long enough to know that you don't really wanna do this."

Robert's body had begun to wear down over the years, and the family worried every time there was a fire in town. He hoped that his children would find some other way to make a living, but he did not know how to assist them.

Luann was even less equipped to help her daughter Megan. She was a single mother living in the rural, in-state town where she had grown up. Every week she pieced together part-time waitressing jobs to feed and clothe herself and her youngest son, for whom she received no child support. Luann could not afford to worry about how her two older children were doing. She told them, "'You can join the Air Force or Army or have somebody else take care of you because I am not.' Otherwise you are hindering them as a parent. Who says I am going to be here tomorrow?"

Twelve sets of parents, who I refer to as bystanders, parented with minimal involvement in the academic and social spheres of college.

It was difficult to detect a gendered division of labor because parental intervention was so limited. Hampered by resource constraints and a lack of familiarity with college, bystanders were not in a position to micromanage or offer constructive advice. They shared some similarities with the "natural growth" parenting style common among working-class and poor parents of elementary-age students.[1]

However, not all bystanders were the same. Six sets of parents, including Robert, made emotional and financial investments in their daughters. Many of these parents were their daughters' biggest fans. I refer to them as *supportive bystanders*. Clustered in the middle and lower-middle classes, these parents believed in the transformative power of college and thought they should help finance a mobility expe-

Table 4.1. Characteristics of Bystander Approaches

Approach	Supportive Bystander	Total Bystander
Division of Labor	N/A, as neither parent is involved	N/A, as neither parent is involved
Interventions	None: Assume college will provide for daughter's needs as part of the cost	None: See daughter as self-sufficient adult and assume access to college services
Early Career Development	Enthusiastic emotional support	Detached
Guiding Gender Model	Pragmatic approach to work and family, emphasizing economic stability	Pragmatic approach to work and family, emphasizing economic stability
Funding	Parental duty to help out during college; promise of future loans thought to keep student focused	No assistance; students may be offering help to parents
Ideal Resources	Moderate financial resources	None
Families and Class	N = 6	N = 6
	MC: Susie and Zack (Emma); Eileen (Karen); Lori (Whitney)[d]	LMC: Jody and Paul (Carrie)[d]
	LMC: Janice (Becky)[d]; Rose (Crystal)[d]; Robert (Stacey)	WC: Diane (Amanda); (Amy)[d]; (Alyssa); (Heather)[d]; Luann (Megan)[d]

Notes: MC = middle class; LMC = lower-middle class; WC = working class.
Amy's, Alyssa's, and Heather's families are included, although no parent interviews were conducted.
[d] = parents divorced or other parent deceased.

rience. They were desperate to see their children achieve and were unflagging in their support—even if they could not offer active guidance.

In contrast, six other sets of bystander parents were removed from their daughters' lives. Gaining access was a challenge, due in part to strained parent-child relations. I was only able to interview parents in three of the six families. They were the most disadvantaged in the study, primarily from the working class. These parents did not root for their daughters or offer financial resources. The adult experience required little from parents, and many had little to give. For this reason, I refer to them as *total bystanders*.

Bystanders, as a whole, did not worry about their limited involvement because they assumed Midwest U was a full-service institution. Supportive bystanders believed they were paying for someone who knew "all of the ins and outs" to shepherd their children through college. Total bystanders were skeptical of higher education but believed universities would minimally "take care of" their students. All of these parents needed college to quickly and directly lead their daughters to economic stability.

On the Sidelines

Lori was the first bystander I interviewed. I had just completed interviews with a number of helicopter and paramedic parents, and had gotten used to the types of questions that prompted detailed response. Lori was a different creature entirely. When I asked if she could remember any issues that Whitney encountered during college, she said, "Nothing that stands out." When I asked about encouraging Whitney to be involved on campus, she noted, "[It's all] her choice. She just does it, then tells me, and I'm like, 'Oh good.'" When I asked about her concerns, she noted, "I've never ever worried about Whitney."

At one point I even apologized to Lori for the sorts of inquiries that I was making. I could tell they were going nowhere and was concerned that I was making her feel inadequate for not doing the things

I was implicitly suggesting parents should do. Hoping to convey implicit approval of her approach, I noted, "Forgive me . . . I keep asking you these questions because it's somewhat unusual that a child is so self-guided." Lori seemed to warm up:

> *Lori:* Yeah, I pretty much just left her alone and she's done fine. . . . You can't teach them anything when they're in college. . . . If they don't have the background and the upbringing and the common sense, you're not going to give it to them when they're eighteen and in school. You just got to hope for the best.
>
> *Laura:* It seems like you did something right because she seems fairly self-sufficient.
>
> *Lori:* Oh, she is. . . . It's really been an easy, quick four years compared to what I hear from other parents where I work.

My interactions with Lori taught me to be less assuming in my questioning and revealed that some parents—even in the middle class—took a strictly hands-off approach.

Lori's impression that there were no issues was telling. Every college student faces at least minor hurdles. Even the most non-interventionist paramedic parents with the most put-together children found it necessary to step in sometimes. Bystanders did not see these moments because they were not looking, did not know what a red flag looked like, or felt unprepared to offer the help their daughters needed. This is what distinguished them from other types of parents, who provided everything from strategic rescues to continual intervention in their children's lives at college.

Bystanders sometimes offered active parenting at earlier ages. For example, Emma's parents were involved in her high school activities. As Susie reported, "When we first went over to high school, [the band director] said, 'They will tell you that they don't want you here. They will tell you that you don't have to go to the contests. They will tell you that you don't need to get involved.' And he said, 'They won't mean it.' I said, 'Okay.' So we jumped right in."

In college, however, they took a different approach—distancing themselves from Emma's education. Zack explained, "At seventeen, eighteen years old, when you're off to college, it's a whole new experience. . . . You can't live for them. You certainly can't be around them like you could when they were in high school." When I asked Susie if it was difficult to step down the level of involvement, she noted, "No, we still had [our youngest child], and he was still playing football. We were so involved in his life . . . it was kind of like, 'Oh yeah, she's [at MU].' She always seemed well adjusted. It wasn't worth worrying about because we think she's okay."

Emma's parents envisioned their new role as that of enthusiastic supporters. They may have left behind their advisory role because college presented a new set of challenges that they were less comfortable addressing. As Susie stated:

> Emma wanted to go into dentistry. We thought that was wonderful. . . . I sometimes wonder if we weren't too excited and kind of kept that alive because we were just like, "Oh yeah!" And everybody would say, "Oh, Emma's gonna be a dentist!" Throughout the family it was just gonna be big, and we'd talk about it and go, "Oh, Emma's gonna go to dental school! It's great!"

Emma's parents did not know what it would take for her to become a dentist. Their lack of involvement was a sharp contrast to the parents of another budding dentist, as discussed in chapter 2: Andrea literally walked Taylor through the steps necessary to gain admission to dental school.

Emma struggled to make dentistry work. She received her "first C ever" in her second year of college. Susie and Zack, trying to cheer her up, told her that this was to be expected: "You're in college, you know. It's something totally different than high school." But what Emma really wanted was guidance on how to balance academics with her sorority's social requirements. She noted, "I think what is most difficult about college is not necessarily the [level of] school work. It's the organizing [of] my time. . . . Giving the right amount of time to what's [important] and prioritizing." She was coming to realize, "The more I saw of dentistry and what it entailed, the more I was like, 'Ew, I don't wanna do that!'" Emma worried that her parents did not see or accept what was happening because "they didn't want me to end up like them."

It was more likely that Emma's parents did not understand the social requirements involved in participating in a top sorority. Susie even cheered on Emma's social success:

> They get all caught up in that rush thing down there. It's a big thing and everybody else is going through it. . . . I remember the excitement when she kept getting through [each round of rush], and she kept getting bids to come back [to top houses]. The excitement just started going [*laughs*]. . . . When she did get in, she really seemed excited, and she really felt that this would be good. Obviously if it's something she wants, then you're all for it.

Susie had little sense of what this decision might cost Emma, in part because she had no personal experience with the Greek system. Zack would eventually come to blame Greek life for Emma's academic trajectory. However, he was only able to see this after the fact.

Susie and Zack had the most resources and advantages of any bystander couple. They were middle class, college educated, happily married, and had several extended family members who attended MU. These factors enabled them to be supportive bystanders, who maintained close emotional ties to Emma, ardently rooted for her, and offered significant financial support. Yet even they did not know how to counsel Emma. They could not tell her what sorority life would be like or give her the tools to evaluate the appropriateness of dentistry as a career. They did not view the C or Emma's efforts to reach out to talk about it as red flags. Their inability to offer detailed guidance or to intervene when necessary kept them removed from Emma's college experience—as outsiders looking in.

Total bystanders were far less affluent and typically had no experience with college. They were even further outside of their realm of knowledge. This made it more difficult to get involved. As Diane told me, "Amanda was so easy to send to college. She did so much of it by herself. . . . I didn't really know, never going to college myself. I didn't know how things worked." In fact, Diane's children inspired *her* to attend a community college. She admitted, "I have to call Amanda, and I'll ask her to help me with my homework." Diane received academic assistance from her daughter, rather than the other way around.

The strained nature of parent-child relations in many of these families also worked against parental intervention. As Paul described, during some semesters he "parented . . . a healthy way [and] talked to Carrie every couple of weeks." Other semesters he "dropped her off and went down there once [more to pick her up]." In neither case did he have an open line of communication, necessary to identify problems that needed to be fixed. Similarly, Heather's parents would not answer her calls. At times, Alyssa was not speaking with her parents.

The daughters of total bystanders were disinclined to ask for help, even when they desperately needed it. For instance, Amy refused to request moving assistance from her father, necessary for switching rooms after an assigned roommate failed to show. As field notes indicated:

> [Amy was] really scared of moving rooms because she was worried about how to move her stuff. Compared to some of the other women, she has only a few things . . . [yet] she was facing having to do it herself. I asked if her dad would have come back to help, and she seemed to think that was the most ridiculous idea ever. This is in contrast to Taylor's parents, who came to help her with [a dental emergency]. Taylor's father was in the hall after having taken her out to dinner.

Amy's father lived in-state, under a two-hour drive away. However, it was virtually unimaginable to her that he would make the trip, due to the cost and time off from work. Amy had already learned that she was expected to be on her own.

Faith in the University

Bystanders shared some faith in the university to provide for its students. It was strongest in supportive bystanders, but even total bystanders assumed Midwest U offered an array of basic services, as part and parcel of tuition costs. For many, this eased their minds and removed a sense of personal responsibility.

Total bystanders thought that financial help would be readily available. Luann, for example, assigned the task of filling out financial aid forms to Megan in part because doing so herself was daunting, but also because she believed that MU had staff whose job it was to assist with this paperwork. The only reason she began to wonder about her daughter's financial situation was that Megan seemed consistently broke. "She doesn't seem to have a lot of money. I know kids that go to college that will get four or five thousand bucks right off the bat and don't even need it. . . . I don't know anything about [the financial aid form]. But she always goes to the people at college to help her fill them out, I think." As far as I was aware, Megan never received instruction on how to fill out her financial aid forms. Nor did she receive the sum that Luann thought she was due.

These parents also looked to the university to offer the comprehensive academic counseling that they were not able to provide. Thus, Luann assumed that Megan would have a skilled advisor to help with course selection. She deflected Megan's attempts to seek academic advice, believing that someone who knew far better would help her daughter make good decisions. Luann explained:

Megan talks about her classes all the time. . . . The best ones to take or if I really need this one or should I do this. But then again, I don't know. . . . So I would just say, "Well, Megan, you can make that decision yourself. Then if you can't, go to someone that is getting paid to do that. There are people there getting paid to help you out so that is what I would do." [Laura: Did she ever end up . . . finding someone like that to help her?] Not that I can remember. I don't know.

It was often hard for Megan to turn to her mother for help because Luann assumed that MU was already offering it.

Supportive bystanders had even more extensive expectations. They believed, for example, that their daughters would receive invitations to meet with professors outside of class—assuming a more intimate learning environment than what actually exists at most state schools. Rose thought that Crystal's mental health issues would be flagged and treated at school. Many parents assumed their children would learn a variety of life skills via classroom instruction. When I asked Zack about teaching his daughter how to budget, he told me, "I'm sure that some of the classes they had in college helped them out in that regard." Zack was also under the impression that Emma could access work-based learning opportunities via the university. He told me that MU enrolled her in a dental shadowing program. Eileen thought that Karen would be offered help in locating a suitable internship. None of these assumptions turned out to be true.

Supportive bystanders also trusted that the social side of college would bolster their mobility projects. These parents (at least initially) believed that Greek houses provided a safe, structured environment. As Robert explained:

Her mother and I were actually trying to lean her in that direction. . . . Sororities have rules, regulations, charters, and pledges, where you're a little more regimented in what you do and what you participate in. It always seems that it's maybe a little better road than some that were taken by kids that weren't in fraternities and sororities.

Sororities were thought to be partially protected spaces, relatively favorable to studying in comparison to unchecked hooliganism. This was not the case.

These were not unreasonable expectations. Affluent parents often send their children to elite private institutions that at least purport to offer more complete care. A carefully crafted social and academic environment, a large and well-trained advising staff, tailored professor-to-student mentoring, expanded career counseling, and job placement services were what many bystanders thought they were getting in MU. They did not understand that these amenities are only available at a price point substantially above what they or their daughters could pay. After all, MU was the most expensive, prestigious school that many working-class, lower-middle-class, and even middle-class families could buy. With limited abilities to navigate their daughters through college, these parents were reliant on MU to offer advice, guidance, and support. Unlike other parents, they could not do it themselves.

Helping Out

Limited levels of involvement linked supportive and total bystanders. They diverged in the other types of support they offered. Perhaps the starkest difference was in the funding of college. Supportive bystanders may have been relegated to the sidelines of college life, but they financially backed their daughters from afar. All of these parents put themselves in considerable debt to cover costs during college. They pulled out loans—subsidized and unsubsidized—secured home equity lines of credit, drained retirement and savings accounts, and collected contributions from family members.

When it came to money, supportive bystanders used a language of assistance. As Rose explained, "I tried to help as much as I could." They worried that without their financial support, college would be unfeasible for their children. As Zack told me, "I recognize that the cost of schooling has gotten astronomical, and [it is] really kind of ridiculous for an individual to try to pay for it, so what we tried to do is cover as much as we could." Getting their daughters to and through college was, after all, their driving purpose. They understood, to some degree, the role that financial support played in ensuring persistence.[2]

Like professional helicopters, these parents did not see the value of working during college. They preferred to keep their daughters focused on academics. As Zack told me, "Emma has not worked since she's been in the school. The reason we did that was because she had a lot on her plate. The biology thing is a lot of work. . . . We want her to really concentrate on school. We want her do well." Similarly, Karen, Whitney, and Crystal were not employed during the school year. Stacey did an occasional stint as a Miller Lite girl, which involved dressing up sexy and marketing beer. She claimed this was more for fun than anything else.

Janice was the only supportive bystander who wanted her daughter to hold a part-time job while at MU. However, Becky had "talked about leaving a number of times." Janice paid upfront rather than risk having Becky drop out. She explained:

> I had at first told both the kids that they needed to pay for their own books and take out loans to the extent that they could. But I have to tell you, I caved with her. . . . I don't think she could've handled it. . . . I tried a lot of different tactics, and I really don't think so. When I say tactics, probably threats. . . . It was like pulling teeth to get her to stay with a job while she was in college.

Becky never managed to hold a job for an entire semester, but, on the other hand, she did not leave MU, to her mother's great relief.

Assistance was not easy to provide. Rose was supporting five girls on her own, with at least two in college at any given time. Emma was one of four children. Her father, Zack, had recently experienced a medical crisis that bankrupted the family. Over time the college-related debt piled up. Lori told me, "Right now, I'm probably twenty-four thousand in the hole with Sallie Mae." Yet these parents did not complain or describe themselves as deprived. As Robert put it, "We're comfortable, but we're by no means wealthy. We're trying to strike a happy medium between getting a college education and being able to afford it. Or subsidize it."

The financial backing offered by supportive bystanders was time limited and focused on getting their children through college. They assumed that their daughters would cover some of the cost after college. Robert explained to Stacey that they would pay up front, "but when you graduate, half of [the cost of college] comes back. We are your primary student loan funder." This was fairly typical. These parents would eventually leave between one-fourth to one-half of college expenses to their children. As Zack noted, "I'm not unhappy with the fact that they came out of school with *good* student loans" (emphasis added).

The promise of loans was thought to be protective, an inoculation against taking one's education for granted. In this way, they were similar to paramedic parents. Zack explained, "The world is not a free ride. . . . Some of the kids that she was in the sorority with that don't have to pay anything have a different outlook on life. They're not as serious about it. They have expectations that are unrealistic in today's world unless you're fully funded for the rest of your life." Robert took a similar stance:

> I've seen wealthy kids who . . . anything they wanted was paid for because they had a mom and dad to write the check. Those kids were the ones who were just D for diploma and party all the way through school. No matter what happened, the parents were there to bail them out. . . . Stacey's mother and I, we're just the opposite of that.

He believed Stacey's stake in her own education would keep her from squandering it.

For total bystander families, the exchange of money and resources had dried up or reversed, flowing from child to parent.[3] Alyssa kept her parents afloat. As she described:

> They're not in the position to where they can give money. They're strapped as it is, and I'm kind of helping them when they absolutely need it now because I'm sitting all right. I mean, I'm upset about it, but there's nothing you can do. . . . My dad was barely getting forty hours a week. . . . They cannot have a credit card, because they're so in debt. . . . I was just kind of like okay . . . I'll make one of their [car insurance] payments, and they need toilet paper. . . . It may not be $500 a week or something like that, but it's just something . . . I can try to contribute.

Alyssa was aware that her parents were not acting as parents of young adults "should" act, at least according to many of her peers. This realization upset her.

Daughters of total bystanders had to work during college. Labor went toward family upkeep, as well as paying personal bills. Many kept punishing hours. Years into college, when she lived with her family, Megan reported:

> I have to feed . . . [the horses] every morning. . . . The way we have our barn, we don't have water out there, so I have to carry it in buckets. When we had all of that snow . . . it was horrible. . . . [At home] I had always cleaned everything, made supper, did everything. [My father's] girlfriend . . . moved in, and she's got five kids. [Laura: You've got a lot on your plate.] I know, I do. I feel like I'm about ready to bust. . . . Last semester I was a TA for Psych 100. . . . That took up a lot more of my time than what I thought because I attended every class. I was taking fifteen credit hours, but it was like I was taking eighteen because I had to go to that class also. . . . Then every Friday, Saturday, and Sunday, I worked. . . . I would get up at five or sometimes earlier, depends if the roads were bad. . . . [Laura: Where do you work at?] It's at a restaurant in [a neighboring state].

It's a half hour from my house. I work 7:30 in the morning until 3:30 in the afternoon. Then I would have class every day. . . . I've just never had time to go out and do stuff.

Students like Megan had none of the free time that so defined the college experiences of others. It was hard to juggle so many responsibilities.

Lacking parental financial support, these women did not enjoy a well-defined young adult life stage. College was not a marker of newfound independence or freedom, but rather a continuation (and amplification) of earlier obligations. Megan explained:

I would consider myself as an adult, I always have. Even in high school, I felt older than what I was. When I meet people [who] rely on mom and dad for everything, and some people don't even know how to do laundry, then I'm like you're still a high school kid. You need to grow up at some point. . . . I had to rely on myself a lot. . . . I was just forced into adulthood.

Women like Megan were adults in college, if not before.

Mercurial Parenting

Most bystanders were dependably supportive or removed. Carrie's and Heather's parents fluctuated. Given that their daughters spent long periods of time on their own, I classify these parents as total bystanders. The difficulties that Carrie and Heather faced highlight problems with inconsistent financial and emotional support.

I was able to interview both of Carrie's parents. Paul and Jody agreed that their contentious relationship disrupted their parenting. Paul explained, "Her mother and I divorced when she was a junior in high school. . . . She probably didn't speak to her mom until maybe during her first semester [at MU]. . . . Her finishing high school [and] me starting my own life on my own . . . that was a pretty difficult time, and I would say that a lot of things . . . got set by the side." Although family resources had always been scarce, Jody was an educator with a college degree. She used her inside knowledge to help obtain college funding for her older children but not Carrie.

Without the promise of scholarship assistance, Carrie's parents disagreed on where she should go. Jody wanted her to attend Midwest U and be provided with some financial support ("You don't drop them like a dead egg!"). Paul, who was to pay the lion's share, wanted Carrie to go to a less expensive commuter school, live at home, and keep her job year-round. The fight continued several years into college, when Paul was still pressuring Carrie to transfer back home. As Jody told Carrie, "'I think it's important that you continue.' When her dad was saying, 'Save money and go to [Local U],' . . . that was one of those moments when I said, 'No, you're not. You are going to continue. I'll figure out a way to pay for this. I've worked three jobs before.'" Carrie ultimately stayed at MU but with an angry primary funder.

Paul initially paid everything for Carrie. But then he stopped. Carrie was not prepared. She had no loans set up, nor did she have a job. In the interim she went hungry: "I have no money, and I have, like, no food. . . . I don't eat breakfast. I don't really eat lunch. . . . The only thing I've bought is milk in the past two weeks. That's like all I've had to drink." Her mind was occupied by food fantasies—in particular, lobster from the expensive grocery store in town. She contacted Paul and told him that she needed money to eat, but the only thing he did was send a small care package with junk food she did not want.

Jody's promise of steady assistance never came through, either. However, one year she sent Carrie $200 for a spring break trip. As Jody noted:

> When she called and said, "Mom would you help?" I said, "Absolutely." . . . When they grew up, honest-to-Pedro, a few times we went to bed hungry. . . . I did everything I could to protect them and to give them what they needed. But definitely no splurges of any type. It just wasn't [possible]. Right now, the job I have is the most

money I've ever made, and they know that if they call, I'll do what I can. I guess it is sort of making up for what I couldn't do when they were young.

This is "windfall child-rearing," typical among low-income families where money is both scarce and unpredictable.[4] Not knowing when they will have money again and wanting to offer their children things they desire, parents may provide bursts of funds for unnecessary extras. In Carrie's case, it contributed to the lack of consistency in support that defined her college experience.

Heather's situation was similar to Carrie's in that her divorced parents did not communicate well about funding, and her father was (reluctantly) in charge of providing financial support. Midway through college, he ended it. Heather recounted:

[My father] helped me pay for school. . . . Then he said "Good luck. See ya later." He's trying to teach me a lesson. Not to take things for granted. Basically telling me to grow up. But I've been working since I was fourteen. I've paid for all my own stuff since I was fourteen. Bought my first car, tons of crap. . . . It'd be nice if I had a little help, 'cause I'm kind of stressed out about money. Not everybody can rely on their dad, unfortunately.

It is hard to know, without her father's side of the story, exactly what happened and why he removed support. However, it was clear that the funding relationship had changed.

Heather's parents also refused to stop claiming her as a financial dependent, even when they offered her no help. She tried to get in touch with the U.S. Department of Education but found herself in a quandary:

I felt really bad because I literally yelled at the lady [on the phone]. I was like, "Listen. I don't talk to my parents. I don't get any money from them. How am I supposed to pay for school?" She's like, "I'm

> sorry; there's nothing we can do for you." . . . They told me to call the
> MU financial aid office, and MU just told me to get student loans.

Many students are likely harmed by the same technicality. Student funding rules and regulations do not reflect the complex relationships that older youth often have with their parents. The real level of parental financial support they receive may bear little relationship to that which parents claim on taxes—especially when there is a significant financial benefit at stake.

Things would have been easier for Carrie and Heather if their parents had transferred financial responsibility to their daughters the first time they decided to cut off aid. Instead, they sabotaged their daughters' efforts to take charge of college finances. When Carrie pulled out a loan without her father's knowledge, Paul intercepted the check, put it in his own account, and did not disperse the funds to her. She had no recourse and resorted to begging Paul to release the funds—which he eventually did, but only partially. Heather had to deal with her mother's unlawful use of her credit after she "took out a bunch of credit cards in my name, without me knowing it. . . . My credit is so bad right now because of her." These events also further damaged women's already poor relationships with their parents.

Pragmatic Work and Family Plans

Bystanders needed their daughters to move rapidly into adulthood, precluding a long career-building phase for women or their future mates. Early economic stability was the central goal. This shaped the types of careers and timing of romantic partnerships they supported.

Parents and daughters alike assumed that people went to college to "be" something. Teaching was the most obvious, direct path to mobility for women in their communities.[5] Thus, five women attended with the intention of becoming a teacher. Their parents understood this choice. As Diane explained, "Most girls want to be teachers because that's something they've been exposed to their whole life. I was in banking, and she wasn't too interested in that, so I think she just went to the only other thing she knew, which was teaching." Three other women wanted to be in health care or social services. These are feminized fields, largely occupied by women, especially in the lower ranks. However, they offer vocations that women can easily enter right out of college.

As a rule, bystanders did not want their daughters to become financially reliant on men. Jody noted, "I would like to see, for all of the girls, that they are able to stand on their own. . . . That I can do this if the situation is such that I have to be on my own. I can do it." Robert told me, "Stacey knows that once she has [her degree] that it's something she'll have the rest of her life, and hopefully [it will] open doors for her and keep her gainfully employed . . . without having to rely on a spouse." These sentiments made sense given the relatively limited economic prospects of less-privileged men in working class towns in the Midwest. As I discuss in chapter 7, these were the men that their daughters dated.

At the same time, however, bystanders did not hold gender-progressive views about family life. For instance, Eileen hoped to see her daughter become a teacher because, as she explained, "It's the perfect job for a wife and mother. You're off when the kids are off." In their own households, mothers held paid jobs but also did all of the cooking, cleaning, and child care. Their daughters (but not sons) were expected to contribute. Thus, Megan would complain about caring for her father and brother between school, work, and farm labor. "I'm doing everybody's work. Doing laundry and everybody's dishes and it just makes me mad. . . . My brother just pops in. He's gonna be twenty-three, and he just comes in and eats and takes a shower and leaves." As the only woman in her father's household, she carried a particularly heavy burden.

Most bystanders married and had children at relatively young ages. Luann told me, "I was married when I was twenty. I had [Megan's brother] when I was twenty-one." Jody got pregnant her freshman year of college. Her parents told her to get an abortion or get married. She did the latter. These women had lived through the difficulties of being young wives and parents. As Luann continued, "If I had to do it all over again I would wait. Wait until *at least* later in the twenties." Nonetheless, bystanders saw marriage before graduation as the norm. As Eileen realistically noted, "It's a lot less likely for a lot of people, after years of school, to wait."

Bystanders were unwilling to oppose a potential match, even if they saw it as unfavorable. For example, Megan was engaged during college twice, to two different men. Luann did not like the second fiancé. She explained, "He came from a generation of the men telling the women what to do and how to do it. . . . I always felt, in the back of his mind, he felt [that] once he got her, he could talk her into not going to school." Rather than tell Megan of her misgivings, Luann convinced others not to say anything. "When everyone here was real negative about it, I told [them], 'This is Megan's life. It is Megan's marriage. We are all going to go to her wedding, and we are all going to be happy because it is what she wants.'" I asked Luann why she kept silent. She told me that she felt it was not her place to speak up. Unfortunately, as I detail later, the marriage would be disastrous for Megan.

Many other parents would have objected to such a pairing. To begin with, the fiancé lacked a college degree. However, bystanders did not judge potential mates on these grounds. Thus, when Emma was in a serious committed relationship with a hometown man in the military, Susie indicated that she was "absolutely not" bothered by the fact he never went to college. This was not relevant for her. What was more relevant was that he had a steady income and benefits, and could supplement Emma's earnings. Early commitment was not viewed as problematic especially if it helped women to build an economic base.

This is the last chapter in part I. In part II, I turn to the *consequences* of parenting approaches, for both parents and children alike. The chapters are organized around parents' satisfaction with what their desired college experience yielded. Each group responded in a unique fashion. Chapter 5 begins with the frustrated pink helicopters, who managed to fund fun but were caught off-guard by their daughters' poor academic performance and continued dependency.

PART II

Parenting Consequences

FIVE

Funding Fun

Pink helicopters succeeded at providing a social experience for their daughters, complete with partying, fun, and the development of social networks. They should have been pleased, as they accomplished what they set out to do. However, anger, bitterness, and frustration filled their interviews. They did not fully understand in advance that the way they parented while their daughters were in college cultivated long-term dependency, both economically and psychologically. The daughters of pink helicopters graduated—but with poor academic records not easy to translate into jobs. These women had little motivation to seek employment, and the jobs that they could get would not sustain their lavish lifestyles.

Drained of money and energy, pink helicopters were ready for their daughters to assume more responsibility, yet the women were entirely unprepared to do so. As Cindy noted with a sigh of resignation, "[This is] what happened with our generation. We worked to support our kids, give them a better life, and then our kids—it's not that they threw it in our face—we didn't realize that they didn't know any better now. They just figured the funds were unlimited. . . . You could say what a fool this mother is." Like other pink helicopters, Cindy worried that her efforts to make her daughter's life pleasurable had backfired. These parents blamed themselves—although they were not pleased with their daughters, either. Only a few had the resources necessary to compensate for these unintended consequences.[1]

Table 5.1. Benefits and Costs of the Pink Helicopter Approach

	Pink Helicopter
Benefits	+ Fun, best-years-of-life experience
	+ Deep and rich social networks
	+ Unlikely to transfer from school of origin
	+ Extremely low risk of drop-out
	+ Leave without student debt
Costs	– Low grades
	– Concentration in easier, media-based majors
	– Potential for "social semester" delays
	– Lack of motivation and ambition
	– Parental job-hunt assistance needed
	– Long-term financial support after college necessary
	– Potentially damaging to parents' economic security
	– May require financial "rescue" by wealthy spouse
Families	$N = 9$
	UC: Connie and Logan (Abby); Alexis and Frank (Hannah)
	UMC: Rachel and Matt (Julie); Cindy and Ed (Naomi); Cathy and Walt (Natasha); Marian and Rick (Nicole); Rhonda (Tara)[d]; Allison and Tom (Sydney)
	MC: Lacey and Arnold (Blair)

Notes: UC = upper class; UMC = upper-middle class; MC = middle class.
[d] = parents divorced or other parent deceased.

The "Best Years"

Pink helicopters watched as their daughters enjoyed the "best years of life" at college. Most of these women quickly moved onto the party pathway, utilizing the social and academic infrastructure built for socially oriented students. All but two women joined sororities. They tended to join elite houses with intense social schedules—partying three to five nights a week.[2] These organizations streamlined the production of fun by pairing sorority and fraternity houses for alcohol-infused parties and socializing. Through this process, ties to other demographically similar students were also created, as houses were de facto segregated along the lines of social class and race.[3] Revelry, with an exclusive set of students, was mass-produced.

Parents had few complaints (detailed later) about their daughters' experiences with the social machinery of MU. As Frank reverently noted, "The big changing point in Hannah's life was the sorority thing. . . . She met some great kids that she has bonded with for [life]." For Frank, the value of the sorority was in its capacity to facilitate close connections with "great kids." Hannah's new friends were exactly like her. As her mother, Alexis, explained—pointing to a picture of Hannah with her three closest friends—they were from affluent East Coast families (and, as I silently noted, all white). The experiences they accumulated together would ensure that Hannah had roommates in her New York City apartment and connections to other families on the eastern seaboard. Hannah would also have the right kind of stories to tell at job interviews, social get-togethers, and eventually play dates with her children.

Admission into a sorority signaled that pink helicopters' daughters had mastered the style of femininity many of their mothers valued. As Rhonda remembered with pride, "When I was in school, [top sorority] was very exclusive and [had] beautiful girls, all blondes, the best. . . . I was real proud that Tara got in there." Her references to "blonde" and "exclusive" have particular racial/ethnic, religious, and social class implications. White, non-Jewish women were most likely to have the light hair and blue eyes that the term "blonde" suggests.[4] "Exclusive" suggests that only women from affluent families were included. Rhonda's comment reflects awareness that a specific type of femininity—which Tara performed well—was afforded highest status on campus. As a measurement of success, climbing to the top of the MU social ladder certainly counted in the eyes of parents like Rhonda.

Only two sets of pink helicopters failed to get the social experience they desired for their daughters. As Matt bemoaned, "In the big picture socially . . . things could have been better. We encouraged Julie multiple times to get involved in some kind of club or something.

She thought about the sororities and that didn't work out." Neither Julie nor Natasha participated in mainstream college activities, like joining a sorority, regularly attending fraternity parties, participating in campus clubs, or cheering on the home team at big-time sports games. As Walt noted, he was "disappointed because Natasha didn't . . . go to a football game or a basketball game. 'Cause I thought maybe that's a way to get a little MU spirit and she didn't. . . . That just wasn't her cup of tea."

These parents' complaints revolve around the importance of forming the "right" type of social ties. Both of their daughters had social lives during college, but they centered on hometown connections and did not involve collegiate activities. Julie lived for years with her high school best friend and struggled with a possessive and depressed boyfriend. Natasha smoked pot with her high school best friend most of the time and dated young men who did not attend college. Cathy wanted Natasha to "make new friends" so that she might leave behind the "lower class of people" she had associated with in high school. Their cases suggest that parents seeking the "best years" were quite specific about the *kinds* of social experiences and social ties that were valuable and which were not.

Academic Underperformance

Parents' elation over their daughters' social successes did not translate into the academic realm. Their parenting approaches, focused on funding fun, had a detrimental effect on students' academic performance. This pattern conforms to an earlier quantitative study of postsecondary students around the country: I found that the more money parents directed to college expenses of any kind, the lower their child's GPA—up to a certain point. Well-funded students tended not to perform poorly enough to warrant dismissal. However, they did engage in a behavior that I referred to as "satisficing."[5]

Satisficing can be described as an intentional but measured dialing down of academic efforts to create time and energy for social activities.[6] It generally leads to lower grades and academic investment, both of which are apparent here: the children of pink helicopters had an unimpressive average GPA (exactly a 3.0), in not particularly rigorous programs of study. The parents of the six students who earned GPAs at or below a 3.0 were incensed. The parents of the three students who earned above a 3.0 were not and did not mention their daughter's grades; these women had not done poorly enough to make academics relevant in our conversation.

However, from my perspective, none of the women discussed in this chapter were performing at their potential. That is, had they put forth more effort, they could have earned better grades. In fact, during the yearlong ethnography, I rarely—and in some cases *never*—saw these women open a book. With two exceptions (Hannah and Nicole), they did not talk about classes or discuss their grades, even with graduate students and a faculty member in their midst. Academics were not their first priority. To be fair, their parents never suggested that they should care about their grades, beyond passing their classes.

Abby provides an ideal illustration of satisficing behavior. She arrived with obvious ability, as suggested by a record of A's and advanced placement classes at a high-performing suburban high school. During college Abby did not exert herself. As she explained, "It's like the 20/80 thing: you can put in 20 percent effort, [and] you get 80 percent of the results. But if you want the 100 percent, you have to put in your other 80 percent effort. I'd just rather keep putting in 20 percent in everywhere and get as much as I can." When I asked Abby what GPA her 20 percent effort afforded her, she noted, "Around a 3.0, about an 80 percent. But that's fine. . . . My grades didn't matter to me that much because it's not worth the 80 percent stress for the 20 percent grade increase. For me, it wasn't. *Half the reason I was in college was not because of school*" (emphasis added).

As she suggested, "school" (i.e., the academic component of college) was only part—and, implicitly, the lesser part—of her time at Midwest U. Students who were less talented than Abby had to anticipate a lower GPA for their 20 percent effort. For instance, Naomi predicted in advance that her GPA would dip below a 3.0 by the spring semester of freshman year, due to extensive socializing. She explained, "My parents aren't gonna be very happy, but they'll understand. . . . I mean, I'm living in a very social dorm."

Many parents, despite what their daughters hoped, did not understand. They expected better than a 3.0 but believed grades were secondary to fun and did not intervene. Anything at or below this GPA, they interpreted as a lack of effort. As Connie commented:

> Abby could have done a lot of things with her life. She was in AP math even in [grade] school. . . . [She] always scored off the board on standardized tests. I always knew that she was really bright. . . . [But now] she has this attitude that she doesn't have to prove herself through her grades. . . . I am disappointed. . . . She just doesn't seem to really care. Sometimes it annoys me and I say, "You know, you're going to an out-of-state school, and it's really expensive. It would be nice if you at least *tried* to get good grades. . . . God, if you really tried you could have gotten an A. I always think you're so capable."

Similarly, Cathy said deflatedly, "I don't think Natasha was very motivated to work real hard in college. I think she's smarter. She didn't apply herself a hundred percent to get good grades. I think she did what she could to get by."

I was surprised by how upset these parents were. It seemed obvious that offering encouragement to socialize and funds to dive into the social whirl, combined with low to no academic expectations, was likely to result in low academic performance. Yet parents had a hard time recognizing, at least before it happened, that funding fun might exact a toll on achievement. For example, when I asked Ed about college partying, he responded:

> That's part of it. Everybody does [it]. Well, not everybody, but was Naomi excessive? I don't know. . . . I know she had a good time. I guess the group of friends that she met was just like her. They

were all . . . marginal students. What's surprising was when she graduated, her and all her friends, there wasn't one of them that was going to graduate school. Not one.

Ed was pleased that the four years were so fun but somewhat puzzled by Naomi and her friends' uninspiring performance. His confusion suggests that parents often had unrealistic expectations for what a good time in college could reasonably offer students.

Part of the problem was that parents like Ed did not understand just how demanding the social scene at Midwest U was. This was not a work hard/play hard school, where there was a culture of pride in being able to rally after a long night of partying to maintain a solid academic performance. Encouraging a social experience at MU helped to place students in the center of the party pathway, which was organized around social demands. Even parents who encouraged drinking, drug use, and revelry came to feel like MU offered too much. As Cindy remarked:

> These colleges are excessive. I just don't remember that we partied [like that]. . . . It would be maybe Friday night and Saturday night. . . . Now it starts Wednesday night, Thursday night, Friday night, Saturday night, so that the only nights they seem to be resting are Sunday and Monday, and maybe Tuesday. I just can't believe it's just Naomi's group.

Had they fully appreciated what it really meant to send a child to a "party school," they might have understood the need to also encourage investment in academics.

In a few cases, children took the social experience way beyond what their parents intended. This was true for the one middle-class pink helicopter family. Lacey and Arnold had pushed Blair to attend MU instead of another in-state school closer to home and had encouraged her to join a sorority so that she might branch out socially. But over time Blair got in deeper and deeper. As Lacey explained:

At first Blair said, "I don't want to go out, and that's all they care about is partying. . . ." Eventually since everyone else was doing it, she was going to do it too, because otherwise she wasn't going to have friends. . . . Then she did start going out all the time. That [last] semester was pretty terrible. She had spent so much money . . . [that] her dad hit the ceiling. And she did terrible in school. She failed her math class.

This account explicitly links high levels of parental funding, partying, and poor grades. Lacey and Arnold might have recalibrated their vision of college; however, it was a bit late, as Blair was nearing graduation at the point of the interview.

Daughters' lackluster grades are notable given the low degree of difficulty of their coursework. They selected majors that allowed them to focus on socializing, without risking academic suspension. All but one opted for "easy majors" characterized by the ease of obtaining a high GPA, as well as little evidence of learning (as reported by Richard Arum and Josipa Roksa in *Academically Adrift: Limited Learning on College Campuses*).[7] Easy majors were a central piece of the party pathway infrastructure at MU because they allowed women to get degrees without detracting too much from their socializing.[8]

A majority of these women were in a communications field (e.g., sports broadcasting, sports communication, telecommunications, or journalism).[9] Media-based majors led to fields with a heavy focus on appearance, personality, and charm—traits that women were already working on in the party scene. Women hoped to translate them into what seemed like glamorous careers in media, fashion, design, music, or the arts. Naomi, for instance, majored in sports communication because she wanted to move into "the entertainment field."

If pink helicopters said anything about major choice, they pushed for the path of least resistance. For instance, Arnold told his daughter Blair that she should select something "that she could not [possibly] struggle with" after she picked a program that he believed was "too hard . . . and hurt her GPA." Most of these parents were primarily focused on graduation and getting the degree. A hard major or difficult class was a hurdle to be overcome or, better yet, evaded—not an exciting challenge or a start to a promising career path.

As Arum and Roksa's sequel, *Aspiring Adults Adrift: Tentative Transitions of College Graduates*, indicates, easy majors—especially in communications—are associated with a higher probability of unemployment two years after graduation.[10] Yet only Naomi's parents seemed to recognize, well after the fact, that what made Naomi "marginal" was, in part, her major: sports communication leads to a few low-paying jobs and does not direct students to graduate school.

Cindy and Ed did not care what major Naomi selected while in college but later began to worry that it might be an issue on the labor market. Cindy lamented, "Naomi really needed a vocation, and that's what she did not get at MU. . . . School of education, she needed to do something like that [or] social work. . . . Something that when she came out she actually had some credentials." Ironically, teaching and social work also qualify as less rigorous fields of study.[11] Both programs, however, required a series of tests for licensing and had language requirements—neither of which Naomi wanted to do.

Graduation (Prolonged?)

High parental financial support may drag down student achievement, but it also offers students considerable protection against stopping or dropping out.[12] The children of pink helicopters never had to worry about how to pay their bills or if they could afford to live on campus for another semester. They did not have to juggle paid employment and school. Parental interventions made their lives smooth and pleasant. Most were having the time of their lives at college: why would they leave the party early?

Pink helicoptering is almost fail-safe with regards to college completion. All nine of the women discussed in this chapter graduated within six years. Not one transferred from MU. They were deeply integrated into the social fabric of the institution, which significantly increased their odds of degree completion.[13] There was, however, a risk of delayed graduation—one that parents typically did not support or anticipate. This could occur for a few different reasons: students did not want the fun to end, or parents lacked sufficient resources to help their daughters meet internship requirements.

Abby, Nicole, and Sydney attempted to get an additional, purely social, semester of college. Two of these women succeeded. Sydney spread required classes into the next year, without telling her parents. When the end of her supposedly senior year came, Tom and Allison were ambushed. As Tom indicated:

> Sydney really likes to be in school. . . . She would prefer to do that indefinitely if that's possible. But it's not possible. . . . We were always on the four-year plan. This extra semester was a surprise. . . . I am of the opinion that, if she really wanted to, she could have gotten those credits and still graduated in four years.

Allison understood that her daughter was motivated by social concerns. She described:

> I happened to be talking to another mom of [Sydney's friend]. . . . She says, "Oh, yes, and [my son] wants to stay an extra semester. . . ." I said it sounded awful familiar. . . . I wonder if they have been cooking this up together. . . . Her dad wasn't too thrilled with the whole idea. It's out-of-state tuition, and he didn't plan on another semester. But she went ahead with it anyway. . . . He hasn't paid the bill yet.

Ultimately Tom paid, despite his frustrations. This exhausted any additional funds they might have had to assist Sydney after college.

Lacey and Arnold faced a different issue that would slow Blair's graduation. Her major required an internship as a prerequisite for graduation, but Midwest U did not offer Blair assistance in finding one. Blair's parents lacked the social connections typical of other pink helicopters, who secured their daughters' media internships. One year after she was slated to graduate, Blair still did not have the internship or the degree. As Blair told me, "My parents are frantic. . . . [They told me,] 'We paid a ton of money; please get your degree.'" A sympathetic teacher would eventually take pity on Blair and count her cold-calling sales position as an internship.

Blair's predicament highlights the fact that the success of a pink helicopter approach lies not only in parental funds, but also with parental ties to potential employers. Her middle-class parents, from a struggling post-industrial city, knew no one who could help their daughter. Easy majors were more likely to include such "experience" requirements. Counting an internship for course credit reduced the academic burden for socially oriented students. However, it also offloaded work on parents, who had to secure appropriate positions for their daughters. As the only middle-class parents attempting a pink helicopter approach, Lacey and Arnold were ill equipped to fulfill their role in this arrangement.

Getting Her a Job

Nearing graduation, parents were feeling that the real work was about to begin. As Ed put it, "[Naomi and her friends] were there for their four years, and *now* they have to make careers." Tom thought that Sydney refused to graduate because she wanted to postpone a looming problem. He explained:

> She just bought herself six months because she never dealt with [the job market] this year. She's going to have to deal with it six months from now. It's the same situation. She's going to have to do some interviews, and hopefully she's going to be able to line up an internship or some kind of a connection during the summer that will give her an angle, or at least give her entrée from an employment perspective. Or give her better credentials in her field . . . if it's possible.

He was less than certain that, at this point, Sydney's record could be resuscitated.

Parents' concerns were warranted. Employers often screen résumés based on institutional affiliation, GPA, and major. Midwest U, as a mid-tier state flagship, was not particularly impressive—especially outside of the Midwest. Neither was a 2.8 GPA. At least a 3.0 is often required to make the first cut. These women's majors could also be detrimental, even for media-based jobs, if employers did not understand what they were. Telecommunications, for example, always required an explanation. As Ed recognized, "I think on paper, just sending a résumé. . . . It'll be tough."

At the time of the interview, parents were also starting to realize that university job-market assistance was not forthcoming. Rhonda explained, "Telecommunications doesn't have a lot of opportunities with people coming to school to interview kids. The Business School does. . . . I'm worried. We're in a recession. Looking for a job is going to be challenging at best." As I discuss in chapter 6, the Business School at MU was highly ranked and selective. It offered intensive career placement services that children of pink helicopters could not access. The schools and programs housing their majors did not provide similar services. As Marian put it, "[The school] didn't do that fabulous of a job guiding them along." Rick chimed in: "At MU, I really don't think they did at all."

Finding a job is anything but easy, and the carefully handled children of pink helicopters were not ready to engage in a job search. They displayed little ambition. For example, Frank was frustrated with his daughter:

Hannah's taken her foot off the pedal. . . . It's, "Oh my God, college is ending, please no!" [Laughs] It's the reality setting in. But I helped her with her résumé, and . . . I'm all over her related to this: "Did you follow up? Did you call? Did you do all this kind of stuff?" I worry about it at night 'cause I'm a worrier, but I would think she would've been sending her résumés, following up with it.

You send out a hundred résumés and hope you get one or two hits, you know? But she is not like that at all.

Similarly, Connie—whose daughter had a social semester planned—was not pleased:

Abby hasn't really been that independent as far as going out and getting jobs. . . . I sit there and look at different companies, and I have sent her links to companies that I think look young and innovative. . . . I said, "Abby, it would not hurt even if you just wrote a letter and introduced yourself." That's personally what I would do. . . . I am going to be definitely pushing her along. . . . I would like to see her have a little more drive. I never felt she really had it in her to go pound the pavement.

As these cases suggest, a heavily interventionist parenting style may impede college students' motivation to manage employment challenges on their own.

Seeing no other option, many parents activated their own job connections. Connie was resigned to the fact that this had to happen. While frustrated, she assured me, "It's okay that your family can open the door as long as when you're inside you do a good job." Ed told me, "I know some people. [And] my older daughter, who's in New York and does what Naomi would like to do, knows a lot of people. So I'm sure that something will come up for her." Frank explained, "I have some pretty good contacts in some of the fields Hannah wants to go into, so [sigh] . . . I think she's kind of counting on a lot of my contacts."

Securing a decent job for a less-than-stellar candidate at the start of the Great Recession was no minor effort. Rates of unemployment, even among young adults with a bachelor's degree, spiked during this time, peaking in 2011. Of on-time college graduates in 2009—the cohort immediately following women in this study—nearly 40 percent were unemployed, underemployed (< 20 hours), working part-time (at 20–35 hours), or in a full-time position paying less than $20,000 a year. Only 26 percent made more than $40,000.[14]

Parents used considerable resources to beat these odds. Frank, for instance, reached out to a friend who knew a CFO of a major sports league and forwarded Hannah's résumé. Hannah reported, "Literally a day later I got a phone call from the[ir] production department." However, in the intervening months the league was gutted and restructured. They were not hiring. Frank persisted. Hannah explained, "Then my dad is on the phone with his friend, and he is putting pressure on the CFO. 'Get her in, get her in!' My dad is crazy about it." The league created what Hannah described as a "permanent" freelance position. At around $60,000 a year, it was one of the best jobs obtained by any of the women on the floor. Five daughters of pink helicopters would be offered, and three would accept, jobs originating with a family tie.

The four remaining families were unable to help their daughters. Cathy, for example, was at her wit's end. As she worried:

And here we are. Graduation. What the hell are we gonna do? . . . I don't know what to do with Natasha, you know? I said if you want [to work with] a paralegal . . . in a law office this summer, I've got some contacts. . . . Her dad doesn't do anything like this. Maybe it is better. He kind of lets her alone to do her own thing. But I said [to him], "You have to help kids get jobs."

Cathy was torn. Should she help Natasha, or was Walt right? Did Natasha need to figure it out on her own? Ultimately Cathy offered the only help she had to give: a temp position alongside a paralegal for the summer in their suburban hometown. It was a far cry from the position in New York City that Hannah would accept.

Lacey and Arnold were in a similar situation. Just as they could not land Blair the internship necessary for graduation, they did not have useful job connections. They told her that she could return home like her older brother James—who, a year out of college, was working part-time at a local restaurant. Blair was angry with her parents:

> When I saw how much [my boyfriend's] parents were so supportive of his interviews [and] job search, stuff like . . . "I have a connection here, I'll e-mail them." Then when I saw this summer how upset my dad was. He was like, "Why doesn't [James] have a job?" It's like, he has no connections, he lives in [a small, in-state town], and he's supposed to figure [it] out?

Her boyfriend's family clued Blair in to the possibility that other parents were much more active in the job search than her own; however, whatever connections Lacey and Arnold had did not extend beyond the town boundaries.

A Financial Bridge

In the transition out of college, women needed access to active labor and marital markets. Large urban centers offered the greatest promise of employment, but these markets were competitive and favored applicants with local addresses. As Cindy reported, "Everyone says that you have to move to New York to find a job. I know that Naomi needs an address for New York."

Cities also held potential to further valuable social connections. Rachel, who worried that her daughter Julie was not social enough during college, noted:

> All the kids go to Lakeview [and the] Lincoln Park area [in Chicago]. There's a ton of kids from MU down there. I keep thinking that this is one area she was a little bit light on in college. If we can help her, then maybe this could be the continuation of the social aspect, because she'd be [in the right areas of Chicago]. So that's why we're doing it. *It's finishing her education for her.* (emphasis added)

For Rachel, socializing was the main purpose of college, but Julie had failed at this task. Rachael hoped Julie would make ties in Chicago, pulling her into circles teeming with well-heeled men.

Getting to the city was much easier with parental financial support. Hannah's parents understood how this worked. Alexis explained, "I know Hannah's gonna want an apartment [in Manhattan first]. Eventually she's gonna get a job." They put her up in a spacious two-bedroom, which she shared with a sorority friend, and covered Hannah's portion of the $2,400 monthly rate. It was located just below the wealthy Upper East Side and near an area with happening young adult nightlife. Hannah was never expected to cover the full cost on her own. Instead, the assumption was that she would meet and marry a wealthy man, eventually transferring her financial dependency to him—a central feature of gender complementarity. This would also relieve her parents of their financial obligations to Hannah's upkeep. As Hannah told me, "[My dad] was really happy when I was dating the I[nvestment] banker. [He said,] 'Marry him right now. Tell him to give you all his money . . . so I can retire.'"

Hannah's parents were unusual in their willingness to fund their daughter, potentially for a very long time. They were also the wealthiest in this group. Most parents balked at the idea of continuing to fuel what seemed like phase two of the party lifestyle. For instance, Cindy told her daughter Naomi that she could live at home and use her stepsister's address until landing a good job. Otherwise, Naomi would have to go "waitress . . . eight o'clock [am] until nine o'clock at night, or [hold] two jobs a day to support herself in New York. There's no way she's going to be able to party like she does at school."

Cindy's reservations were rooted in financial concerns. The prospect of extending a financial bridge all the way until marriage was daunting. As she explained:

[My kids] have expensive tastes. I worked all of my life and my husband worked all his life [to support them], but I don't work anymore. That's another issue . . . that the kids don't understand. I'm on a retirement pension. My eighty [thousand in salary] used to pay for all of their fun things and help their college. I don't have it anymore. All that fun stuff, our vacations, our eating out. . . . They've always had this good life so they haven't been able to accept it [won't keep going]. I keep telling them I don't have it, and they think we're teasing. . . . They want me to go into my pension to pay for their life.

Cindy and Ed ultimately covered an apartment for Naomi, until she could get settled in a more desirable job. In her new position as an executive assistant for a large media company, she was only making around $35,000 annually—not enough to fund her lifestyle in New York. Her parents made up the difference; however, every year Cindy's pension would shrink.

For four sets of parents, no amount of scraping or shuffling would allow them to finance a big-city move. Nicole's and Sydney's parents had opted to pay out-of-state tuition in search of the perfect social experience for their daughters, without cluing their daughters (or themselves) in to what this would mean for financial support after college. After her mother lost her job, Nicole ended up responsible for loans equivalent to 15 percent of the total cost of college. Had Nicole gone in-state, she would have left debt free. Blair's and Natasha's parents were similarly drained after four years of subsidizing fun.

Parents with depleted resources were frank about their plans to end assistance. As Arnold snapped, "If Blair thinks that we're going to continue to support her, then she's wrong. It's over with! [Laura: That'll be a rude awakening.] It's going to be extremely rude. She needs it." He continued, "I think it was probably a huge mistake . . . not making them pay for their college—at least some of it. I don't think they realized how fortunate they are to come out of school owing nothing. . . . Not owing anything kind of reduces the drive they might have to find work."

These parents were calloused about their daughters' post-college circumstances. They did not see it as their job to offer more support, as resources had run dry. The goal was for children to experience hardship, with the hope of motivating action. As Allison noted matter-of-factly:

> I don't think Sydney can move out until she has a job that she can afford to move out [with]. [Our older son] Oliver moved out. He lived downtown the first year . . . in a [seedy Chicago] neighborhood, which is awful. He called me one night and said, "I'm lying on the floor and there's shooting out in the street." I said, "You stay on the floor. That's a good spot."

Similarly, Lacey expected Blair to end up "in the ghetto" of Chicago but figured she would learn a lesson that way.

The women with the worst employment outcomes had parents who could not offer valuable job connections or build a financial bridge to the city. Blair made it to Chicago, but in the aforementioned cold-calling position and a less ideal neighborhood. Natasha became a bank teller in her hometown. Neither job required a BA. Sydney was unemployed for nearly a year and fell into a depression. She avoided family outings where relatives overwhelmed her with questions about her future. Nicole was financially stranded at home and forced to come up with a new plan. Her mother, Marian, suggested she attend a nearby college for her MA in teaching. Because Marian never was entirely onboard with a social experience (see chapter 1), she happily set up the entire scenario—from researching the appropriate schools to filling out the paperwork. However, Nicole constantly fought with her parents over her desire to get to the city. As she anxiously told me, "None of the boys [back home] have steady jobs," making marital rescue from her economic plight unlikely.

As these stories indicate, parental resources in the transition out of college are essential to transform the pink helicopter approach into economic security. This parenting style strips women of two essential resources: an internal locus of control—necessary for motivation and ambition—and valuable career credentials. As a result, daughters are

FUNDING FUN | 137

not prepared to fend for themselves after college. Parents must have deep financial reserves and dense social networks to remedy the situation, and they often do so begrudgingly.

Why Didn't They Know?

Pink helicopters are not alone in their myopic focus on socializing. Universities like Midwest U send messages about the value of "fun" when they build bigger recreation centers, invest money in college sports, place stately Greek houses on their brochures, and aggressively pursue well-heeled out-of-state families with a social agenda. It is hard to escape the notion that college is supposed to be a four-year drunken party when popular media plasters it across the television and Internet. In many ways, the social experience now defines college in the United States.

Why would parents be immune to these pressures? Like youth who clamor for college fun, parents are cultural consumers. However, they are handicapped by love for their children and much parental guilt. Many want to offer their children access to the so-called quintessential college experience. They enjoy seeing their children happy and do not want to fail as parents. This is a classic case of short-term gratification supplanting long-term satisfaction, made all the more powerful in the name of one's children.

Furthermore, dominant parenting advice through the 1990s and into the 2000s emphasized parental intervention and investment. It was, and still is, the era of "concerted cultivation."[15] Without clear instructions on *how* or with *what* to assist, pink helicopters were, in many ways, doing exactly what professional helicopters were doing—intervening in their daughters' lives, but to a much different effect. Pink helicopters did not recognize that their efforts were the wrong kind of cultivation, at least for producing strong academic records and economic self-sufficiency.

These parents also failed to understand that their children would read a secondary focus on grades as complete unconcern. They did not realize that they needed to ask their children to perform well academically, instead assuming this would happen automatically—while fun, they believed, would not. The important role of academic accountability in translating parental funds into academic success was not apparent: giving a lot was not enough and could even be harmful, if youth perceived it as a free gift, with no strings attached. Nor was it clear that socializing and grades were as tightly linked as they were at MU, where involvement in the social whirl typically came at the cost of achievement.

It is also hard to fault parents for assuming that any four-year degree would open doors for their children. They might have been aware that Midwest U did not carry the weight of a more prestigious institution. Yet it is only recently that researchers have recognized the extent to which schools are internally stratified.[16] For example, college majors can vary considerably in the earnings and occupational status that they offer graduates.[17] Certain programs, such as business and engineering schools, often provide direct ties to employers or industries, making it easier to locate ideal positions within a given field. In a single graduating class, many students will move relatively smoothly into solid jobs. Others will require considerable financial and practical assistance from their parents in order to obtain low-paying, lower-status positions—a situation that few parents fully anticipate.

To make matters worse, pink helicopters' daughters started college in a strong economy and graduated at the start of the Great Recession. As Cindy warned, "I think gas [prices are] going to rise. I think food prices are going to go up. . . . I don't think you guys are going to make the amount of money that we made." Parents could not have predicted this downturn. Their children entered MU in one of the best economic times in decades. Even major political and economic actors failed to see what was coming. Evidence suggests that this unfortunate timing will have lasting consequences on the career opportunities of young adults.[18]

Changes in the life course also caught these parents off-balance.

They planned on creating ideal homemakers, not high-powered career women. But they did not fully realize the financial implications of the lengthy gap between graduation and eventual marriage.[19] Most knew their daughters would wait longer than they did to marry and thought they were in for two to three years of partial support. In actuality, it is likely that many were looking at five to ten years of heavy support—if their daughters were able to make the matches on which they were counting, an issue I return to in chapter 8.

Pink helicopters best exemplify the decidedly non-strategic nature of many parenting approaches. Parents often do not have the luxury of making decisions with full information. Nor do they always make rational calculations in raising their children, instead operating on emotion, instinct, and habit. It is somewhat unrealistic to assume that parenting decisions are different from other life decisions, most of which are not tackled systematically or with prescient knowledge of the outcomes. In the next chapter, however, I turn to two groups of parents whose approaches yielded strikingly better results.

SIX

Predictability or Possibility

Professional helicopters and paramedics tied for the distinction of happiest parents. Both groups were pleased, even ecstatic, about how college unfolded. They differed, however, in the nature of the success that they enjoyed, which flowed from their distinct approaches. Paired together, they offer a study of predictability versus possibility.

Andrea and Keith were professional helicopters, who zeroed in on their daughters' career development. Keith was convinced that Andrea's careful engineering led to positive academic and career outcomes for both Taylor and her sister, whose strong records would carry them to dental and medical school, respectively. As he remarked, "I'm happy because the way we did it worked out in terms of them being admitted to the graduate programs they wanted. . . . I think the decisions we made were the right decisions. . . . It seems that it worked." In leaving nothing to chance, professional helicopters ensured their daughters against risk—as long as they had the resources necessary to effectively execute their approach.

In contrast, Debby and Bob were paramedics who stepped in only in the case of emergency. Their focus on autonomy was a gamble. Without parental micromanagement, the threat of failure was real, but so was the potential for high-functioning independence. As Bob boasted, "My daughters . . . balance their own checkbooks. They pay their own bills. They get good grades. They drive. [They] can cook a darn good meal. They do their own laundry. They're not dependent on us, and I don't want them to be. . . . I'm quite certain that if Debby

Table 6.1. Benefits and Costs of Professional Helicopter and Paramedic Approaches

	Professional Helicopter	Paramedic
Benefits	+ Solid academic performance	+ Solid academic performance
	+ Select more rigorous majors	+ Select more rigorous majors
	+ Risks engineered away	+ More likely to attempt bold career moves
	+ Unlikely to transfer from school of origin	+ Display independence across a wide array of arenas
	+ Extremely low risk of drop-out	+ Eventual peer marriage likely, but not necessary
	+ Smoothly move into professional career	+ Reduced financial and logistical burden on parents
	+ No financial reliance on future spouse	
	+ Leave without student debt	
Costs	− Parents commit to longer-term financial support	− Higher risk of drop-out
	− Youth remain dependent on parents in other ways	− Risky decisions may not have economic payoff
		− May accrue some student debt
Families	$N = 6$	$N = 12$
	UC: Gayle and Roger (Brenda)	UC: Debby and Bob (Brooke); Sally and Alan (Lydia)
	UMC: Carol and Nate (Alicia); Denise (Bailey); Anna and Steven (Erica); Andrea and Keith (Taylor)	UMC: Darci and Russ (Brianna); Molly and Vern (Lisa)[d]; Trudy (Madison); Renee and Peter (Morgan)[d]; Sherry (Sophie); Theresa (Tracy)
	MC: Alice and Jim (Mary)	LMC: Tami and Charlie (Alana)[d]; Betsy (Michelle)[d]; Don (Valerie)
		WC: Tina and Kenny (Monica)

Notes: UC = upper class; UMC = upper-middle class; MC = middle class; LMC = lower-middle class; WC = working class.
[d] = parents divorced or other parent deceased.

and I died in a plane wreck tomorrow, all of our children would fare well."

In this chapter, I compare and contrast the consequences of professional helicopter and paramedic approaches. I highlight similar outcomes, such as in the academic realm—where both groups shone, as well as differences in *why* their daughters performed well. Much of the chapter examines the ripple effects of encouraging versus limiting autonomy in the lives of young adults. The frequency of serious mistakes, boldness of career moves, degree of financial self-sufficiency, timing of romantic coupling, and development of adult competencies are all shaped by this dynamic between parents and children.[1]

Making the Grade

The academic achievers of the book are clustered in this chapter. The average GPA for the six professional helicopters' daughters was a 3.3. The average GPA of the ten paramedics' daughters was slightly higher, at a 3.4—excluding two dropouts.[2] Standout students in both groups were in the 3.6 to 3.8 range, despite the fact that many selected more rigorous majors. Nine women earned solid GPAs in fields of study that were more difficult at MU, including accounting and marketing in the competitive Business School, biology, classics, English, political science, and psychology. Two majored in nursing and education, pragmatic vocational fields that led directly to careers. Only five were in media- or entertainment-based majors (e.g., communications or tourism) frequented by children of pink helicopters.

For the daughters of professional helicopters, this was direct result of parental cultivation. As Andrea described, referring to Taylor's hard-earned 3.6 in biology:

> *Working with Taylor*, some semesters were rougher than others. She would never not hang in there, but she would get very upset because she would be exhausted. There's no fluff in that major. . . . [I would] cheer her on. Support her. Tell her she'll get through it, just a course at a time. . . . She did it, and she hung in there, and made choices that let her have all of these options [after college]. (emphasis added)

In talking with Andrea about Taylor's academic progress, it was clear that she had also experienced it: every hurdle Taylor had to clear was one that Andrea helped her to manage. Andrea and Keith were proud of what Taylor had done at MU; however, her success was not particularly surprising, as it represented the culmination of their long-term plans.

Andrea helped Taylor to stay on a pre-dental track that separated her from most of the women on the floor. Professional helicopters supported the development of stronger academic records in part by hand-selecting the institutional environment that their daughters encountered. Most ensured that women were in the most selective, rigorous majors and programs, took classes with tenured professors, and got involved in the right clubs and activities for their résumés. They took advantage of the professional pathway at MU, as it is designed to move students smoothly into well-paid professional careers and graduate programs. The professional pathway was hard to enter and difficult to navigate without assistance.

For example, Anna and Steven opted for Midwest U's well-ranked Business School, even though there was a good public university system in their home state. This was the only condition under which Erica could go to MU. They made sure that she met all of the qualifications. Anna and Steven had to stretch financially to pay for this. They would end up servicing loans for ten years, when they could have had no loans at all. However, it was a sound choice. As Anna explained, "When Erica went there, she started working hard, and taking the academics more seriously, and really becoming a lot more driven than she was in high school. She was on a path." In that environment, Erica began to perform very well.

The Business School required that students maintain a minimum GPA. It also had a rigorous academic peer culture, encouraged professionalization (the best-dressed students on campus were from the Business School), and was known for its weekend testing—putting a wrench in Friday and Saturday party plans. At MU, being on the professional pathway took on even more importance than it might have at a school with a less developed party pathway. Professional helicopters' efforts to navigate students into particular programs protected their offspring from social temptations, discouraged majors with a poor payoff, and fostered achievement.

Professional helicopters also made arrangements to ensure that funds went primarily to enrichment, not socializing. Recall that, unlike pink helicopters, they set up an accountability contract with their daughters: As Anna noted, "If you're supporting them, you have to have some expectations. Place some minimum standards." This contract changed the meaning of the financial support parents offered. To some extent, children had to earn it, which may have protected them from negative academic outcomes. It was not only the *amount* of funds that mattered, but also how they were administered and what they signified.[3] If women failed to meet the standard, professional helicopters promised to pull their support. This was a conversation that none of them had to have. As Alicia's father put it simply, "I think that it worked."

In contrast, paramedic parents, whose interventions were limited to emergencies, did not oversee academics. They were genuinely surprised and effusively congratulatory when their daughters did well. As Tami happily recounted:

> I think Alana did excellent, absolutely phenomenal. Better than I would ever have expected. I have always been very proud of her for the grades that she has gotten. Sometimes even surprised that she continued to keep it up even through pretty difficult times. She knew she had to push herself to do it, and in the end it was really a great accomplishment for her to know how well she did.

Tami's language offered a striking contrast to Andrea's discussion of Taylor's GPA. Tami emphasized how Alana pushed herself and made the decision to prioritize grades. She also saw the greatest rewards as internal and accruing primarily to Alana.

Paramedics believed achievement was a desirable side effect of sharing the financial burden of college. Most of their children held part-time jobs that were not too taxing, but also prohibited them from spending too much time in the party scene. As Betsy noted, "I knew [a job] would be something that would make Michelle a little more responsible. She couldn't be partying as much if she knew she had a job to go to the next morning. I think it did teach her to manage study time, play time, work time." Betsy's explanation of why Michelle performed well runs counter to the approach taken by professional helicopters, who assumed paid employment could only detract from academics. For paramedics, a (manageable) job was one way for students to be invested in their education, as it offered structure to college life.

Paramedics rarely focused on grades for grades' sake and were thus less instrumental than professional helicopters in this way. Instead, good grades were an indicator of holistic self-development, just like balancing one's checkbook or learning to cook a good meal. These parents believed that women needed to learn an array of cognitive, emotional, and social skills in order to care for themselves after college without much parental assistance. Therefore, the *process* behind academic achievement—and what women learned along the way— was just as, if not more, important than achievement itself.

For example, paramedics reported that women discovered what their talents were when they selected their own majors. As Theresa described, "Tracy really did a lot on her own [academically]. We talked, but it was mostly just cheering her on in her choices, where she felt her gifts [lay], and the coming to the surface of English and writing." Paramedics let their daughters discover how to balance the social and academic, valuing the lesson in self-control as much as the resulting grades. Sally noted, "Lydia learned how to get the grades. I know she loves her parties, but she also figured out how to study too. [Socializing] is just part of life, and I want her to have that—but I didn't want her to tank her grades. Once she finally sorted through that and figured out how to make it happen, it was good." Lydia's realization allowed her to stay on the professional pathway, in the Business School accounting program.

Had Lydia faltered for too long, however, Sally probably would have intervened. Rescues were an important part of the paramedic recipe for success. As noted earlier, Alana's 3.5 GPA, despite a serious back injury, was partly a function of Charlie's money-for-grades incentive program. When Madison's struggles to fit in at MU impacted her academic performance, her parents encouraged her to transfer, even though it would add a year. It was effective. As Trudy told me, "She's turning out to be a great student. It's just amazing. . . . I've seen a lot of maturity over the past few years. She's taken a turn and really worked at things." Similarly, Betsy managed Michelle's early inclination to bail on MU by fielding many sobbing phone calls in the middle of the night, until Michelle was more stable.

Potential for Risk

There were very few ways that a *well-executed* professional helicopter approach could fail a student, particularly one compliant with parental advice. These parents protected women from institutional hazards, such as a robust party scene and easier majors. Student abilities and motivations were managed. Erica, for instance, was not a stellar high school student and socially oriented, but still had a 3.4 in the Business School marketing program. This approach, like that of pink helicopters, was remarkably successful in carrying students to degree completion at the school of origin. All professional helicopters' daughters obtained degrees at Midwest U within six years. A few students took more than four years. However, any delays were for academic reasons (e.g., a major switch or double major). Decisions about academic programs were made collaboratively with parents and did not catch them by surprise.

The paramedic approach posed greater risks. The mistakes that paramedics allowed their children to handle on their own could become too hard for parents to fix. Rescues did not always work or could come too late. It is not incidental that two daughters of paramedics left Midwest U entirely, and neither one was on track to complete a four-year degree when I interviewed them five years from their first year at MU. This kind of outcome was unthinkable for professional helicopters.

Brianna's story illustrates the potential issues that paramedics' daughters faced. She was a straight-A high school student athlete who had experimented with drugs and alcohol. Her father, Russ, was a lawyer familiar with MU. He worried about the party scene: "[Partying] goes on seven nights a week down there. . . . I've had colleagues at the med school whose kids have gone off to Midwest U, gonna go be a lawyer, gonna be a doctor, and at the end of their freshman year of college that is not gonna happen." Initially, he planned on sending Brianna elsewhere. "We thought that she should apply to several small liberal arts colleges, but I also offered her the opportunity to take a post-grad year at [an elite New England boarding school]. . . . MU's a great school, but it's a bad fit for some kids who don't have their feet on the ground 'cause there's too much social life."

I thought it likely that Russ would have been fine with a low-intervention, career-oriented approach, as described in chapter 1. This might have worked well at the schools he had in mind. However, his wife insisted that Brianna make her own school choice. Darci had struggled financially before marrying Russ and wanted to foster Brianna's independence. Darci and Russ seemed to reach a compromise on a paramedic approach, knowing that Brianna might need some help at MU, but—for different reasons—neither was interested in hovering over her.

Within the first year, red flags emerged. Brianna's grades fell. She lost interest in hobbies she used to love and built ties with drug users. Darci and Russ attempted a rescue. They pulled Brianna out of MU and brought her home, where she attended community college. When she wanted to go back, they told her, "Fairview is toxic for you. You can't handle the social scene there," but they still allowed her to return. She ended up hospitalized with an alcohol overdose and was arrested on a felony drug charge. As Russ noted with resignation, "We expect that she's gonna be in jail at some point. We don't know when it will happen. We're hoping it's really short, but I think she's gonna do time, at least a short period of time."

Brianna's parents chose to respect her autonomy—as many other paramedics might have done—despite their initial sense that MU was not a good fit for her. There is no way to know if things would have been different for Brianna with the assistance of a helicopter parent watching her every move, likely at a different school. I suspect that her troubles would have been smaller in magnitude, although probably not absent. Her story, however, underscores a crucial difference between the two parenting approaches compared in this chapter: the paramedic approach is inherently uncertain and in some cases may lead to disaster.

Morgan and Sophie offer less extreme examples of women who did not fare well with paramedic parents. As described in chapter 3, they lacked internal motivation. Both graduated from MU, but barely managed a 3.0 and left with little intellectual or social growth. As Morgan put it during our final interview, "I think I'm still the same person . . . as the first time you interviewed me." Sophie ended up redoing several years of undergraduate credits at a community college on her own dime, in order to make progress toward graduate school.

However, as Sophie noted excitedly, a year after graduating from MU with a communications degree she could not use: "I'm doing really well [in my science classes now]! Which makes me actually feel like this is what I was supposed to do, because these classes are coming so easy to me and I'm actually enjoying them, and it's like, wow, I found my niche finally!" Sophie's case suggests that she (and Morgan) were capable of more. Sherry could have saved her daughter time and money had she been willing, or able, to be a more hands-on parent in college. Sophie might not have been developmentally ready to manage the level of independence that her mother desired of her during college. She needed more active guidance, at least at that stage. It was only after college that Sophie came into her own.

Stick to the Plan or Make a Move

In the transition out of college, professional helicopters found that much of the work was already done. For example, Taylor was reaping the benefits of her parents' early academic and career interventions. As Keith explained:

> At the three [dental schools] Taylor applied to and interviewed with—[she] got offers from all of them. She got involved with the things that are important to dental schools. You can tell what those are by looking at their websites. She got involved with the [charitable] Foundation and did one of the mission trips. She was a Big Sister for a girl. She got involved in the pre-dental club [and] the Cavity Free Zone in her sophomore year. They set up a program with Crest, and that led to her becoming the president of [the club]. The big thing was just to let our daughters know what was possible and then help them to understand the kind of things that they needed to do.

When she arrived at dental school, Taylor realized that not everyone had this advantage. As she told me, "I think the average age in my class is twenty-five or something, because a lot of people just don't know to do [all the scouting work], so it takes them two or three times to apply." She admitted that her parents "played a big role" in her admission to a Top 15 dental school. Based on the starting salaries of graduating students, she anticipated "$90,000, and then I think it can go pretty high from there."

Professional helicopters' initial efforts to place their daughters on the professional pathway also paid off. As Anna raved about the Business School:

> I know exactly how Erica found [her job]. She found it because the School of Business did [it]—and I knew this about them, okay? I knew the kind of jobs people who went there came out of with. . . .

They had mock interviews her whole junior year. She got all sorts of feedback. . . . And they did an amazing job bringing in recruiters. . . . They do it in the fall. That's what's so fabulous. So it's all settled before [graduation]. Parents don't have to worry, 'cause it's all taken care of. . . . I can't say enough about the Business School. To tell you the truth, when Erica found her job, I sent an e-mail to one of the advisors saying that you guys have done everything right. You linked employment to students' studies. Maybe some people think that isn't what it's about, but it is. *It is for parents who spend that kind of money to send their kids to college.* (emphasis added)

Anna understood that by getting (and keeping) her daughter in the Business School, Erica would have access to the type of experiences and services necessary to get a good job. She believed that such help was due to Erica, in part because of how much they spent on her education—implying that not all students should receive equal consideration and assistance.

As Taylor's and Erica's cases suggest, the daughters of professional helicopters could expect employment in a job requiring a college degree or entry into a graduate program. Even Alicia, who ignored parental advice and made a mistake barring her from entry to the Business School, was in a full-time, salaried merchandise coordinator position with benefits. She was disgruntled, living at home, and not highly paid (at $30,000 annually). But it was not a worst-case scenario.

Only Mary, the daughter of middle-class professional helicopters, experienced the worst-case scenario. Had her parents been better informed about what admission to a ranked law school required or understood their daughter's academic limitations, they might have recognized the need to take a different course of action. Instead, they pushed her to double major rather than work on bringing up her 3.0 GPA. As they explained:

Jim: Her fields of study are what's going to get her in. It will when she finds the right university.

Laura: So she's hoping to sell her psychology and criminal justice [double majors]?

Alice: Yes, and that she's worked with kids. At church camp or scout camp, and she's done a variety of things; she's been in videography. . . .

Jim: And they want a class of different people in it.

Alice: Yeah, they don't want all political education majors or whatever. They don't want just that. . . . I'm very strong in God. . . . If that GPA, if it's too low . . . he'll have those people see the other qualities, and they'll override it.

It was hard to imagine affluent helicopters making similar assumptions—or hoping for divine intervention. After a torrent of rejection letters, Mary was unsure how to proceed. She took a job delivering pizza in Fairview. Her experience highlights the problem of employing a helicopter approach without the right educational, cultural, or financial resources.

Mary was an exception, as the daughters of well-resourced professional helicopters had largely predictable trajectories. These women offered a striking contrast to the daughters of paramedics, who made self-generated, often surprising, post-college choices. By granting their daughters more space, paramedic parents enabled moves that otherwise would have been blocked by risk-averse parents.

During college Betsy watched as her daughter pursued her love of journalism. After graduation, she assumed Michelle would seek full-time employment and start paying off student loans. But Michelle had different ideas, as Betsy explained:

Michelle found this advertising school, up in [a city] where her friends are. . . . She even went over the Christmas break and made an appointment on her own. [She] went in and toured the school and talked to a few people. She's going to apply. It's a two-year program. I've looked at the website; it's very amazing. . . . It's going to cost her. She's going to be in debt big-time if she does this. . . . I'm thinking we need a Plan B.

Betsy was dubious about the wisdom of this plan. However, Michelle was adamant: "She told me, 'I think I've got the talent. I've got the drive.' I said, 'Do it. You're only going to know [if it will work] if you put forth the effort. . . . If this is what you want to do . . . get it done.'"

Like Betsy, I was worried. "Ad" or "portfolio" schools like the one Michelle attended are designed to give students an advantage in the competitive advertising industry, but they do not offer a degree of any kind. I did not know if Michelle would be able to break into the field, even with portfolio school experience, because her parents had no industry connections. I would later learn that Michelle's instincts were right. After graduating from ad school, she obtained a job as an art director for a digital advertising agency, in the city that she loved, making over $70,000. It was an enormous success for this first-generation college student.

Lydia, another daughter of paramedics, turned down a certain job for the possibility of one that suited her better. Her father, an accountant, had helped her land a prestigious internship at a "Big Four" accounting firm office in her home city the summer before her senior year. Her parents fully expected her to leverage this into a postcollege career. As Sally described:

I remember sitting with Lydia at a football game for my son [after her last day at the internship]. . . . I said, "Did they offer you a job?" [Lydia said,] "Yep." I said, "What did you say?" [She responded,] "I said no thank you." I remember saying, "Are you nuts?" And she said, "Mom, I don't want to live in [our home city]. I want to live in Chicago." I said, "Okay, and how are you going to make that happen?" She said, "I'll interview and I'll get a job." I thought . . . she may not start right out with an accounting firm. She may end up waiting up tables or something, but she'll get there. A couple weeks later, she called and said, "I got an offer from [a Big Four firm in Chicago]." And I was like, "I don't believe it!" But that's Lydia. . . . She tells us in hindsight that she was scared to death that she wasn't going to get it.

The job Lydia took was closer to friends, and it offered greater potential for upward movement. It was not the choice that Sally or Alan would have made, but in taking the leap, Lydia saw considerable rewards.

Bold decisions did not always lead to professional careers. For example, Monica decided to leave MU during her first year. She saw herself changing as she began to spend time in the party scene and worried about the consequences of continuing on this path. Monica returned home, worked as a hairdresser, and married a man who would support her progress toward an associate's degree in nursing. Despite the turn of events, Kenny was pleased. "[Monica and her husband] are going to be absolutely fine. I think they are good money managers. They seem to have made wise decisions. . . . They are both hard workers . . . [who] seem to have a real zest for life and . . . care about each other. That's what's important."

In another case, Alana's love of the outdoors would lead to a series of tourism jobs in a beautiful community in the western United States, alongside her forest-firefighting boyfriend. The positions were not high paying and did not require a college degree. However, her parents were excited for her. As Charlie noted, "I think they are both adventurer types. . . . Alana wants to see world and to experience more things. . . . I think she'll find her way to do whatever she would like to do. When she is presented with a problem, she can figure out a way to resolve it or a way to overcome it. Those, to me, are the skills that [matter]."

These assessments reflect paramedics' privileging of independence, which is often connected to economic security but not synonymous with career success. Paramedics deemed the cost of college worth it if, at the end, women were competent, contributing, and content members of society. It is possible that the positive views of Monica's and Alana's parents were linked to their less affluent class positions. However, affluent paramedics echoed similar themes. As Alan put it, "My decision on whether I am happy is whether Lydia is happy."

Overall, great variance characterized potential career paths for paramedics. There were professionals earning a solid salary, women who seamlessly moved into graduate school, those who eventually found their way there, happy but low-earning women, and at least two miserable women: Morgan, who was working as a bank teller, and Brianna, who was just trying to stay out of jail. Ceding control to women could lead to great success but also increased the likelihood of unconventional or rocky paths into adulthood.

Long-Term Support vs. "Smart Money"

Helicoptering had a long-term impact on parents' own finances. While most professional helicopters shifted to *partial* support after college, they did not let up until their children were making enough money to live at least a middle-class, but preferably an upper-middle-class, lifestyle. This was consistent with a more extended commitment to primary parenting.

Taylor's parents, for example, would finance half of her dental school costs. When I asked Keith why they made this choice, he assumed I was asking why they were not doing *more*:

> We're trying to balance the fact that we want to retire early against how much we're going to help and the fact that they're going to come out with careers that will be more lucrative in the long run. . . . The loans won't be a burden to them. But sometimes the expenses run more than that. [We don't want them] to try and take out the maximum so we're still helping out. [Also,] they're still on our car insurance, cell phone bills, and there are still a lot of things

that we absorb just as a matter of course that are an in addition to doing some of the direct school funding.

Keith's interpretation of my question was telling. He felt the need to explain why they had pulled back, but I was focused on the fact that they were still heavily supporting Taylor.

Professional helicopters based the length and level of support on how established their daughters' careers were. For instance, Steven believed they would only need to give Erica a car and, in the short term, pay a few bills because "she'll be making pretty good money working, and she already has an apartment that she'll be sharing with her sister." In contrast, Bailey's parents chose to cover her rent and pay her bills while she looked for a better job. This allowed her to find a marketing position for a sports team in a saturated market, translating her sports communication major into a secure position. Her case bore similarities to those of pink helicopters' daughters— except Bailey did the months' long search on her own, impressing her parents with her tenacity.

Not all professional helicopters could afford this level of post-college subsidy, and it mattered for their daughters' abilities to launch careers. Both Mary and Alicia left with weaker records than others. If Mary could have relocated to an urban center after her failed law school attempt, she probably would not have ended up delivering pizza. Yet leaving the small-town Midwest was unthinkable to Mary or her middle-class parents. Similarly, Alicia's parents, although upper-middle class, had strained their finances with out-of-state tuition and could only welcome their daughter back home. Alicia's relatively low-paying position, which offered little room for advancement, reflected the job market near her house. In each case, with funds and valuable social ties, parents could have compensated for academic deficits.

Paramedics, with their focus on crafting autonomy, perceived life after college to be their daughters' financial responsibility. This was, after all, what these parents had been working toward. Peter explained:

I'm not trying to sound cavalier, [but] my expectation is that they step out and they become themselves. They become self-sufficient. That's what they've been doing [in college]. This is what we're preparing for. . . . [They]'re not trust fund babies, where Mommy and Daddy are going to take care of everything. It doesn't work like that, nor should it. You need to carve your own way.

Paramedics did not offer lifestyle supplements. As Bob remarked, "If they go, 'Oh my God, I'm spending more than I'm making,' they better change that. You better find a way to make some more, get some overtime. Go back to graduate school . . . [and] take out some loans. . . . Whether I've got the money or not, I think you need to be responsible."

It would be incorrect to say, however, that paramedics completely ended financial support after graduation. Instead, they interjected in moments of need. Lydia would refer to this tangible, strategic support as "smart money." She explained, "I think the money they gave me was smart. . . . I couldn't go blow the money they gave me. It's good that they could start me out comfortab[ly]."

Smart money often took the form of needed material goods and was typically confined to one-time events. For example, Brooke's new job with the federal government required moving eight hours away from home. As she described, "[My parents] really set me up. Granted, it's only a studio apartment. They only had to buy so much [furniture]. But they were so generous about that and then paid my first month's rent. That was huge. . . . Now I have enough money to do all the basics." It may not have been possible for Brooke to take this job without her parents' assistance. Such financial decisions were made for particular purposes and offered women the equipment, or put them in the position, to begin supporting themselves.

Significant start-up costs were easier for affluent paramedics to cover. In contrast, the less affluent offered financial infusions in the $500–$2,000 range. For instance, Michelle's parents bought her the iMac that was a prerequisite for her design program. Such assistance was important, just not as potentially course altering. Women from less-privileged paramedic households also carried some debt with them after college, while others did not. However, in comparison to many bystanders' daughters (discussed in chapter 7), their burden—generally less than $10,000—was relatively minor.

Paramedics from all class backgrounds offered their daughters a long-term safety net, just in case. As Bob put it, "Hopefully I'll always have the means to help my kids if they get in trouble." Similarly, Charlie noted, "I don't really anticipate her [asking]. . . . But obviously if she asked me for help, and if it made sense to me at all, I probably would be willing to go along with it." For less-privileged women, this was a guarantee of assistance in times of need that most of their low-income peers could not expect.

On Independence—Ties to Men and Parents

There are many different ways to think about independence. Professional helicopters viewed it almost entirely through the lens of career development. They wanted their daughters to build successful professional careers in order to become financially secure. Women had to devote time to self-enrichment *before* marriage in order to ensure that they could both become and attract a well-credentialed, solid earner.

Professional helicopters were largely successful on this front. A majority of their daughters were developing professional careers, single, and in no rush to seriously commit—exactly what this approach demands of women in their early twenties. As Erica put it, "Whether that's based on what my parents have instilled in me or what. . . . I've always been someone who wants to have my own money, have my own career. . . . I just don't see myself being someone who marries young and lives off of some boy's money." This freed women to focus on their own futures, before considering the needs and interests of others.

Only two women in this group were close to marrying. Their parents pushed back. Roger refused to give Brenda and her fiancé his blessing unless they agreed to live apart for a year while she launched her nursing career. Brenda acquiesced. Denise was worried about Bailey focusing too much on the career of her live-in boyfriend (a former college athlete) and was campaigning for later marriage: "I would have thought she would get married when she was twenty-six or twenty-seven. . . . Jump into her career and get some money going [first]." Their efforts ensured that this space was preserved for longer.

In other ways, the daughters of professional helicopters were strikingly dependent. For example, it was hard to imagine Taylor not calling her mother for advice on problems she encountered. During the parental interviews, Taylor and her older sister, who was several years ahead and in medical school, popped in and out of the house, grabbing food and hanging out. I am fairly certain that this was what Keith, and especially Andrea, wanted—despite the ongoing work it entailed for her. I could see Andrea happily helicoptering any future grandchildren. Being a highly involved parent was how she defined herself as a mother and as a person.

Professional helicopters understood that, in some ways, this reliance was not ideal and could not continue indefinitely. Roger explained:

> [We're] gonna really have to kinda back off. Make more suggestions versus [saying], "You need to do this." It's gonna be, "Should you do this?" I gotta change in that respect. I had to do that with my oldest daughter. And that was hard. That was really hard. 'Cause it worked pretty well when we would always just tell her to do something.

Many were developing plans to pull back. As Anna noted, she would be handing over the managing of bills to her children: "I'll show Erica how to go online and do it, and so I'll give her a little mentoring. [Laura: Did you just feel like it was time to transfer that to them?] Well, don't you think? [*Laughs*] [It's] the healthy thing [to do]. Oh my God, I was married at twenty-two." She suggested concern for Erica's abilities to manage adult tasks and noted the distance from markers of adulthood—such as marriage. By privileging career development, Anna necessarily delayed her daughter on other fronts.

In contrast, paramedics made no effort to pace (or end) women's romantic entanglements. Their daughters were more likely to have some sort of relationship during the final interview wave. In most cases, however, women were actively managing these relationships on their own in order to preserve space and delay marriage. For example, two had relationships that they refused to publicly acknowledge, lest they prove too time-consuming or demanding. As Michelle noted, "When he walks through the door, he's my boyfriend, and when he walks out the door, he's not. He'll come over and tell me that he misses me. I don't say it back." Four were in relationships that were headed toward marriage but had built-in buffers. Lydia, for instance, insisted on living apart from her college boyfriend for a year, then together for a year before engagement (although at that point, as she told Ethan, she wanted a ring). Only Monica was already married; this made sense in the rural, less-privileged community to which she had returned.

Daughters of affluent paramedics, in particular, expected peer marriages, even without parental coaching. A potential mate had to be at least college educated, financially secure, and have a professional career. Women claimed to be "picky." Lisa and Lydia, for example, refused to date anyone seriously until their senior year in college, when both met men whom they deemed equals. With sufficient time, it seemed likely most of these women would marry men who were at least as successful as they were. Through continued communications, I learned that Lydia married three years after graduation. Ethan's business-consulting job paid even more than her accounting position. Others were in position to follow suit.

Paramedics' daughters, however, did not need to marry to be secure. Nor were they dependent on their parents. With few exceptions, they were well situated to fend for themselves. It was hard not to attribute this, in part, to parenting style. These women could subsist without financial support. They knew how to budget and pay bills on time. They had an internal locus of control that aided them in managing crises, navigating new cities, and living on their own. They called home less frequently, not because they had strained relations with their parents, but because they were busy and did not need assistance. As Betsy told me, "Michelle's definitely grown into being her own person. That's what I've seen in the four years of her being at college. She's learned how to make those decisions and how to make good decisions."

Daughters of affluent paramedics ascribed their autonomy to parental efforts to hold back resources. Unprompted, Lydia praised her parents:

> There were times I was frustrated because I would have friends who were getting cars and just being given things. I know you have the money. Why aren't you giving me things as well? But, in the end, I think it's really smart. Now I can appreciate it more that I have my own money, and I feel like it's made me want to work harder. . . . There are people who are not as motivated because they have always been given things. . . . [In that case,] I definitely think you're not going to be as independent right after college. You're probably still going to be expecting Mom and Dad to do everything for you.

She drew a direct connection between independence, motivation, and having "skin in the game." Ironically, providing less—not more—was what Lydia saw as her parents' best decision.

Daughters of less affluent paramedics were, in contrast, effusive about their parents' efforts to, at strategic moments, offer the help they needed. As Michelle put it, "My mom, if I ever really needed anything, I knew I could count on her." What Lydia's and Michelle's quotes suggest is that women recognized and valued elements of parenting that were unusual or took particular effort, given their family's class background. Parents' counter efforts may have balanced out problems associated with highly intensive or less involved approaches typical among more affluent or less affluent families, respectively.

The experiences of paramedics' daughters underscore the importance of both support *and* space for high levels of autonomy, demonstrated in multiple ways, across several arenas. Even professional helicopters could not expect their daughters to immediately move into adulthood after graduation; many would likely continue to offer substantial financial and emotional support to their children for another five to ten years. However, as I discuss in the following chapter, it was possible to have too much space. Bystanders' daughters needed active guidance, as well as financial and emotional support, to survive and thrive during and after college.

SEVEN Failed by the University

Bystanders *often had high hopes for Midwest U. Their daughters beat the odds to attend the state flagship—bypassing the for-profit* and community colleges frequented by youth in their hometowns. Midwest U was the most prestigious school in the state. Initially, it seemed an auspicious choice. Parents who went on tours and interacted with MU staff were reassured that this was a good place for their daughters. As Robert explained, "[At orientation] the people were very nice, and they portrayed everything as a big bowl of cherries. . . . Anytime you need help with anything, it's all just right there at your fingertips."

During college, however, bystanders began to feel a sense of betrayal. Robert told me that MU did not offer his daughter Stacey all of the support and assistance that he was led to believe would be available. He explained: "The reality is that help wasn't around every corner, and some of the help she got . . . wasn't all that great. . . . It was a little deceptive, you know, in what they said and then what they produced. It's kinda like the stuff that works on TV, and then you get it home and it doesn't really quite live up to the expectations." Sighing, Robert continued, "I'm an outsider. I'm not directly involved with everything that transpired, but . . . it's never been flat ground. It's always an uphill road."

Robert, like other bystanders, saw himself as an "outsider" because he was not knowledgeable about college life at a school like MU; he felt that his own educational and career experiences were not useful in this setting. These parents could not provide active guidance or

Table 7.1. Benefits and Costs of Bystander Approaches

	Supportive Bystander	Total Bystander
Benefits	+ Avoid financial struggles during college	+ No burden on parents
	+ Access to emotional support	
	+ More likely to persist to degree	
Costs	– Lack access to vital academic and social guidance	– Lack access to vital academic and social guidance
	– More likely to churn through majors	– More likely to churn through majors
	– Low grades	– Low grades
	– Costly immersion in party scene	– Social isolation from peers
	– Greater risk of transfer from school of origin	– Serious financial struggles during and after college
	– Increased time to degree	– Greater risk of transfer from school of origin
	– Accrue student debt	– Increased time to degree
	– Unprepared for financial independence after college	– Risk of drop-out
	– Unlikely to see mating benefits from college	– Heavy burden of student debt
		– Unlikely to see mating benefits from college
Families	$N = 6$	$N = 6$
	MC: Susie and Zack (Emma); Eileen (Karen); Lori (Whitney)[d]	LMC: Jody and Paul (Carrie)[d]
	LMC: Janice (Becky)[d]; Rose (Crystal)[d]; Robert (Stacey)	WC: Diane (Amanda); (Amy)[d]; (Alyssa); (Heather)[d]; Luann (Megan)[d]

Notes: MC = middle class; LMC = lower-middle class; WC = working class.
Amy's, Alyssa's, and Heather's families are included, although no parent interviews were conducted.
[d] = parents divorced or other parent deceased.

effectively intervene when problems arose. Their children needed the skilled advising and caretaking that other youth had in-home. Bystanders often expected MU to offer these services. Instead, they found the university inattentive to their daughters' needs.

Many bystanders identified inadequate academic counseling,

the provision of inappropriate majors, and a hostile climate as road-blocks for their daughters. Other complaints varied with the *type* of bystander. Supportive bystanders, who offered financial backing and emotional support, were upset about the diversionary party scene—as their children had enough funds to participate. In contrast, total by-standers, who did not offer much support to their offspring, were frustrated with the lack of financial assistance the university provided.

These barriers had a meaningful effect on women's college and career experiences. As a group, bystanders' daughters earned lower grades, churned through different majors, and faced lengthy roads to obtaining their degrees. Transferring out of MU seemingly offered a way off of the "uphill road" that Robert described, but the process seemed designed to frustrate families. Most women also left college with debt (in several cases, to their surprise) and were hampered by problematic relationships. Some bystanders saw their daughters persist to graduation at MU; however, this was far from a guarantee of mobility, or even economic security.[1]

Academic (Mis)Guidance

When I asked Robert to provide examples of ways that the university let his family down, he pointed to the first- and second-year academic advisors. "The biggest thing we were disappointed with is she goes to her counselor and she's trying to stay on track and . . . the right hand doesn't know what the left one's doing. You have inexperienced counselors [who] can't provide the guidance that is desperately needed." To understand why he was so frustrated, it is necessary to look at his daughter's experience with her advisors.

Upon arrival, Stacey and her roommate Heather, also from the same town, did what they assumed college students should do—look for interesting classes and try to figure out a major. Unfortunately, none of the classes they selected met general graduation requirements. They were never informed of this fact, and it set them back at least a semester of coursework. When I asked Stacey what she would redo about her first year if she could, she responded. "Classes. I'm gonna recommend my kids to take general classes like psychology. Stuff that you're gonna need for a lot of different majors. . . . I regret taking so many [major-specific] classes last year. I'm never gonna use them."

It is interesting to parallel Robert's and Stacey's interpretations of what happened. He unequivocally blamed the counseling staff for Stacey's inability to select courses appropriate for any major she might declare. After all, he believed this to be a central responsibility of an academic counselor. Stacey implicitly blamed her parents for not passing on critical information. She did not put much faith in counselors but saw how effective other parents were. Thus, Stacey assumed the breakdown in communication was on the parental, not university, side.

Part of the confusion that Robert noted (e.g., "the right hand doesn't know what the left one's doing") also had to do with non-credit remedial classes that Stacey was required to take before enrolling in credit-bearing classes. Robert did not realize that Stacey was near the bottom of her MU cohort, due to poor academic preparation in her less-than-stellar high school, and would need remedial classes to catch up to her peers. Remediation often set disadvantaged students up for failure.[2] Neither Robert nor Stacey understood that these courses would not "count" because no one clearly explained how the process worked.

The major choice process also frustrated bystanders. MU directed students away from the highly pragmatic, vocational, and mostly traditionally gendered majors they envisioned. For example, Eileen was upset when Karen left home planning to be a teacher but was encouraged at college to select another field. She explained:

Karen went [to MU] for elementary ed[ucation]. When you're going through the orientation, they're going, "Most people change their major five times." And they make it sound like it's no big deal. . . . She start[s] hearing all these exotic-sounding majors, which I'm not sure quite what jobs they're going to end up with. Then she went to see the advisor to make plans for her sophomore year, and they're going, "What's your passion?" To me, that's more what you do for a hobby. Most people, that's not what their job is. She said she likes sports. So she went into sports communication.

Eileen believed that college majors should not be "hobbies" but instead reflective of future "jobs." College was expensive for her family. They could not afford for it to offer Karen fun diversions rather than skills that she might use to make a living. Thus, Eileen was displeased with the fact that less pragmatic majors were available and advertised by the advising staff.

Despite her worries, Eileen did not feel comfortable counseling Karen to stick with an elementary education major because "what if . . . we were wrong?" The fear of being wrong rarely plagued well-educated professional helicopters. Yet Eileen's intuitions were correct. Karen came to her parents halfway through college, worried about her ability to get a job in sports media and asking if she could switch back to elementary education. As a supportive bystander who offered her daughter financial and emotional support, Eileen told Karen she would "back her a hundred percent." The late switch would require nearly two additional years of college.

At one point, seven women declared a less rigorous major tailored for affluent, socially oriented women. Bystanders did not trust their gut instinct to steer their daughters away or were similarly seduced by these glamorous majors. Amanda blamed her mother for not stopping her transfer from elementary education to tourism: "[My mother was] like, 'You could be teaching [by now].' I was like, 'Shut up. You should have told me not to switch.'" Eventually, most women would realize that these majors would not pay off for people like them—only those with family money or social ties. They moved into teaching, nursing, counseling, or other pink-collar vocational fields. These fields fed directly to jobs. But the process rarely went smoothly. Stacey, for example, churned thorough five total majors.

Along the way, women became discouraged. Midwest U was already Carrie's second choice, after she failed to get into the architecture program at another school. Early admission to competitive programs often favored women with highly involved parents who could help tailor their applications. Carrie did not have this assistance. Thus, as her mother, Jody, described, "Carrie settled on interior design at MU [which starts with open enrollment]. Things were going well. She was nervous . . . but that was Carrie. . . . Then she was rejected from the program [when they made their initial cuts]. She was led to believe all along [that it would be okay]."

After wasting a year, Carrie transferred to education. A conflict arose when Carrie was shadowing a teacher in a local classroom:

> This very poor teacher left the room to take a phone call and said, "Here, take over the math lesson." Carrie looked at her and said, "But I'm not prepared, and I don't want to stand up unprepared in front of these students." She did the exact, correct thing. That teacher held it against her. [Her instructors] brought her in and told her that she didn't have a passion [for teaching]. They reduced her to tears.

This incident put Carrie's student teaching credits in jeopardy and shattered her already shaky confidence.

Jody saw the interior design dismissal and the heavy-handed teaching critiques as a pattern of mishandling her daughter. As she told me, "Carrie's been crushed at this university a couple of times. . . . You literally are a number; it's hard for them to really understand that you're a real human being." Better-resourced parents generally found problems with major selection and academic programs to be fixable—either by direct intervention, transmission of skills and knowledge, or post-college compensatory actions. In contrast, Jody, like other bystanders, saw Carrie as being at the mercy of the university.

The Social and Political Environment

Robert, like many other bystanders, assumed Stacey would find herself in an environment that supported their family's values. He was mistaken:

> Midwest University embraces gays and lesbians, which is just absolutely against the grain of Christianity. . . . That was one of the reasons [her brother] came home. He had a good background in religion. Sometimes in class, say they were talking about Darwinism, he would disagree and talk about some of the things that are written in the Bible. Holy cow, it raised quite a stir. Even one of the professors said, "You shouldn't say this. . . ." Once you realize that the university in general embraces that kind of a lifestyle . . . which completely goes against the grain of everything they'd been schooled on religiously as young children, it becomes kind of an uncomfortable environment.

I understood that Robert saw his deepest beliefs as under attack. Other parents from working-class towns like Robert's shared similar sentiments. Most espoused conservative religious beliefs and expressed unease with racial, religious, or sexual diversity.

It was easier to sympathize with Robert when thinking about what many affluent, well-educated parents in my sample often took for granted. Most (although not all) would have been horrified if their children encountered explicitly anti-gay sentiments at MU.[3] They assumed—perhaps naively—that direct and explicit instances of prejudice would be rare on campus and unlikely in a classroom. The idealized social environment at MU, that which administrators and student affairs staff attempted to realize, mirrored highly educated, upper-middle-class political sentiments. On numerous dimensions, MU felt like home for these families.[4] In contrast, for those from socially conservative in-state towns, the school seemed foreign and hostile. This contributed to Robert's sense of MU not being what it seemed.

Diversions in the Party Scene

The two types of bystanders, as detailed in chapter 4, varied in their funding levels. This had consequences for the types of challenges their daughters faced at MU. Supportive bystanders offered financial support with the hopes of facilitating academic achievement. However, these funds allowed their daughters to dabble in the party scene. Here, women were surrounded by affluent students and encountered social temptations. Parents were angered when campus social life led their daughters astray but were unable to intervene.

Lori's daughter Whitney joined a top sorority. When I asked what most occupied Whitney in college, Lori replied, "As [far as] I can tell, she'd go over to one of, whatever fraternity it is, I can never keep them straight. And basically just party." Lori saw this as connected to Whitney's academic choices. She complained, "I was disappointed 'cause at first she wanted to start out at [the competitive Business School], and then she right off the bat [decided] that will be too hard. That upset me." As a college-educated, middle-class parent, Lori had exposure to a greater variety of career options than most bystanders. She thought her daughter "would be a great lawyer or doctor. But if she won't do the Business School, she sure won't go to law school, so I can kiss that good-bye too."

Lori's assessment of her daughter's abilities was sound. Whitney barely studied and used her near-photographic memory to achieve straight A's in her easier major. With her 3.85, she had one of the highest GPAs of all the women in the study. She was direct about her choice to do less work so that she could party more. If Whitney had chosen to apply herself, she could have managed to utilize MU's professional pathway with far greater ease than most students. When I asked Lori if she did anything about her frustrations, she noted that she could have "said something smart-alecky like 'You shouldn't be lazy' or 'That's why you're there at school, to get the jobs.' [But] what good is that going to do?"

Zack was in a similar situation but directed much of his frustration at MU's sorority system. He remarked, "I was a little disappointed in Emma's first semester in the sorority because I think it took her a while to understand that sorority life is not the future. I think her grades suffered. . . . [The sorority] impacted her ability to do well in that school." When I asked him to elaborate, he explained:

> You get into a sorority, and if you try to live beyond your means, which a lot of those girls . . . their parents provide them with way too much, and so the expectation was [that it] doesn't matter what school does. When we get out, we'll do whatever Mom and Dad can afford for us to do. I think that there are a lot of those kids that Emma was hangin' around with, and maybe [she] had to learn the hard way. . . . During the semester you can't spend your time partying. A lot of those girls were in classes that were not near as difficult as what Emma was in. She tried to run with them and do the things that they did, and I think that affected her. Her grades showed that.

As Zack astutely observed, he could not afford for Emma to approach college in the same way as students from more affluent families. School had to "do" something for those who did not have family financial resources or job connections.

However, social life on campus was not organized around the concerns of those with more pragmatic goals. It was easy for these students to get distracted by the party pathway. Like Whitney, they often downgraded their majors to those that required less effort in the short term but would be harder to translate into careers in the long term. They were pulled into the party scene, like Emma, as they attempted to find friends and fit in. The organizational infrastructure at MU nudged women in this direction—even if they did not arrive with a heavily social focus, and even if they had big career goals at the start. Supportive bystanders did not know how to push right back or, in many cases, even recognize the need to do so.

Semesters of partying pulled down the grades of most supportive bystanders' daughters—leading to an average of 3.0. While at MU,

Becky, Karen, and Stacey did not meet this benchmark. In fact, Karen's GPA was only 2.5. Even Whitney, an extreme outlier with her high GPA, was performing below her potential in her business-lite major. These women responded to parental funds in the same way as the daughters' of pink helicopters: for a time, they engaged in satisficing behaviors, dialing down their academic efforts to make more space for socializing.[5] As Robert put it, "[Stacey and her friends] like to party maybe a little too much. Perhaps A's and B's weren't as important because it takes some of their social time."

Financial Troubles

Total bystanders did not believe it was a parent's job to pay for college and looked to MU to offer financial assistance. They felt like the university did nothing to help. At the same time, these parents were relatively detached when their children struggled as a consequence. The students in the worst circumstances, however, were those whose parents unexpectedly withdrew aid partway through college.

Diane was very vocal about her financial frustrations. As she told me, Amanda never received any scholarships. "I resent that part of it. Maybe the school could have a program where parents could have gone and gotten [information] on how you do scholarships. To me it's just so out there . . . that I'm like, I don't know how to grasp getting the scholarships." She understood that obtaining scholarships required special information and skills that were not available to her family. She or Amanda might have taken advantage of programming that offered such assistance.

Federal funds turned out to be no easier to acquire. Amanda could not figure out how to fill out the student loan paperwork, so Diane tried. Her efforts were ineffectual: "Everybody liked the FAFSA. We thought we'd get some financial help. We got nothing. So I kind of got discouraged, like we're not going to get anything, so why even bother. I never knew what the income [guideline was], 'cause I tried figuring that all out. I'd spend hours. We don't really make that much money.

Definitely not." Without clear guidance, Diane stopped trying to figure out how to get subsidized loans. Consequently, Amanda would take out unsubsidized loans at exorbitant rates.

Limited financial assistance contributed to social isolation and academic fallout. Parents were callous toward (or unaware of) these problems. For example, Diane knew that "Amanda was the only one [of her college roommates] that had to work, so she felt like an outcast. They were always doing this and that, and no, she had to go to work, so that made her feel different." Yet her sympathy was limited at best. She continued, "Amanda was maybe resentful toward us. She would tell me it made her mad. But even when we were at orientation, they said it was best for students to get a job . . . because it gives them more focus. . . . So I never caved in to her. Sorry about that [said with sarcasm]." Here, she quickly moved from relaying Amanda's plight to defending herself—even invoking the authority of the school.

Luann was not aware of Megan's financial circumstances relative to her peers. When I asked her if Megan ever mentioned the wealth on the floor, her eyes widened and she responded, "No, I never heard her say one thing about anyone having money. . . . Aren't they flamboyant? Aren't they real showy, some of those women?" It had not occurred to Luann that Megan, who spent all of her time working for pay, might be socially isolated. Luann did not understand the vast class divide between Megan and many other MU students.

Total bystanders also overlooked academic issues. For instance, Amanda had the worst GPA in the study—a 2.10 at the time of the last interview—in large part because she was also working fifty to sixty hours a week. Diane was in the dark. As she told me, "Amanda always had good grades and it came pretty easy to her, so I wasn't too worried about her going up there partying and just wasting time. I'm not afraid to go in there and look at her grades. [But] she's probably doing fine." Her assessment was, of course, not correct. Amanda was on academic probation at the time of the parental interview, and this was not due to partying—an activity for which she had little time or money.

While Amanda's GPA was unusually low, long hours spent at work, worries about buying food and paying bills, and a bone-weary tiredness took their toll on the grades of total bystanders' daughters. As Megan explained:

> This one girl I met, she was in a sorority, and . . . she was like . . . "All I have to do is go to school. I don't really have to work, and my GPA is a 3.2 so that's good." I'm like, all you have to do is go to school, and you only have a 3.2? Are you serious? What do you do? I just can't be around those kind of people.

Megan was whip-smart. Although she received the highest GPA in this group (a 3.5—well above the 3.0 average), she could have done better with more financial support.[6] Yet Luann was dismissive of Megan's concerns. As she grumbled, "Megan complains about stress and everything all the time. And that is why I told her, 'Relax. You need time to relax and get away from school because you dwell on it too much.'"

Diane's and Luann's inabilities to connect with their daughters over the difficulties of being low-income students are interesting. Both mothers faulted the university for not making financial aid more forthcoming or clear. However, when it came to discussing the actualities of their daughters' lives, they seemed defensive or uninformed. Perhaps they were worried that they would be judged for not offering more help. Maybe they did not see it as their business to pry into their daughters' affairs—after all, the women were adults. In any case, they did not offer the sort of emotional support other bystanders provided when life at MU proved difficult.

Of all the women in the study, Carrie and Heather fared the worst. Their parents had withdrawn financial support before they could obtain the loans and jobs necessary to survive at college. These women scrambled, mid-semester, to put a plan in place that would allow them to stay at MU. But, in the meantime, they faced severe hardships. Carrie, as noted earlier, often went hungry. Heather was nearly evicted from her apartment, as it took a few days to get a job and even longer to get her first paycheck. She cobbled together holiday gifts from extended family to pay her angry landlord. Their situations suggest that inconsistent parental aid can be more damaging than none at all.

In emergency situations like these, it was not easy for students to get help from the university. There were no food banks on campus for hungry students. Many students were probably unaware that there was a local food bank in Fairview or lacked the necessary transportation to get there. Loans that students might apply for mid-semester were not widely advertised. I never saw such information posted in the dormitories. The phone queue for the financial aid office was frequently so long that students got disconnected. In fact, I had the same experience when I tried to call recently. Regardless, any loans they might access would probably not come in time for pressing housing or food needs. Students without the ability to access parental funds, especially in times of need, were thus extremely vulnerable. There seemed to be limited recognition that such students existed on campus.

A Rocky Road

Movement among different institutions characterized the college careers of five (possibly six) women discussed in this chapter. This is consistent with research on students from less-privileged backgrounds: They are more likely than others to experience interrupted academic trajectories.[7] Alyssa, Karen, Megan, and Stacey all transferred to four-year campuses closer to home. Heather moved into an associate's optometry program. Amy left so abruptly during her first semester at MU that it was impossible to follow her academic trajectory. Three other women filled out paperwork to transfer, although they ultimately did not do so.

Bystanders were angry about how the transfer process unfolded. For example, Eileen was incensed when she realized that Karen's sports communication classes would not transfer—even to a school in the same state system. "Now it's going to take two more years, because nothing transfers. The school knows that. They make it sound like no big deal to change [majors]. But yeah, they're making big bucks by kids changing." Eileen believed she had been swindled out of two years of tuition.

For Robert, Stacey's transfer away from MU was the final insult. He indicated that Midwest U handled the situation poorly:

> The main campus doesn't really communicate well with [regional] colleges like MU Northwest or MU Northeast. . . . They shouldn't even call it MU because it's like different colleges. . . . Different classes and different majors, and that doesn't work 'cause you didn't have this, and this doesn't work 'cause you didn't have that, and this doesn't connect, and we can't count that. I mean, what the hell is that about? . . . It seems like things could be better coordinated between (a) the counselors on campus and the students and (b) the campuses and the satellite campuses.

Robert's trust in MU, and in universities in general, was worn thin at this point. However, he did stop Stacey from opting into a two-year program, like her roommate Heather, because he still saw the benefits of a four-year degree.

Parental interviews occurred four years into college, shortly after several women made school transfers. Therefore, I do not have parents' reactions to regional campuses. However, in *Paying for the Party: How College Maintains Inequality*, there is a detailed discussion of less-privileged leavers versus those who stayed at MU.[8] On every dimension, student experiences improved. Tuition and living costs were more affordable, easing the financial burden on women and their parents. Social integration was smoother, as new campuses were filled with students from less affluent backgrounds working toward pragmatic goals. There was no robust party scene to derail women; consequently, GPAs increased. Women easily found vocational majors in the teaching, accounting, counseling, and health professions. I imagined that, in the years to come, their daughters' positive experiences on regional campuses would likely only sharpen bystanders' critiques of the flagship institution.

Transfers added time to the degree. For two daughters of supportive bystanders, this would amount to two additional years of schooling each. However, all were still slated to receive four-year degrees within a six-year window. In this regard, parental financial support was protective: Women could be waylaid in their progress, but they were likely to eventually obtain bachelor's degrees. Supportive bystanders, whose mobility dreams hinged on this fact, made sure of it. There was no way that Eileen was going to abandon Karen, nor would Robert stop funding Stacey, when their daughters were so close to the finish line.

In contrast, daughters of total bystanders faced serious degree completion issues. Not one obtained a four-year degree within a four-year window. Timely progress through college was nearly impossible. As noted above, a few abandoned ship—opting for more cost-effective two-year degrees or potentially no degree at all. Others would recalibrate expectations, anticipating a five- to eight-year stay at college. The great irony was that the longer they were in school, the more it cost. By moving to regional colleges, several women hoped to mitigate this expense. The worst option was to slowly toil away at high-priced MU.

Debt and Denial

The daughters of total bystanders carried the most student loan debt, as their parents offered little to no financial assistance. Their debt ranged between $15,000 and $50,000. For instance, Carrie, who stayed at the costly MU campus, anticipated paying $500 a month for around eight years, to cover her $44,000 dollars in loans. As she told me, "It's emotionally hard for me thinking about that, just the weight of it, but I had to do that to get an education. So it was worth it, I guess.

But it's hard thinking about that much money, and a lot of it is interest." With a degree in elementary education and a job after college as a day-care provider, servicing her student loan debt would absorb a sizable chunk of her take-home pay for the rest of her twenties.

These women were concerned about the debt they carried and the impact it would have on their lives after college. Their total bystander parents were not. See the following exchange with Luann.

> *Laura:* At this point is Megan aware of what her loans are?
> *Luann:* Yes, very aware of it. It is a worry [for her]. I told her, "Don't worry about it. You are in the same boat as millions of other people with college loans. You can just work and pay them off when you can. And who is to say—by then, you could inherit money. You don't know what the future is going to bring. . . . [Worrying] is a lot of negative energy."

This may have been a coping mechanism, as getting anxious about the situation would not change it. However, Megan could have used some practical advice.

Supportive bystanders shielded their daughters from college costs during school but not after graduation. The total debt these students faced was smaller, but they were ill prepared to take it on. When I asked Susie if Emma knew how much she owed in student loans, she replied: "I would guess not [*laughs*]." Janice similarly told me Becky was unaware of what she had to pay back. She felt it was useless to inform youth earlier because "you can talk to your child until you're blue in the face . . . and until they start seeing the bills themselves. . . . [Now] she's seeing how fast that money goes." This approach toward financial matters was intended to relieve women of monetary worries as they obtained four-year degrees. However, after college women were often shocked to learn what they owed.

In one case, a parent maintained complete silence about her daughter's loans during college. Lori told me that Whitney would have around $10,000 to $15,000 dollars of student debt. Yet when

I asked if Whitney knew this, Lori noted, "I don't think she does. I never mentioned it to her." Indeed, Whitney later complained, "I didn't know that I did [have loans], but thanks, Mom, for taking that out in my name." Whitney lived rather lavishly in college in order to fit into her sorority. Dues alone cost thousands of dollars a year, which came from loans. Had Whitney been aware of this, it is possible that she would have made different choices. Not involving women in college cost calculations meant that they had little control over what would, in many cases, be their own post-college debt.

Problematic Partnerships

Partnerships with solid earners who could share financial responsibilities might have improved women's economic circumstances. Many were in serious relationships and headed to early marriage. However, the hometown men they paired with had limited levels of education, held traditional gender views, and posed barriers to women's career development. Women's bystander parents did not intercede.

Several years into college, Megan married a local man who was not supportive of her career goals. As detailed in chapter 4, her mother, Luann, disapproved of this match, worrying that he would stop Megan from pursuing the education that Megan wanted. Yet Luann chose to remain silent about her misgivings. Megan's husband isolated her from her family, was verbally abusive, and engaged in physically threatening behaviors. At times, even our interviews felt risky, as he disapproved of her talking to me. After he smashed her windshield in a rage, she fled. Megan was forced to leave her regional school mid-semester and lost credits. She would eventually divorce her husband, as Luann predicted. It seemed unlikely that this would have transpired for the daughter of a professional helicopter, whose mother would have engineered a troublesome suitor out of her daughter's life—or at least said something.

This was not an isolated case. Most of the men this group of young women dated had little to offer. They had limited income; some were engaged in illegal activities. Several were abusive. They were not the partners that bystanders hoped their daughters would find. As Amanda reported, Diane used to tell her, "You're in college, and there's twenty thousand guys on campus. . . . Come on, you have to find somebody. . . . Hang outside the chemistry building." However, with no better candidates in sight, bystanders did not help their daughters to leave relationships that were pulling them down.

Alyssa's case offers an illustration. For several years, she financially supported her unmotivated fiancé. He consistently failed and retook entry-level courses at the local college. "Meanwhile [he was] unemployed. . . . It's not cool." Alyssa asked her mother for help:

> I've never broken up with someone. . . . And I don't know how to go about the whole process. [My mother] wasn't willing to help me and didn't give me a whole lot of guidance. Every time I'd try to make a move, she would always be like, "What about this? Did you talk to him about this?" And I'm just like, "Do you think I want to call up every single day and see how he's doing and check on him?" It just got to the point where I couldn't talk to her. . . . [Eventually] I kind of made it on my own, and trying not to involve her, so she doesn't have to deal with it.

It was not just that Alyssa had no practical advice on how to execute a breakup. Alyssa's mother wanted to see her daughter married and already thought of the fiancé as "her son." This would create a rift in her relationship with her daughter.

Bystanders' daughters did not acquire ties to economically secure, supportive men from their time at Midwest U. Instead, they drew from the mating pools in their hometowns, as if they had never left. As Susie reported, "Emma met Joe, who she went to [high] school with [but] didn't really hang out with. . . . They came back full circle to [this post-industrial town]." These women's social networks, even those in sororities, never expanded deeply enough to facilitate the romantic benefits others would likely reap from college.[9]

Eventually, their parents seemed resigned to this fact. By the time that I interviewed her, Diane believed that "you usually follow with your class of people . . . [and] naturally grow into the class that you're in. Wealthier people are usually drawn to other wealthier people." These mating patterns would likely have consequences for women's future class positions, as they could not rely on a steady and substantial second income.

Post-College Struggles

By the final round of student interviews, only five of the twelve women discussed in this chapter had graduated. These women—Becky, Carrie, Crystal, Emma, and Whitney—stayed at MU. Seemingly, they should be the success stories. However, in the first year out of college, only one woman secured a job that required a four-year degree.

Emma graduated with a biology major, even though she had abandoned her plans for dental school (see chapter 4). Zack assumed everything would work out. As he noted, "I expected her to continue on and get into a field that she wanted to be in and succeed in it. Excel in it." However, this did not happen. Zack explained:

> Emma wanted to get into microbiology, which would have required her to go on and get her master's. . . . . She wanted to work in a lab situation for the CDC. . . . She looked into a training class through one of the local hospitals that would provide an opportunity to work in that field. . . . I think her overall GPA may have had some influence on that because they only take four out of a hundred. She just found out that she was not going to get into that. I think she's kind of struggling right now as to what she wants to do.

Zack had come to realize just how much Emma's mediocre record would hurt her. Her 3.0 was not sufficient to compete with the large numbers of biology students who did not gain admission into medical, dental, or veterinary schools and were thus seeking lab positions.

Emma would end up taking a position as a dental assistant, making $11 an hour. The job did not require a college degree. In fact, she was the most educated person in her office, outside of the dentist himself. Zack was upset:

> She ended up working in the dental field again. The thing that she didn't want to do. At a level that's well below her capabilities, and I just think she's got a lot more talent and a lot more to give than what she's able to do in that particular job. I would have loved to have seen her have an opportunity to get a good, solid career started. That just hasn't happened. It hasn't happened for a lot of college kids, I think.

Still believing in the power of schooling, Zack hoped that Emma would "continue her education" and move out of this "stop-gap" situation. It was possible this could happen, and that Emma's situation would look different five years out. However, her college record would limit what she could do. In any case, she was already at least two years behind her graduating cohort in making progress toward a more lucrative career.

Janice was also worried about her daughter's job prospects. Initially, she "was really hoping that Becky would get a teaching degree," but Becky struggled with depression in college. In order to keep her in school, Janice abandoned her preference for a practical major. She told Becky, "If you feel like there's so much pressure on you, then just choose something that you think you'll love and get a degree." Becky opted for classical studies but graduated with a 2.9 GPA. At this point, Janice realized that "Becky's best prospect is probably in sales. That's what I'm in, and it's like the last thing I would want either one of my kids to be in"—especially because many such jobs did not require a college degree.

Even sales would be better than what Becky would do immediately after college. As Janice explained, "She's working as a waitress at two jobs right now. I hope that's not going to be her life either." Janice was concerned about the sustainability of such an approach: "She is at a point right now where she can be on my health insurance. She only has another year. She has got to get a job where she gets benefits. She has to." Like Zack, Janice held out hope that Becky would "go back and get a master's" in order to establish a more promising career path. However, this was exceedingly unlikely. Classics is a highly selective field for graduate study. Even if Becky chose a different field, her 2.9 GPA was too low to receive serious consideration.

Why did bystanders' daughters face such dismal prospects upon graduating from MU? Certainly, their weak records left them with limited career options. However, pink helicopters' daughters looked no better on paper, but many managed to secure higher-paying jobs requiring a college degree. What made the difference?

Bystanders lacked the kind of contacts that might be useful to their daughters. Lori, for instance, did "not see anything wrong with [providing an in] as long as your kid isn't stupid." Her only personal tie, however, was through her ex-husband's wife. "She works somewhere with a surveying company, and they offered to get Whitney a job. Like standing out [Laura: as the cars go by . . .] sweating, and then the orange [vests]." We both laughed at this image, knowing how uncomfortable stylish Whitney would be in such a situation. The surveyor job, however, was the *best* potential connection that any of the parents in this group had to offer their daughters.

After college, bystanders—of both types—did not, and often could not, build their daughters a financial bridge into new careers. For example, Paul told me:

I think Carrie has got to find out on her own how much it costs to eat, how much gasoline she is going to use in her car. She probably doesn't realize that when I was her age, and her brother was born, we didn't do anything. If we went to McDonald's, that was a treat.

She is finding out the same thing. . . . I want her to learn a few lessons. . . . I think that everybody needs to go through that.

I was somewhat surprised by Paul's statement, given that Carrie had
been on her own through much of college. When I asked if there were
forms of support that parents *should* provide, he noted, "The only
thing that I do for them, really, is I have painted their apartment[s].
Each of them, I gave them a piece of furniture for their first place. . . .
Carrie has this room [in her sister's apartment]. I gave her a really nice
[used] queen-size bed, and I gave her a television."

A bed, television, and painted walls were useful comforts. However, Carrie did not have the kind of financial support she would need
to pick up and relocate to cities where she could land a teaching job.
While the market was dry near her hometown, larger cities offered
positions. But Carrie could not get to them, even for an interview.
This is how she ended up as a day-care provider. Paul staunchly believed that he was doing right by Carrie, and all of his children, in
forcing them out on their own. Other parents would offer a free place
to stay, potentially for years, as their daughters attempted to enter
the labor market. However, none of these parents—even supportive
bystanders—had any more to give.

Whitney's situation after college, by far the best of this group,
highlights the difficulty of managing without parental support. She
landed a position that paid $40,000 a year, but these funds did not go
far in Chicago. Lori thought it ludicrous that Whitney tried to leave
home. As she commented, "You go right ahead, see if you can have an
entry-level job and live in Chicago. In her efficiency apartment under
the L [transit system] [*snickers*]. Under my breath I will say, 'I told you
so.'" Indeed, Whitney did not live in the nicest neighborhood. She was
living "paycheck to paycheck." She would struggle to meet the dress
code necessary for her workplace. Whitney told me that she was even
"pulled into HR . . . and they said something to me. I was in tears. . . .
It's suits all the time, but I can't afford a lot of suits." This was not the
glamorous city life experienced by daughters of pink helicopters.

Who Is to Blame?

Bystanders' stories are depressing. Some saw their dreams of family mobility crushed. All formed a deep distrust of the university, based on their daughters' experiences.[10] The notion that a college education is the "best investment" rang false for bystanders and their daughters—at least in the context of MU. By graduation, the group of women remaining at MU was considerably smaller. Of those who managed to persist, only one was poised to experience upward mobility. How do we make sense of this situation?

Some readers will blame the women themselves. It is true that women often arrived at Midwest U unprepared academically. They were not well informed about college. These characteristics, however, can be attributed largely to class differences in primary- and secondary-school quality, available educational resources, and prior upbringing.[11] The fact that many of these women managed to make it to MU at all is a testament to their abilities, especially relative to those in their surrounding communities. For total bystanders' daughters, who also lacked financial and emotional support from their parents, attendance at the state flagship was nothing short of a miracle. At college, these women showed sheer grit and determination well beyond that displayed by any other women on the floor. Their struggles at MU were not rooted in a lack of effort.

The daughters of supportive bystanders, who had financial backing from their parents, were in a somewhat different situation. Admittedly, they were not dragged kicking and screaming into the party scene. Some readily confessed that they just did not want to work that hard—or rather, they really wanted to play hard. This makes them, if anything, remarkably similar to a majority of their peers at MU. Yet their peers often managed to emerge from college unscathed and ready for professional careers. Even those who left MU with poor academic records, after having loads of fun, sometimes saw no penalty. The differentiating factor was parental intervention. Those with involved and well-resourced parents were more likely to land solid jobs or secure positions in graduate programs.

We might, then, blame parents for their daughters' problematic college experiences and limited educational returns. One total bystander even ended the interview with what sounded like an admission of guilt: "I probably under-parented. . . . Dropping them off and picking them up in the spring, I don't think is necessarily the right way." Paul acknowledged, even in a small way, that his parenting approach was not ideal. He seemed to understand that Carrie would have been better off if had he managed to be a more active parent during college. This is likely true. All of the women discussed in this chapter would have probably fared better with professional helicopters or paramedics at their side. However, this was not plausible for parents who had little to no experience with college, limited economic resources, and were frequently dealing with other family crises (e.g., divorce, bankruptcy, illness, etc.).

Having a bystander parent did not have to cost women so much. Things could have been different in a different institutional context, as women's experiences at regional schools suggested. The problem was that bystander parenting approaches aligned poorly with Midwest U—a relatively expensive school with weak academic advising, an array of majors of varied quality and market value, and a seductive party scene. Students could not effectively navigate such an institution on their own, without encountering serious roadblocks to mobility. As Robert's tale of betrayal suggests, most bystanders came to view their daughters' situations as indicative of institutional failure. The school did not provide the services that they saw as essential to student success.

What organizational infrastructure would work for bystander parents? Their families needed a functioning mobility pathway, which did not exist at Midwest U. A mobility pathway levels the playing field for students who lack family advantages. It offers long-term and emergency financial aid, ideally in the form of grants, for those who need it. It is built around majors that do not require family interventions to meet requirements or secure jobs after college. This pathway can intersect with the professional pathway, but it is focused on training students to move directly into vocations (e.g., teaching, nursing, or accounting). It does not distract students with a thriving party scene. Campuses with a strong mobility pathway often have enough first-generation and low-income students to normalize these statuses, rather than making them a source of stigma. Advising is holistic, dealing with students as complete people—just as parents do with their children. This requires financial aid, academic advisors, residence hall staff, faculty mentors, and others to work together in helping students solve social and academic issues or prevent them before they arise.[12]

A healthy mobility pathway reduces the importance of parents for students' educational and career success, rather than penalizing students who lack parental guidance and support. Unfortunately, taking on responsibilities that might otherwise be assigned to parents runs counter to the current trend at many public universities. As I discuss in the final chapter, schools are coming to rely heavily on parents to solve institutional problems posed, in part, by the privatization process. College is effectively being outsourced, in ways that are likely to exacerbate the plight of bystander families.

College Outsourced

G*etting a child to college is not the end of the road, as parenting con-* tinues to matter well past age eighteen. In fact, how parents approach the college years shapes the life chances of young adults— sending youth on fundamentally different trajectories. Parents' own satisfaction and economic security also hang in the balance. Even the modern public university depends, in part, on the availability of parental support and labor. College parenting is thus vitally important to the post-secondary enterprise.

This chapter addresses the outsourcing of responsibilities, tasks, and functions associated with colleges and universities to parents. I discuss the academic and career advantages that accrue to students with involved and well-resourced parents, synthesizing findings from chapters 5 through 7. These benefits, enjoyed by an exclusive set of families, are one consequence of the new "partnership relationship" between parents and universities, which is driven by privatization. There are, however, high costs to this arrangement for most parents and students—especially those from disadvantaged backgrounds. Looking forward, I suggest three policy solutions to ease parents' burdens and equalize class disparities, turning to the market, status-based processes, and the state.

The Parenting Advantage

Professional helicopter and paramedic approaches systematically benefitted students, particularly in the context of MU. Recall that pro-

fessional helicopters funded heavily and carefully orchestrated career development for their children, while paramedics privileged autonomy but offered financial support and emergency interventions.
These two approaches had a few features in common: they asked parents to contribute *at least* a moderate amount of labor and required
specific cultural, financial, and social resources to execute properly.

From a class reproduction standpoint, professional helicopters
won. Most of their daughters earned solid grades, persisted at the institution of origin, graduated in a relatively timely fashion, and moved
into jobs that required a BA or entered graduate programs. There was
little doubt that these women would eventually be self-supporting—
not reliant on their parents or a future spouse. Their success had less
to do with women's talents or drive than it did parental efforts. They
were good but not stellar high school students (which is why they
ended up at MU), and several were socially oriented. Most of their
mothers used class-based resources to engineer social, romantic,
and academic risks out of the equation. This approach worked well
as long as women complied with parental efforts—although it was
both labor intensive and expensive for parents.

Why were professional helicopters generally so successful? They
offered the parenting trifecta: savvy parental involvement, high
levels of funding, and investment in a gender-egalitarian model of
women's economic security, at least in the career realm. Only parents
who could manage to do all three saw good returns. For example, Andrea, a college professor, understood exactly how to navigate Taylor
through MU and prepare her record for admission to dental school.
She had the funds to fully support Taylor's career development and
fiercely resisted traditional gender arrangements. Removing any single piece of this puzzle posed an issue for academic and early career
performance.

Here, Janet's case is illustrative. As detailed in chapter 1, she was
an exception at MU—a wealthy parent who believed in and financially supported a career-building experience but maintained a low-
involvement approach. Her daughter, Linda, was not the type to be

Table 8.1. Indicators of Parenting Success

Parenting Approach	Women's Outcomes During College		Women's Outcomes After College		Parents' Outcomes	
	Academic Record*	Persistence	Post-College Employment	Financial Independence	Labor and Expense	Satisfaction
Professional Helicopter	3.3 GPA; 50% opt out of easy majors	Remained at MU; 66% graduated in four years; all in six	All but one in BA-requiring jobs or graduate school	Set for future independence and peer marriages	High labor for mothers; costs taper over time	High; all went according to plan
Pink Helicopter	3.0 GPA; only one easy major opt-out	Remained at MU; 66% graduated in four years; all in six	44% in BA-requiring jobs or graduate school	Highly dependent on parents or future spouse	High labor for mothers; high and continued costs	Low; angry at self, disappointed with daughter
Paramedic	3.4 GPA; 60% opt out of easy majors	75% at MU; 75% graduated in four years; 83% in six	58% in BA-requiring jobs or graduate school	Self-sufficient and secure, affluent set for peer marriages	Moderate shared parental labor; bounded cash infusions	High; pleased with daughter
Supportive Bystander	3.0 GPA; 40% opt out of easy majors	66% at MU; 66% graduated in four years; all in six	Only one in BA-requiring job or graduate school	Pushed into self-sufficiency but unprepared	Low labor, high expense during college	Low; angry at MU
Total Bystander	3.0 GPA; 33% opt out of easy majors	50% at MU; no one graduated in four years; 50% in six	Future looked promising for those who left MU	Self-sufficient by necessity, not secure	Low labor and expense	Detached but frustrated with MU

*GPA averages and major information do not include women who dropped out in the first or second year of college.

seduced by MU's party scene; she refused to drink underage. Linda also self-identified as a "nerd" and had unusually bookish tastes. Still, she floundered at MU academically, unable to find her niche.

Linda decided to stay in college an additional year to acquire a French major, alongside international studies. She turned to her parents, but they only offered money and uninvolved assurances. Linda explained, "[My parents] are the most frustratingly supportive-of-what-you-want-to-do people you will ever find. I'm very indecisive. I can never make up my mind. They are like, 'Whatever you decide is good with us.' I'm like, 'Why don't you decide for me?'" In her fourth and fifth years of college, Linda was toying around with plans to teach English in France, joining the FBI or CIA—which she believed would require learning Arabic (necessitating more college), and "sav[ing] the world in the Peace Corps." She had a 2.9 GPA. Only the first plan was remotely possible, at least right out of college; yet no one had seemingly informed Linda of this.

At MU parenting approaches organized around career development necessitated careful hand-holding. There was a professional pathway available, complete with rigorous academic programming and career assistance—for select groups. But without parental guidance, identifying and getting into those programs was difficult. Linda's story suggests that the notion of parents as distant funders of young adulthood is flawed—at least in the context of a school like MU, where there were many ways to go wrong and not many institutional safeguards. Here, involvement was key.

However, involvement was not enough. What parents chose to cultivate in their daughters was equally important, as not all investments contributed to academic or career success. Pink helicopters' focus on funding fun and the development of normatively feminine traits led women to engage in satisficing behaviors, dialing down academic efforts in favor of time spent socializing. Many of their daughters were creative, smart, and capable. Yet as a group, they had lower GPAs and were likely to select Midwest U's least rigorous majors, often in media-based fields. After college, most were unable to translate this record into a career requiring a four-year degree. Others did so only on the backs of their parents, who needed industry connections and extreme affluence to ensure class reproduction.

Pink helicoptering was the most resource-dependent approach; however, potential downward mobility could occur for *any* helicopter family lacking resources. Being a middle-class professional helicopter was particularly ill fated, casting doubt on the notion of "concerted cultivation" as a broadly middle-class parenting style—at least for older youth.[1] For example, Alice and Jim encouraged Mary's dual JD and PhD dreams without a levelheaded assessment of her capabilities. Nor did they understand what she would need to do to fulfill her dreams. These parents could not smooth Mary's way financially or offer connections to facilitate alternative careers. At the last interview, Mary was delivering pizza. Middle-class parents like Mary's might have been able to manage concerted cultivation when their children were younger, but doing so successfully in college requires upper-middle-class funds, social ties, and cultural knowledge.

It is tempting to say that parents who cannot be professional helicopters should simply be paramedics. For the parents in my study, being a paramedic meant less worry, bounded levels of involvement, reduced expense, and a more egalitarian division of parenting labor. And on many dimensions paramedics' daughters fared well. There were notable exceptions, but on the whole, their grades were high, persistence and completion rates strong, and job placements after college good. Those from affluent families were also headed to peer marriages.

If we broaden our criteria for evaluation, it is even possible to view the paramedic approach as having the *best* returns. Most paramedics' daughters stepped off of campus and into near-immediate financial and emotional self-sufficiency. They were well-rounded, capable adults, with an internal locus of control and strong problem solving skills. It was easy to see these competencies as serving women well into the future.

This is not to say that being a paramedic is attainable for most parents who find professional helicoptering to be impossible. Paramedics had to be able to accurately assess and remedy serious threats. They required knowledge of how the higher education system works. Surplus funds were necessary; targeted cash infusions allowed women to make important career moves after college. Paramedics did not hover, but they watched—a task that was challenging for full-time employees with limited career flexibility. This endeavor necessitated at least a baseline level of familial resources.

In sharp contrast to either paramedics or professional helicopters, the stories of bystander families illustrate the limitations of low-involvement approaches at a school like MU. Supportive bystanders offered money and uncritical emotional support. This ensured eventual graduation; however, it also put the party scene in reach. Parents did not know how to address the resulting academic fallout or steer their daughters toward majors they could use to secure jobs requiring a BA. Total bystanders provided virtually no financial or emotional support. Their daughters' time at college was often punctuated by stress, poverty, and menial paid work. It was a hard road. If these women managed to persist, the best thing they could do was leave for a regional university.

It is certainly possible that the career circumstances of bystanders' daughters will change over time. Many were still finishing their four-year degrees. Those who were struggling five years after the start of college might begin to look more like their peers ten years out. However, at the time of the final interview, bystanders' daughters were not well positioned to make up ground—given that many of their peers were already gaining experience, forming connections, and obtaining more training in their desired fields.

What makes a bystander approach problematic is not inherent. It is not irrational to think that eighteen-year-olds should be "grown up" (in fact, at one point in time, most were).[2] Or that tuition should include more complete services. The issue lies, in large part, with the institution. As much as administrators and staff at schools like MU might complain about helicopter parents, they implicitly assume that students arrive with helicopters by their side. Students with parents who parent intensively, or at least strategically, are rewarded.[3] Only a small slice of the college-going population arrives with parents who can manage to do so effectively.

While affluent parents might adjust their parenting approach to avoid downward mobility, it is not easy for less-privileged parents—who often lack funds, time, social connections, and an intimate understanding of higher education—to be more involved. As Herbert Gans realized in his 1962 study of Italian Americans in the inner city, "us[ing] middle-class values to help low-income populations solve their problems" is generally not a wise or tenable approach.[4] Intensive parenting approaches only work when paired with considerable class resources. Ignoring this reality is likely to disadvantage those with limited resources and make them the targets of blame for their own misfortunes. Instead of attempting to "fix" parents, we might turn our gaze to the post-secondary system that asks so much of them.

A New Relationship with Families

Recent years recall an era in which a small set of affluent families supported an American higher education system still in its infancy. In return, schools provided elite families with an exclusive social playground, necessary to solidify social and professional networks. Each served the other well—at the cost of the many non-white, poor, and immigrant families who were excluded from the social contract.[5]

Universities once again depend heavily on families. An ongoing process of privatization, or the replacement of public funds with private dollars, is at the heart of this relationship.[6] The problem has been exacerbated by the rapid growth of administrative positions, contributing to rising costs.[7] Tuition dollars have been used to fill the financial hole. Net tuition now rivals state and local appropriations as the primary funder of public higher education.[8] In this equation, affluent parents become a crucial source of financial support during their children's college years—and even after, as donating parents of alumni.

Parental contributions are also needed for students to focus on young adult self-development projects, unhampered by heavy work or family obligations.[9] Four-year schools structure their classes, activities, and living options around traditional students and expect parents to do the work of maintaining them. Many parents in the middle to top stratum of the class structure—precisely the parents that universities target—readily accept these tasks. They believe that a college experience is something that "good" parents offer, even as the financial, physical, and emotional costs of doing so continue to escalate.

The new "partnership relationship" also recruits parents into the labor of producing successful students and workers.[10] Affluent, well-educated parents—typically mothers—often dive headlong into the roles of academic advisor, career counselor, therapist, and life coach. They have flexible careers that allow for emergency visits, ties to professionals in industries where their children show interest, a savvy understanding of higher education, and money to smooth over every hurdle. In the end, however, their efforts become invisible—student achievement is attributed to individual talent and hard work. Mitchell Stevens refers to this process as "laundering privilege," as the evidence of family advantages is washed away.[11]

Parents even mediate the translation of a college degree into a job. Top-tier investment banks, management consulting firms, and law firms look for markers of status that parents cultivate in their children—for example, skill in upper-class extracurricular activities, a narrative of achievement and actualization, and delicately honed interactional skills.[12] Universities rely on families to transmit (and deeply embed) these traits, as the degree alone is not enough to secure top jobs. Internship and job placement services are also outsourced to parents, who help ensure the career outcomes for which universities may become increasingly accountable.

It is little wonder that children from affluent families are highly

desired by elite schools. Their parents may, in fact, be the real assets to prestigious colleges and universities. In order to compete for
these families, moderately selective public universities must provide
them with special benefits. For example, many schools have shifted
away from offering large need-based scholarships to awarding numerous small merit-based packages. These tend to go to wealthier
families, whose class advantages have earned their children stronger
records—a process that some refer to as "financial aid leveraging."[13]

Universities may also be increasing investments in targeted programs with competitive admissions, such as MU's Business School.
Honors colleges offer another example. Early screening mechanisms
ensure that most students in academically oriented programs come
from privileged families. Internal stratification within colleges and
universities guarantees that these students, but not others, find help
around every corner.[14] Professional parents paying top dollar expect
at least this level of assistance from a school—otherwise they would
go elsewhere.

Wealthy families seeking a social experience also have their own
demands. They want control over where their daughters—and presumably sons—will live and with whom they will socialize. They
want institutions to offer a rich catalog of easier majors. They clamor
for big-time college sports, Greek life, and a robust party scene. And
universities provide these perks—despite the fact that, for most students (even most of those who seek it) this particular organization of
campus life is detrimental.[15]

These benefits are not free for parents. They come with heavy demands and other costs, as detailed below. However, well-resourced
parents are advantaged when parental labor is built into the very
form and function of the university. This is a game they that they can
win, simply by out-strategizing and out-funding everyone else. At
a school like MU, many students arrive underprepared, lacking parental support, and unable to receive compensatory university assistance. Affluent, well-educated parents and their offspring have a
distinct advantage. At elite institutions, it may be harder to beat the

competition. The bar for admission is higher, virtually all parents are well equipped to assist their children, and university support systems may be richer. Here, intensive parenting may be taken to even more extreme levels.

The Costs

The shift toward a privatized public higher education system exacts a toll. It reinforces the importance of parental class background for college success, supports gendered college experiences, and extends youth dependence on their parents—at a great financial and psychological cost to families.

The Centrality of Family Background

University outsourcing to parents increases the salience of family background for post-secondary success, exacerbating existing inequalities. If research on younger youth is any indicator, we might expect growing gaps over time in post-secondary educational achievement between those from rich and poor families.[16] Racial disparities are also likely to persist, as a substantial proportion (although not all) of the variation in educational success can be explained by differential access to class-based resources.[17]

Many cash-strapped families are being priced out of state flagships, even regional universities. The average annual cost of attending college (including tuition, room and board, and fees) has increased significantly. Families in the bottom income quartile are now paying 59 percent of annual income, after taking into account grant aid, to send a child to a four-year public school. The two middle quartiles are also significantly impacted, at 31 and 25 percent of annual income, respectively. Only the top quartile can reasonably afford it, spending 16 percent of annual income.[18]

Social class impacts students' abilities to obtain a four-year degree. While rates of college completion increased 18 percentage points for high-income cohorts born around 1980 relative to the early 1960s, corresponding low-income cohorts only saw a 4 percentage increase.[19] Even if they make it to college, low-income students struggle to stay—currently, only one-third complete their bachelor's degrees by age twenty-five, compared to two-thirds of more affluent students.[20] Class-based inequities also contribute to significant racial/ethnic gaps in college completion: only 39.5 percent of full-time black students and 50.1 percent of Latino students (compared to 68.7 percent of Asian students and 61.5 percent of white students) graduate from four-year institutions within six years.[21]

In the parenting arms race, less-affluent parents simply cannot keep up. Nor will universities, so dependent on parental funds and labor, organize around the interests of these families. Indeed, meeting the needs of *all* less-privileged students who qualify for admission is expensive and offers little financial return. These students often arrive requiring extensive academic, social, and professional help. Increases in student service spending over the past decade suggest that four-year public universities are at least attempting to respond to these challenges—although there is some question as to which students and what activities these dollars are directed.[22]

Most schools maintain programs geared toward a select set of low-income, first-generation, and minority students—those who display high levels of academic potential or are at the highest risk for academic failure.[23] Creating these programs and showcasing them visibly in university promotional materials are necessary steps for legitimating the entire enterprise.[24] Without such programs, the extent to which the deck is stacked against less advantaged students is distastefully apparent.

If the goal is to narrow the gap in educational opportunity, universities need to provide disadvantaged youth with the same tailored guidance and financial support that affluent, highly educated parents provide for their offspring. This seems unlikely without the more extensive advising and deep pockets characteristic of elite schools, where *per student* endowment amounts run in the millions.[25] Unfortunately, the higher education system is highly stratified, ensuring that those least in need of resource-rich environments are most likely to access them.[26]

Class background may also shape the returns students see on their four-year degrees. Older data suggest that colleges largely mitigated the relationship between class origins and destinations for those with only a four-year degree.[27] However, there are reasons to believe this might be different for youth graduating in the early 2000s, especially during and after the Great Recession.[28] Patterns may also depend on institutional context: the higher education system is continuing to expand and internally differentiate, meaning that not all bachelor's degrees have equal value in the labor market.[29] Gender and race may matter for the returns students get from *the same* college or university—nuances not well captured in much prior work.[30] Recent evidence also suggests that securing an elite job or a spot in a graduate program hinges heavily on parental social class.[31] Thus, the question is still open of whether college remains the "great equalizer."

The Gendered College Experience

It is easy to blame student peer cultures for the emphasis on women as social and sexual companions that pervades many college campuses. However, universities build and support an infrastructure around a gender inegalitarian party scene in no small part because a powerful contingency of *parents* wants it—sometimes more than their daughters. If these same parents led the charge against a sexist Greek system, pushed for more women-in-STEM programming, and showed disapproval for majors designed to build gendered traits, change would happen.

This is one of the problems with a public university system driven by the private market: it reflects the interests, habits, and practices of the highest bidders. Affluent families are not ideal partners for public universities if the goal is gender-progressive practices and policies. Indeed, women's most rapid gains in higher education—in terms of representativeness at four-year colleges and in majors typically filled by men—occurred during periods of heavy state and federal support.[32]

Although traditional femininity may buy women status on campus, it prepares them for work heavy in emotional labor and leaves them reliant on looks, charm, and sex appeal. Jobs labeled as "women's work" are associated with less pay and prestige, and women workers experience hiring, wage, and promotion penalties when status characteristics mark them as feminine.[33] Building normatively feminine traits—in lieu of other skills and credentials—may hurt women's status on the job market.

Gender complementarity does not pose the same risk for men, as performing normative masculinity often comes with career and social benefits after college.[34] Men are not penalized for being strong, athletic, confident, aggressive, and even domineering.[35] In fact, those who are collegiate athletes do well in the job market, despite poor grades, as they are rewarded for the very traits they honed in college. Women athletes get the same boost, but only because they push against normative femininity.[36]

Preparing for gender complementarity puts most women in a position of economic vulnerability. Few parents possess the funds and connections needed for their daughters to gain entry into media or entertainment fields where feminine attributes have some value. Furthermore, marital rescue may not be a possibility. Less-privileged students, for example, will not see the same marital benefits from college as those from more privileged backgrounds, for whom education increases the likelihood of marrying and marrying well.[37]

Yet the continued viability of a postponed MRS for *all* women is rapidly decreasing. Today men and women use the same factors to select their spouses; education and income are at the top of the list.[38] High-earning, well-educated individuals partner with each other.[39] In many heterosexual pairings, beautiful and socially skilled women may be desired—but are also expected to bring economic contributions to the partnership. Attempting to use traditional femininity to "marry up" is a risk, only feasible for women whose parents can afford to infinitely support their daughters.

Notably, university outsourcing may pose a different set of gender-related disadvantages for men. Some scholars have implicated family socialization processes in helping to produce the college performance and completion gap favoring women—parents often raise their boys to have more independence than girls, over whom they exert social control. This problematic dynamic may, ironically, end up creating educational benefits for some young women, who respond to parental supervision by spending more time on schoolwork and learning to model behaviors that schools reward.[40]

Although I did not study men, it is possible that parents are much more likely to helicopter daughters—or to helicopter them more thoroughly. It may not be coincidental that the most intensive professional helicopters in my study had daughters only. Among paramedics, it appeared that parents were slightly more proactive, financially forthcoming, and watchful of their daughters. For example, I thought it unlikely that Debby and Bob would have let Brooke join ROTC to pay for college, as they did with their eldest son.

Reliance on parents may have the effect of magnifying problematic gender differences in how parents approach young women and men. Women are harmed by the content of the gender complementary lessons that some parents provide and universities reinforce. However, men, especially those from relatively disadvantaged backgrounds, may be the least likely to see the kinds of parental assistance that lead to academic achievement and persistence.[41] These disparities may contribute to men's struggles to perform at college, although more research on this issue is needed.[42]

The Price of Extended Dependence

Parental support of all kinds is a strong predictor of how youth fare during the young adult life stage—which is crucial for their subsequent class placement.[43] On this count, media hysteria surrounding college helicopter parents is dead wrong. Today's youth need parental assistance in order to engage in an increasingly essential period of self-development.

However, the primary reason that young adults do better with parental help is the lack of other support systems. This does not speak to the usefulness of extended parenting as much as it does to the problems with limited federal, state, and institutional support for older youth, including college students. Thus, we might question the price of extended dependency on families, even for those who can seemingly manage the burden.

Parents have been forced to extend intensive financial support further into their children's (and their own) life course. In the early 1980s, parental spending was roughly consistent across children's age; now spending is highest for young children and those over eighteen.[44] Parents drain their retirement accounts, refinance their homes, and take out home equity loans to pay for college. They are asked to do heavy financial lifting for their children at the same time they are supposed to be building their own financial security. Many put themselves in precarious financial positions in order to ensure that their children get the most out of their college years. The debt that parents acquire makes them vulnerable to unanticipated events such as unemployment, divorce, and illness.[45] Even anticipated events, such as retirement, may be delayed.

Today's parents also endure the social and emotional pressures of primary parenting for longer, which can diminish mental health.[46] Research shows that mothers of younger children who engage in intensive parenting pay a particularly high price, experiencing high levels of depression and stress.[47] As helicopters, college mothers invest time and energy into their children for two and a half decades or more. Many build identities around this role; however, it is likely to impact their well-being, as well as their careers.

Extended dependence may be a necessary coping strategy for youth, but it is also clear that they lose something in the process. This is particularly true when parents do not relinquish some control over their children's lives. Concerted cultivation, as detailed by Annette Lareau, is assumed to be an effective parenting style in large part because parents model behaviors for their children that youth eventually assume on their own.[48] They are to become their own high-powered micromanagers, who can skillfully move through upper-middle-class environments with ease. This transfer of responsibility from parent to child is crucial; otherwise, offspring may be indefinitely dependent on their parents.

Here, the trade-offs between the daughters of paramedics and those of helicopters are instructional. Most paramedics made the transfer of responsibility, using the young adult years to scale down many different forms of assistance. Their daughters faced some risks, as paramedic parents did not anticipate and prevent their daughters' mistakes. However, as noted earlier, most of these women left college as self-sufficient adults, capable of getting a job, caring for themselves, and working within a budget.

In contrast, helicopters (of both types) did not use college to significantly step back. Many helicopters' daughters thus had little practice managing the challenges of adulthood. Even the wealthiest of their parents were concerned about potentially missed life lessons and skills. As Frank, a member of the upper class, noted, "If you have to do a lot more, would you learn more for the future? You probably would. . . . Was it a disservice to make it that much easier or comfortable for them? That's something I've thought about." At least some helicopter youth will continue to be psychologically and financially reliant on their aging parents, whose resources and willingness to help may wear thin over time.

As a recent survey of college students suggests, the limited ability to effect self-determination may be at the root of higher levels of depression and lower levels of life satisfaction among children of helicopter parents.[49] Intensive parenting can also help to create performance stress and anxiety among college students, as suggested by reports of overcrowded mental health centers on many campuses.[50] This level of distress may be most common among students whose parents are seeking the "cultivation of excellence" experience, detailed in chapter 1. This group was notably missing on a Midwest U party dorm floor—as it was not an obvious location to pursue nationally renowned intellectual or artistic achievement. Such a vision of college may lead parents to combine heavy interventions, high levels of surveillance, and expectations of extreme success. Add a pressure cooker, such as an elite college campus, and youth may suffer mental health emergencies.[51] Success in highly competitive environments may demand such a parenting approach—but the price is potentially quite high.

Regardless of the parenting approach, research clearly shows that many youth are staying in their family homes longer today than in the past, as job opportunities disappear and societal safety nets fray.[52] Most women in my study viewed this form of help as a last resort because it represented a "failure to launch"—even though it was a logical response to economic conditions. Research also suggests that parental financial assistance may be linked to depressive symptoms and decreased self-esteem among young adults, especially those who are otherwise occupying adult roles.[53] These negative responses, even feelings of personal inadequacy, may be more likely to occur when economic success is assumed to be primarily about individual intellect and determination, as is the case in the United States.[54]

Moving Forward

Higher education need not exact such a price. Below I address three possible solutions to provide relief for families and help level class differences associated with parenting. I look to the market, status-based processes, and the state.

Market-Based Solutions

Given the problems introduced by privatization, it is ironic to think about turning to the market. Yet game-changing advancements in technology, new "big data" sciences, and the urge to innovate on an outdated model have opened up conversations about higher education that were unthinkable just ten years ago. What role might market-based processes play in reshaping the relationship between families and universities?

Currently, there is a push to disseminate clear and complete information about the real costs and benefits of attending different institutions.[55] This might be thought of as a *Consumer Reports*, or caveat emptor ("buyer beware"), approach. It imposes market principles on the already privatizing post-secondary system. Ideally, *all* families could easily access such knowledge and use it to decide how to best invest their time and money. If the process works efficiently, schools with high costs, limited services, and a poor record of serving students will lose families. In contrast, those with a strong track record will draw more.

However, even if we could reduce class-based information asymmetries, parents would still be differentially positioned to use such knowledge to their advantage. Affluent parents, who have greater familiarity with higher education, as well as more time and money, are better equipped to be model consumers. This approach also runs the risk of putting responsibility back on parents—especially if they do not choose their purchases well.

And choices there are. Everything is being questioned, especially as market alternatives develop. Do students need to be enrolled in a given college to access its classes? Do they even need to be in a classroom at all? Does an education require a set-aside period of development? What should it cost? How do students best learn? Who should teach them? What is the best way to measure progress?[56] There is potential to restructure education in a way that helps relieve parents of their heaviest burden—supporting four to six dedicated young adult years at brick-and-mortar institutions.

But markets are oriented around profit, not social justice—leaving low-income families vulnerable to exploitation. For-profit schools, for example, seem to offer desirable features to non-traditional students, such as flexibility in scheduling and the ability to attend class from home. However, only 14 percent of students graduate from for-profits within six years, in comparison to 55 percent of those at four-year public schools.[57] For-profits have the highest rates of federal student loan default.[58] Recent research also suggests that employers treat applicants with for-profit coursework little to no differently than those with high school diplomas.[59]

Why is the value potentially so low as to be non-existent? The answer lies, in part, with the disadvantaged class background of most for-profit students, on whose grants and loans these schools rely. We do not know what for-profits actually offer in terms of knowledge and skills. But even if these schools provided something revolutionary to less-privileged families (a premise that is questionable at best), the for-profit credential is unlikely to gain worth without the buy-in of affluent families.

It may be unrealistic, therefore, to assume that the market will rescue low-income families. Instead, the possibility for increased class stratification is real. Affluent, well-educated parents will not stop sending their children to elite residential universities. These schools will adopt the sleekest versions of market innovations, for example MIT's interactive data labs, replacing traditional lecture halls.[60] In contrast, less-privileged families will continue to turn to lower-status alternatives.[61] Those who remain in the public system will likely see stripped-down versions of technological "advances" trickle down, such as the Udacity-run online classes attempted by San Jose State—with poor results.[62]

Status-Based Solutions

Status systems offer a useful point of intervention. Institutional status is best captured by the *U.S. News & World Report* ratings. Schools are under enormous pressure to improve their numbers, as rank shapes the size of the applicant pool, perceptions among donating alumni, and employer interest. However, rankings do more than just reflect school "quality." They are social constructions that actually shape the hierarchies they purport to assess.[63] Schools model their policies and practices around criteria that will optimize their standings.

Unfortunately, existing criteria work against disadvantaged families. Nearly a quarter of the *U.S. News* rank depends on *overall* six-year graduation and freshman retention rates.[64] This may serve as a deterrent to enrolling low-income students who, on average, have lower graduation rates—due, in part, to limited parental funds and guidance.[65] Also important is student selectivity (at 12.5 percent).[66] There is little incentive to attract, or gain a reputation for serving well, disadvantaged students whose parents may be limited in the help they can provide.

Yet if it paid status dividends to invest heavily in low-income families, more institutions would do so. Including measures of less-privileged, first-generation, and minority student representativeness, programming, funding, and graduation rates in status ranking criteria would reshape what schools must do to remain at the top of the hierarchy. Schools seeking prestige would immediately take notice.

Recent years have brought some efforts to this end. "Best schools" lists for low-income and minority students are beginning to surface. CollegeNET and PayScale have developed the college Social Mobility Index (or SMI), designed to identify schools that "provide pathways for social and economic mobility."[67] These may prove useful tools for disadvantaged families. However, alternative ranking systems are unlikely to motivate change, as schools like MU can ignore them with little cost.

In contrast, when top schools adopt a practice, it becomes a marker of status. This is how a racially diverse student body, once a threat to prestige, became a source of it.[68] Elite institutions, in responding to civil rights pressures, began to compete for the nation's best black (and eventually Latino) students. Now, being (or appearing to be) a nearly all-white institution is undesirable. Similarly, schools invest in football—even in the face of financial losses—in part because that is what universities of a certain caliber do.[69]

Selective schools must be compelled to address disadvantaged student populations, otherwise schools that do so may be marginalized in the sector. This will require the most powerful ranking system in the country to get on board. The *U.S. News* rating report has shied away from this issue, as a significant number of top schools refuse to release useful data, such as Pell Grant recipient graduation rates.[70] Penalizing or refusing to include schools that fail to comply would send a strong message.

A fundamental change in how status is accrued might be freeing for schools like MU. Many are reliant on affluent, out-of-state families not only for financial support, but also rank. These families tend to provide students that help universities' *U.S. News* rankings, as they often hail from strong suburban schools. Moderately ranked schools often race to attract them with a Greek party scene, big-time sports, recreational centers, and lazy rivers. None of these features improve the quality of education. They also come with undesirable side effects: sexual assault, drug and alcohol abuse, hazing, and racist outbursts. Shifting criteria may redirect university resources to academic support.

"Socialist" Solutions

Many countries—including Argentina, Brazil, Denmark, Finland, France, Germany, Greece, Iceland, Ireland, Italy, Norway, Scotland, Slovenia, Spain, and Sweden—provide free or relatively low-cost higher education.[71] In this sense, the United States lags far behind. Currently, college is a personal edification project that American parents must enable—not something that the state owes, or can benefit from providing for, its citizens.

History suggests we might be at a turning point. Childhood and adolescence, once the province of the wealthy, were eventually bolstered with governmental protections and funds—normalizing these life stages and widening accessibility.[72] For instance, the comprehensive high school, developed in the early twentieth century, coincides with the formal study of adolescent psychology as reflecting a distinct life stage.[73] With greater backing, public higher education could play a significant role in supporting the young adult life stage.

Recent proposals highlight how. For example, in 2015 President Obama recommended that the government provide two free years of community college. His plan drew, in part, from a more detailed proposal developed by Sara Goldrick-Rab and Nancy Kendall, which offers students two free years of college at any two-year *or* four-year public university, including all costs associated with attendance (i.e., tuition, fees, books, supplies, and living expenses).[74] This model of college financing does not depend on family resources.

Nor would increased support for the public sector necessarily require more federal funds. Currently, for-profit and private schools drain resources that might otherwise flow to public schools. For example, for-profits generate the majority of their revenue from Pell Grants, military education programs, and federally subsidized student loans.[75] Similarly, private schools receive a disproportionate amount of Pell Grants, Supplemental Education Opportunity Grants, and work-study funds, relative to the number of students that they enroll.[76] Private schools also see the most individual and corporate contributions and earnings from endowments—which are not taxed by the federal government.[77]

Repurposing federal support dedicated to higher education is only one possible funding model—and not part of Obama's plan. However, this approach does highlight the extent to which federal dollars are not always directed to public goods. This is particularly problematic in the case of "high-Pell, high-net-price" private schools that collect taxpayer dollars and then still charge low-income families extravagantly.[78] Or when considering for-profit schools that only graduate a small fraction of their students.[79]

Although two-year plans have been discussed, a four-year plan would be ideal. However, this would also necessitate shifting state funding priorities. As the #SchoolsNotPrisons campaign points out, California houses 5.6 times the number of prisoners as in 1962, when the crime rate was similar. Since 1980 twenty-two prisons have been built but—despite increasing demand—only one school was added to the University of California system.[80] For many states, a burgeoning prison system has affected investments in education, health, and other community needs. This is the result of political, social, and economic choices.

Less-privileged families would benefit from a "socialist" solution to higher education. However, they would not be alone. Currently, young adults from middle-income families have a higher risk for debt than those from low- and high-income families.[81] Their parents are just above income qualifications for many existing support programs, but below the level of income needed to comfortably support their children during college. Affordable college plans would provide financial relief for a wide swath of American families.

Recently, I had a conversation with a UK-based reporter. He reminded me that such a change might have wide-reaching effects. Coming from a different system (although it is rapidly converging with that of the United States), he was confused about a few things. How is it that many American parents never talk to their children about college costs? Why do many students assume their parents will pay? What does an active college parent do, exactly? Does a book on parenting individuals who are essentially adults even make sense?

The reporter's questions laid bare the basic premise that many Americans take for granted—that college is a central parenting project. In a 2010 survey, nearly half of Americans (48.6 percent) indicated that funding college was a parental responsibility. Thirty-four percent cited students themselves, and only 17.6 percent pointed to the federal or state government.[82] Recent evidence suggests that the responsibility attributed to students is being siphoned off to the government. However, the share of the population citing parents as primary funders remains high.[83]

The assumption of parental responsibility for college—financial and otherwise—shapes everything from parent-child relationships, to family finances, to the onset of adulthood, to the structure of universities. It gives some youth an advantage at the cost of others, is easy to take for granted, and comes at a high financial and psychological price for family members. Unfortunately, in the existing American higher education system, this book makes all too much sense.

Methodological Appendix:
Studying Parenting

Complex relational dynamics form the foundation of family life. Most qualitative research on parenting relies on a single point of access—typically interviews with primary parents, occasionally reports from children, or rich ethnographic observations. All of these methods are valuable and were utilized during the course of this study. However, in isolation they may yield an inaccurate or anemic portrait of parenting. One strength of this research is the reliance on multiple, rich sources of data, from several family members.

During my fieldwork in the 2004–2005 academic year, I observed parenting in action. After move-in day, some parents maintained a regular physical presence on the floor, even from out-of-state. They arrived with care packages, clothing (in one case, hand-selected outfits designated for each round of Greek recruitment), dinner plans, and emergency care for sick or stressed daughters. Most stayed in the campus hotel or other accommodations in Fairview; however, one low-income mother spent a few days on her daughter's floor. Through these interactions, I met a number of mothers, as well as a few fathers. I also observed their long-distance parenting attempts, mediated by technology.

In the following years, I established deep relationships with women from the floor. I interviewed them on an annual basis, asking questions about parental funding, involvement, and interactions—as well as all other aspects of their lives. As these young women grew up, their ability to articulate feelings about their parents and to compare parenting approaches became more sophisticated. They revealed, sometimes unintentionally, consequences that their mothers and fathers could not see. Upon learning more about their personalities, I also gained insight into why otherwise successful approaches sometimes failed.

By the time I began preparing to interview parents, I had already known their daughters for four years. I was privy to many details parents were not, such as romantic/sexual entanglements, pregnancy and STD scares, and brushes with the law. For many women, I was more of a mentor or older sister, rather than a researcher. Given the nature of these ties, I prioritized women's comfort and consent. I spent time in fourth-year interviews talking about the possibility of interviewing both, one, or none of their parents, and assessing how they would feel about each of these scenarios. I promised to maintain confidentiality during interview sessions, not revealing information they shared with me to their parents. I explained that I would grant their parents the same courtesy.

Only eight women were uncomfortable with a parental interview. Two were from less-privileged households, and their parental relations were strained precisely because of limited assistance. I included them in the parent-child study—as well as Amy, for whom I only had ethnographic data—in order to ensure that I did not systematically exclude less involved parents.[1] In these cases, I relied entirely on women's reports of parenting. The other six women were dispersed along the class structure and parenting spectrum, and did not offer consent for idiosyncratic reasons unrelated to either. I had enough data on similar families to warrant not incorporating these women's interviews.

High participation rates among parents are due, in large part, to their daughters' lobbying efforts. Women who agreed to parental interviews also served as relationship brokers. When asked by their daughters, parents—with few exceptions—agreed to be interviewed. In no case did both parents of a willing daughter opt out.

In this way, I gained access to many parents who would have never been involved in a study of this nature. Several informed me of this fact. The preexisting tie also ensured that I entered interviews with a baseline level of trust. Parents knew that their daughters were fond of me and had accepted me into their lives. They understood that I was already knowledgeable about their families and could be trusted with sensitive information.

The majority of parent interviews were conducted at locations of respondents' choosing, typically in their homes and workplaces. I clustered these interviews by location—Chicago, New York, several neighboring states, and regions within the state. Out-of-state trips came earlier, in-state trips later. Timing mattered for how far along women were into their job searches when I spoke to their parents. Affluent, out-of-state parents were often anticipating graduation, while in-state parents could discuss post-college life in greater detail—assuming their daughters were on a four-year clock.

Face-to-face interviews were important to this project. It was easier to ascertain parents' emotional reactions; I could see when parents cried, or if they clenched their fists in anger. I also gained a great deal of insight into familial class position. Little details, like the southern flagship logo gracing the glass wall of an expensive Manhattan office, as mentioned in chapter 1, conveyed a lot of information. Cases where families were on the border between two class categories were resolved by examining the surrounding community, the size and décor of the home, and parents' own style of dress and demeanor. I even learned something about parent-child relationships by entering homes: some parents constructed virtual shrines to daughters' accomplishments while others were in the process of converting former bedrooms into more usable space.

Much research on parenting, both qualitative and quantitative, comes from the perspective of mothers. There is a good reason for this: mothers often know more about their children, are more involved, and carry the heaviest parenting burden. However, I needed the perspectives of both mothers and fathers in order to understand dynamics between parents. Involved mothers of older children did not talk about their extra labor, using the grand "we" to refer to parenting efforts. Ironically, it was only through fathers' lack of knowledge and willingness to admit inactivity that I learned just how unequal the gendered division of labor was in helicopter families. Paramedic fathers offered a refreshing contrast.

I ended up interviewing more mothers than fathers (thirty-nine vs. twenty-three); this was due, in large part, to women's wishes—many granted permission to interview mothers but not fathers, who they deemed as irrelevant (despite my arguments otherwise). There were also cases of fathers who claimed to be "too busy." Such fathers are still represented in the sample, however. Enough mothers managed to wrangle these men into at least a short interview. In one case, a defeated father invited me to his office, only to abandon me for thirty- to forty-five-minute intervals while he attended to business. This experience helped me to better understand his daughter's frustration with his inability to offer focused time.

I asked to conduct parental interviews separately. My concern was that in joint interview situations one parent would monopolize discussion and make it difficult to ascertain the views of the other. Only three couples expressed strong preferences for joint interviews: Marian and Rick (Nicole's parents), Alice and Jim (Mary's parents), Gayle and Roger (Brenda's parents). At times this context proved surprisingly fruitful (see chapter 1). However, as I suspected, one parent tended to do more of the talking. Fathers dictated the flow of conversation—even though they were not the most involved parents.

By speaking with most mothers and fathers separately, I had more time to delve into their familial and class histories. I had not expected to do this. My interview guide did not initially ask parents to reflect back to their youth; they did so without prompting and often in great detail. I learned that parenting is an intergenerational process; individuals do not leave behind their past when they become parents. Instead, they borrow from cultural understandings acquired over the course of their lives, sometimes creating new culture. Parents often engage in this process as a couple. The minutiae of these negotiations are crucial to identifying parental approaches that are neither un-involved nor highly involved.

Parental interviews were holistic in nature and implicitly informed by my knowledge of their daughters. I asked parents to recount the transition into college, college choice process, move-in day, and adjustments in the first year of college. Daughters' friends, social life, engagement with the Greek system, romantic and sexual relationships, and employment during the school year were covered. I sought to determine the depth of parents' knowledge of their daughters, but also to reveal understandings of the ideal college experience and views on parental intervention in each sphere of college life. Parents were asked to discuss their beliefs about financing college (i.e., how, why, and how much). I also ascertained expectations for post-college support, daughters' transition into jobs, and the timing and centrality of marriage and children. Questions were designed to bring forth parents' own feelings and experiences of parenting—not just to recount their daughters' histories.

As I noted in the introduction, I began parental interviews when I was visibly pregnant with my first daughter. I also conducted some after giving birth. My status as a soon-to-be mother of a daughter positioned me perfectly to solicit a wide array of parenting advice, some of a gendered nature. I do not believe that parents would have talked as freely to me if I did not share, in some way, that status.

However, it also helped to be a novice. Parents assumed I knew nothing and needed a great deal of guidance. I was happy to be advised (with the exception of birth horror stories, of which I got many), as I learned more about how they parented throughout infancy and into the college years. My insights into when and how gendering in the family occurred were greatly facilitated by this fortunate confluence of a central life event with my research.

After parental interviews, I had the opportunity to conduct a fifth wave of interviews with women, a year after most were slated to graduate. I tailored these interviews based on insights from parents, allowing me to go deeper. At this point, I could often triangulate information from three interlinked nodes, which allowed me to establish the veracity of family narratives. However, in a few cases, it seemed I might have accidently interviewed three people from three different families. I sought to understand the circumstances that generated this disagreement, as well as the consequences.

Parenting to a Degree: How Family Matters for College Women's Success is told primarily from the perspective of parents, unlike my first book, coauthored with Elizabeth A. Armstrong. For example, in *Paying for the Party: How College Maintains Inequality*, wealthy socialites (a group of women invested in college social life) are discussed as reproducing class status. Yet here we see the steep consequences of such an approach for their *parents*, most of whom are pink helicopters. Taking into account parental satisfaction, producing a socialite seems decidedly undesirable. There are other moments in this book where women come across differently viewed from the perspective of parents, or in light of more information about what their parents were trying to achieve.

In writing this book, I chose to tell the stories of whole families. I understand that many family members will now be able to identify each other in the book. It may be difficult for some daughters to learn how their parents felt about their actions during college or for some parents to realize how their daughters suffered as a result of their actions. I knew women might complain about their parents, but I had not expected parents to be so open, honest, and raw. Field notes from the time record my shock and disbelief. However, all of the parents I spoke to cared deeply for their children, in their own ways.

Maintaining the integrity of the data was important for the conclusions of this book. Understanding the patterned but messy ways in which class and gender intersect to produce parenting approaches required preserving the accuracy of the details. I feared that in creating composite families or blurring the specifics, I would unintentionally alter the theoretical framework and empirical results. Furthermore, there was authenticity in the interplay between parents and their own children that I sought not to undermine. I tried to explain the context in which parents or youth made potentially hurtful statements, and part of this was the relational dynamic within a family. Stripping statements of this history, in some cases, could make them ring false or vindictive when they were not.

I chose not to involve parents and/or daughters in producing the book. It seemed unethical to engage them in a potentially painful social scientific analysis of their family lives and relationships. I do not intend to foist this knowledge on families that have shown no interest. Most will never read this book, and I will preserve their ability to make that choice. However, some parents were intrigued with the notion of the final product. A few said they hoped to see me on *Oprah* one day, despite my assurances that this was highly unlikely. I will share copies of the book with the families who made such a request. After all, it was only through their generosity and kindness that it came to fruition.

Appendix A:
Parents and Daughters

Helicopters (Chapters 2, 4, 5)

Professional (N = 6)

Parents	Daughter	Class
Gayle and Roger	Brenda	UC
Carol and Nate	Alicia	UMC
Denise	Bailey	UMC
Anna and Steven	Erica	UMC
Andrea and Keith	Taylor	UMC
Alice and Jim	Mary	MC

Pink (N = 9)

Parents	Daughter	Class
Connie and Logan	Abby	UC
Alexis and Frank	Hannah	UC
Rachel and Matt	Julie	UMC
Cindy and Ed	Naomi	UMC
Cathy and Walt	Natasha	UMC
Marian and Rick	Nicole	UMC
Rhonda[d]	Tara	UMC
Allison and Tom	Sydney	UMC
Lacey and Arnold	Blair	MC

Paramedics (Chapters 3, 5)

Paramedics (N = 12)

Parents	Daughter	Class
Debby and Bob	Brooke	UC
Sally and Alan	Lydia	UC
Darci and Russ	Brianna	UMC
Molly and Vern[d]	Lisa	UMC
Trudy	Madison	UMC
Renee and Peter[d]	Morgan	UMC
Sherry	Sophie	UMC
Theresa	Tracy	UMC
Tami and Charlie[d]	Alana	LMC
Betsy[d]	Michelle	LMC
Don	Valerie	LMC
Tina and Kenny	Monica	WC

Bystanders (Chapters 4, 7)

Supportive (N = 6)

Parents	Daughter	Class
Susie and Zack	Emma	MC
Eileen	Karen	MC
Lori[d]	Whitney	MC
Janice[d]	Becky	LMC
Rose[d]	Crystal	LMC
Robert	Stacey	LMC

Total (N = 6)

Parents	Daughter	Class
Jody and Paul[d]	Carrie	LMC
Diane	Amanda	WC
—[d]	Alyssa	WC
—[d]	Amy	WC
	Heather	WC
Luann[d]	Megan	WC

Notes: UC = upper class; UMC = upper-middle class; MC = middle class; LMC = lower-middle class; WC = working class.

[d] = parents divorced or one parent deceased.

There were 41 families total. Janet, Linda's mother (UMC), and Barb, Mara's mother (UMC), are not included in this table. See chapter 1 for a discussion of these families.

Acknowledgments

Parenthood can bring otherwise accomplished, stable, functional human beings to their knees, incapacitated with love, worry, frustration, and pride—sometimes simultaneously. I am profoundly indebted to the parents who opened their homes and hearts to share such moments and emotions with me. Their stories are the soul of this book, and without their candidness, it could not have been written. When I face parenting decisions, both big and small, I draw on their combined experiences.

The book also relies on data from the ethnographic and five-year interview study of college women featured in *Paying for the Party: How College Maintains Inequality*. Women were willing to entrust me with their parents—despite my knowledge of legal, romantic, sexual, and academic details of their lives that are decidedly *not* the sorts of things that college students want their mothers and fathers to know. I did my best to protect this trust. These women shared a tumultuous, confusing, and transitional period of their lives with me. My academic career has, in many ways, been built through their narratives. All are now adults in their own right, and some are even parents. I continue to think of them often.

A team of researchers assisted in ethnographic and interview data collection for the college women study, including Sibyl Kleiner, Evie Perry, Brian Sweeney, and Amanda Tanner (who were graduate students at the time), and undergraduates Teresa Cummings, Aimee Lipkis, and Katie Watkins. Their investments and insights were crucial, particularly in the early years of the project. The Spencer Foundation made the longitudinal college women study possible, providing crucial financial infusions to my co-director, Elizabeth A. Armstrong, at both the inception and completion of the project. Pamela Jackson generously offered financial support for transcription of women's interviews when funds ran dry.

The combined parent-child data set, on which this book is based, would not have been possible without Elizabeth A. Armstrong. She did much of the logistical groundwork and initial conceptualization for the college women project (which started as about hookup culture, only later moving to a class focus) while I collected a majority of the ethnographic and interview data. We joined forces to write *Paying for the Party*, in one of the most enjoyable and rewarding intellectual experiences of my life.

Elizabeth nudged my interest in a separate parenting project along and offered financial support, logistical advice, and a critical eye— even when she was swimming in her own (and our shared) commitments. We spent many hours talking about college parenting, particularly as her son neared this transition—blending, as so many of our conversations do, the personal and the intellectual. When I needed serious space to write this book, away from our joint obligations, she created it. When I reemerged, she was there. In the last stages of the book, she painstakingly provided detailed commentary over the course of several multi-hour conversations. Elizabeth has always believed in the potential of this project and the potential in me. We support each other intellectually, emotionally, and interpersonally. I have come to realize that synergies such as ours are rare and only happen once or twice in a lifetime—if at all.

This book, and my work as a scholar, is very much a product of the Indiana University sociology department. Some of my fondest memories are from the period I spent as a graduate student at IU, in a warm, caring, and supportive community. I can always count on my close friends from graduate school, David Blouin, Brea Perry, Michael Rosenbaum, and Brian Sweeney, for their love and encouragement.

The moments we share now—while too rare—have helped sustain me through this project.

My undergraduate mentor at DePauw University, Nancy Davis, was right—IU was a place that I could not only survive, but thrive. I would not have gone to graduate school without her involvement. Nancy delivered me to IU and into the hands of Robert Robinson, who would later become one of my dissertation committee members. At my dissertation defense, Rob insisted that this was a book that must be written. I had my doubts, especially in the midst of writing my first book, but I never forgot his words. Nancy and Rob have ushered me through several crucial life transitions and supported me for nearly fifteen years of my life. They offer a beautiful model of how to live rich, whole lives as human beings, while also producing top-quality scholarship.

At IU I found my academic father—Brian Powell. Brian has many such children and miraculously manages to care for us all. In the stress of data collection and dissertation writing, I landed in his office crying more often than I like to admit. Thankfully he always had a supply of tissues and (expired) headache and cold medicine to share. It was from Brian that I learned how to craft an intellectual argument and make it sound. He taught me to carry a narrative through a piece of work. Brian is a stickler for details—an absolute perfectionist. To please Brian, evidence has to be rock solid. I am who I am as a scholar because of him. Despite his manic schedule as IU's chair of sociology, he found time to devote careful attention to this book, even helping me to solve the problem of the title. His multiple reads of this manuscript were crucial, and the book—like all of my work—bears his imprint. His emotional support has been equally important: Brian knows the keystone moments of my life almost better than I do (e.g., my birthday, wedding date, and children's birthdays). If I do not know what to do about something, work or non-work related, I consult him. Over time he has managed to let down his guard enough to also become a cherished friend—just as parents often become with their grown children.

Many other IU faculty played crucial roles in the development of this project. Eliza Pavalko convinced me—over the course of a several-hours-long conversation—that I could be both a person and a scholar at IU. As a dissertation committee member, she offered insights that later were incorporated into the book. Donna Eder stopped me from dropping out of graduate school by encouraging me to develop my interests in qualitative research and gender. Her interventions set me on the course to write this book. William Corsaro offered the technical expertise that formed the foundation of the yearlong ethnography—I always tell people that I was trained by the best. Pamela Walters's stellar sociology of education graduate course sealed my fate as a scholar of higher education.

This book was written mostly during my years as an assistant professor at the University of California, Merced. My colleagues during those years—Paul Almeida, Irenee Beattie, Kyle Dodson, Tanya Golash-Boza, Zulema Valdez, Nella VanDyke, and Simón Weffer— were unflagging in their support. They ensured that I had all of the time, space, and resources necessary to embark on such an undertaking. Occasionally they would stop by my office to ask about the book, gently nudging me to get it completed. I feel grateful to belong to such a collegial (and growing) department of outstanding scholars.

As it turns out, California is a great place to do work on higher education. I have benefited from a supportive network of scholars in my new home state. Amy Binder and Steven Brint have played increasingly important roles with each passing year. Both are among a small group of scholars who think about higher education from an organizational perspective. I have learned much from their work and insights.

I also owe a great intellectual debt to Mitchell Stevens. He has urged me to think about the ways in which families get pulled into the form and function of higher education, building on seminal ideas in his book *Creating a Class: College Admissions and the Education of Elites.* Mitchell's generous invitations placed me in conversation with scholars and administrators thinking about and reacting to rapid changes in the post-secondary system. Mitchell has also adopted me as one of his own, offering a wealth of career and life advice.

My editor, Elizabeth Branch Dyson, was the *exact* right person for this project. She convinced me that it needed to be done, perhaps sooner than I might have otherwise. We are both relatively young, ambitious, and energetic—and meshed immediately. Elizabeth offered sage advice every step of the way. She provided input on the labels for parent groups, offered ideas for the organization of chapters, and helped me to draw out the most important themes. *Parenting to a Degree: How Family Matters for College Women's Success* is more compelling, theoretically rich, and soundly written for her involvement.

When I was in the thick of analysis and writing, and just wanted to give up, my new friend Vilna Bashi Treitler pushed me to keep going. She has shown me that beautiful friendships can develop in adulthood and happen when you least expect them to. She and her family are an unforeseen source of joy in my life. Susana Rameriz and Kristopher Unger, the neighbors everyone wants to have, are also newfound friends. With four children between our two households, I have experienced the joy of raising children in a village of sorts. I am a better scholar and parent for the (partial) sanity this affords.

In writing a book on college parenting, it is perhaps not surprising that I thought a lot about my own parents, Melody and Edward Hamilton. They fit most closely with the supportive bystander group, in that they offered a lot of emotional and financial support, but were not familiar enough with academia to be helicopters or paramedics. Given the mentorship I received at DePauw University and later at IU, they did not need to be. I feel blessed to be so deeply and thoroughly loved, and only hope that I can manage to offer the same to my children. My sister, Ellen Johnson, and brother, Eddie Hamilton, also cheer me on from my birth state of Indiana.

It is difficult to convey the integral role that Kyle Dodson—my partner, colleague, and friend—has played in the data collection and writing for this book. He accompanied me on every trip to collect parent interviews, as I was in the early stages of pregnancy with my first daughter and quite ill. We have spent years talking about the families portrayed in this book. Kyle suggested the labels for pink helicopters and paramedics. He has coached me through moments of extreme frustration and will be the first to celebrate the book's publication with me. Our lives together are busy; two tenure-track jobs and two children are a hefty combination. The only reason it works is because Kyle and I are equal partners in our endeavors, in every sense of the word. He continually reminds me to slow down and savor life.

Our two little girls, Lane and Sage, are the heart and soul of our family. It would have been impossible for me to write this book without being a parent myself. There is no way to understand the intensity and complexity of emotions that come with parenthood without experiencing them firsthand. One day my girls will most likely go to college. I am not so sure they will appreciate having a parent who literally wrote a book on college parenting. I am thankful, however, to have some insight into this potentially stressful transition, years in advance.

Notes

Introduction

1. Midwest University, or MU, is a pseudonym. This book could be set at many different large, mid-tier, residential public universities across the United States.

2. Stevens (2007).

3. See Weis, Cipollone, and Jenkins (2014) for more on the tactics that middle- and upper-middle-class parents use to gain admission to prestigious universities.

4. This phrase was coined by University of Georgia professor and former administrator Richard Mullendore. See Robbins (2006).

5. Vinson (2012) details (in footnotes) the many labels assigned to this group of parents. Along with "helicopters," these terms have also been used: "invasive parenting," "over-parenting," "aggressive parenting," "smothering mothering," "snowplow parents," "lawn-mower parents," and "Blackhawk or Kamikaze parents."

6. Strauss (2006). For other media examples of the supposed harm caused by helicopter parenting, see Acocella (2008); Dell'Antonia (2013); English (2013); Gibbs (2009); Henderson (2013); Marano (2008); Ozment (2011).

7. Zink and Colavecchio-Van Sickler (2006).

8. Strauss (2006).

9. Nikolopoulos (2013). Silva (2013) discusses the media's negative characterization of the Millennial generation.

10. For examples, see Bruni (2015); Deresiewicz (2014); Lythcott-Haimes (2015).

11. Prescott and Bransberger (2008); Schofer and Meyer (2005); Windolf (1997).

12. Leroux (2008); Lombardi (2007).

13. Western Interstate Commission for Higher Education (2012).

14. Piketty and Saez (2003); Reardon and Bischoff (2011).

15. Furstenberg et al. (2004).

16. Dudley (1994); Goldin and Katz (2008); Kalleberg (2011); Sennett (1998); Silva (2013).

17. Settersten and Ray (2010); Settersten (2012).

18. Settersten (2012) highlights the historical nature of this process, which started in the 1970s–80s. Commentators are often tempted to blame current conditions entirely on the Great Recession.

19. Grubb and Lazerson (2005); Rosenbaum (1997).

20. College Board (2013a).

226 | NOTES TO PAGES 5-8

21. Jaquette and Curs (2013).

22. Charles and Bradley (2002), (2009).

23. For classic examples in the status attainment tradition, see Blau and Duncan (1967); Coleman (1988); Downey (1995); Sewell and Hauser (1976). Also see Bourdieu (1984); Lareau ([2003] 2011): in this research, parents use classed resources to carefully cultivate the cultural tastes, social skills, and dispositions valued in schools. They do so through both intent and habit—the absorption of a family cultural environment.

24. Robinson and Harris (2014) offer a rare dissenting view. Also see Milkie, Nomaguchi, and Denny (2015).

25. Rosenfeld (2007). Also see Arnett (2004) and Furstenberg, Rumbaut, and Settersten (2005). Settersten and Ray (2010) is an exception.

26. Charles, Roscigno, and Torres (2007); Hamilton (2013); Paulsen and St. John (2002); Radford (2013); Steelman and Powell (1989).

27. In a notable and unpublished exception, Shoup, Gonyea, and Kuh (2009) use the National Survey of Student Engagement (NSSE) to study "highly involved" parents, but come to mixed conclusions.

28. Loss (2012).

29. Horowitz (1987); Schofer and Meyer (2005); Windolf (1997).

30. Settersten and Ray (2010).

31. Stevens (2015). As Stevens, Armstrong, and Arum (2008) point out, postsecondary education is a "hub" where multiple institutional domains intersect.

32. Berman (2012); Geiger (2004); Loss (2012); Price (2004).

33. Desrochers and Kirshstein (2013); Loss (2012); Lucas (1996); McPherson and Shapiro (1998); Mettler (2014); Postsecondary Education Opportunity (2012); Price (2004).

34. Desrochers and Kirschstein (2014); Ginsberg (2011).

35. Bickel and Lake (1999); Lansley (2004).

36. Under FERPA, postsecondary students control the rights of access to their own records. Personal information may not be shared with parents unless the student signs a waiver or meets a health and safety exception. University of Pittsburgh (2014) has one of the better summaries of how FERPA works, from the perspective of a college parent.

37. Bickel and Lake (1999).

38. Levine (1980) was an early predictor of the market model of higher education. See Berman (2012); Geiger (2004); Giroux (2014); and Loss (2012) for more.

39. Goldrick-Rab and Kendall (2014).

40. Levine (1980); Loss (2012).

41. Loss (2012).

42. Horowitz (1987, 261).

43. Stevens (2015).

44. Arum and Roksa (2011).

45. Bickel and Lake (1999); Lake (2013). Also see recent media on college rape, fraternities, racist incidents, hazing, and drug/alcohol-induced accidents.

46. See U.S. Department of Education (2015).

47. SHEEO (2015); Stevens (2007) found that admissions' officers even referred to such applicants as "free." Stevens studied an elite private school, but what he found also applies to public schools.

48. Hoover and Keller (2011).
49. See Doherty (2013) for *New York Times* coverage of this phenomenon.
50. Cutright (2008). Also see Coburn (2006).
51. I asked women to provide contact information for their primary parents. Virtually all referred me to biological mothers and fathers. However, the sample also includes one adoptive family and two stepfamilies. Three families with no parental interviews are included. Parents in these families had virtually no involvement in their daughters' lives and often were not on speaking terms with their children. It was crucial to include them in order to represent the full spectrum of college parenting.
52. Some parents were interviewed before graduation and others after, based on scheduling and availability. See the "Methodological Appendix" for more details.
53. See the "Methodological Appendix" for a discussion of the families not included in this study.
54. All individuals in this book—mothers, fathers, and daughters, as well as any relatives, friends, and romantic partners—have been assigned pseudonyms.
55. U.S. Department of Labor (2014).
56. Deil-Amen (2015). Also see Levine and Cureton (1998) for more on the "new majority."
57. This book is grounded in a growing body of research applying an institutional framework to studying inequality within the postsecondary sector. See Armstrong and Hamilton (2013); Arum and Roksa (2011); Bastedo (2009); Bastedo and Gumport (2003); Berger and Milem (2000); Binder and Wood (2012); Brint and Karabel (1989); Chen (2012); Ro, Terenzini, and Yin (2013); Rosenbaum, Deil-Amen, and Person (2006); Smart, Feldman, and Ethington (2000); Stevens (2007); Stuber (2011).
58. Institutional selectivity is defined according to the 2005 Carnegie Classification of Institutions, as used by the National Center for Education Statistics. Categories correspond to the twenty-fifth percentile ACT-equivalent scores of students accepted for the institution. The score range for the "moderately selective" category was between eighteen and twenty-one.
59. Buchmann and DiPrete (2006); DiPrete and Buchmann (2013); Conger and Long (2009).
60. DiPrete and Buchmann (2013).
61. Hamilton (2014).
62. See Tatum (2003). At the start of the study, only around 4 percent of MU students identified as black and 4 percent as Asian. There were even smaller numbers of Latino students.
63. It is possible that one student's mother identified as Latina; however, I was only able to speak with her father, who identified as white. Only two women identified as lesbian or bisexual. All parents identified as heterosexual, with one exception—a father who came out after his children were grown.
64. Scholarship on family life is beginning to push for an integrative model—one in which class and gender, as well as race and sexuality, are viewed as intersecting systems of power. For a critique of Lareau ([2003], 2011) on these grounds, see Choo and Ferree (2010). For an example of intersectional research on parenting, see Bodovski (2010). For more on how sexuality might shape parenting, see Stacey and Biblarz (2001).

65. Lareau ([2003], 2011). Also see Lareau (2002).
66. Lareau (2011). Also see Lareau and Cox (2011).
67. See Settersten and Ray (2010).
68. See Kohn (1977) and Rubin (1976). Lareau also draws heavily on Bourdieu (1977, 1984).
69. As Kingston (2000, 134).argued, "Class distinguishes neither distinctive parenting styles or [sic] distinctive involvement of kids."
70. See Maier, Ford, and Schneider (2008). They found the middle class to be far more heterogeneous than Lareau suggests, making it difficult to spot distinctive parenting practices.
71. Chua (2011).
72. Druckerman (2012).
73. Skenazy (2009).
74. For example, Lareau ([2003], 2011) selected families that met her criteria for poor, working-class, and middle-class families.
75. See Streib (2015) on cross-class marriages, and Roksa and Potter (2011) and Streib (2013) on the importance of parents' own class of origin.
76. Furstenberg et al. (2005); Osgood et al. (2005). See Swidler (2001) on culture in unsettled periods. Adolescence and childhood, as life stages, went through a similar stage of development. See Kett (1977); Zelizer (1985).
77. Goldscheider, Thornton, and Yang (2001) discuss the considerable confusion surrounding how parents should financially support their older children.
78. Patton (2013). Also see O'Connor (2013) for her comments in a press release.
79. Patton (2014). It is hard to imagine a similar book by a father gaining this much attention, without a much stronger backlash.
80. And yet existing accounts of how classed-linked tastes, beliefs, and interactional styles are transmitted in family life typically do not address gender. McCall's (1992) resuscitation of gender in Bourdieusian theory is an exception and heavily informs my work. This lack of attention to gender is surprising, given the extensive family scholarship on gender socialization. See Raley and Bianchi (2006) for a review. Also Eccles, Jacob, and Harold (1990); Etaugh and Liss (1992). Notably, however, the omission goes both ways: gender socialization literature also tends to overlook social class.
81. McCall (1992); Ridgeway (2011).
82. Coontz (1992); Ostrander (1984).
83. Becker (1991); Tolman, Striepe, and Harmon (2010).
84. Friedman (2013).
85. Schwartz and Mare (2005); Sweeney (2002); Sweeney and Cancian (2004).
86. Clarke (2011); Crowder and Tolnay (2000).
87. England (2010); López (2003).
88. Armstrong and Hamilton (2013); Musick, Brand, and Davis (2012).
89. Hamilton (2014). Despite the fact that the masculinities literature has long recognized multiple ways of performing masculinity, the literature on femininity has been slower to develop a similar framework. See Bettie (2003) and Wilkins (2008) for empirical exemplars.
90. Hays (1996, 8).

91. Also see Hochschild's classic (1989) book, *The Second Shift*, for more on the gendered division of parenting-related household labor.

92. See Burawoy's (2009) extended case method.

93. Figure I.1 depicts parents' visions of college at the individual/couple level. At the aggregate level they are equivalent to "class projects," as discussed in Armstrong and Hamilton (2013)—although here I suggest that they are more variegated. Universities are most responsive to the class projects of constituencies that solve pressing problems, such as solvency.

94. Parenting approaches are actually strategies of action in the Swidlerian (1986, 2001) sense, but also see Bourdieu (1977): that is, they are patterned actions inflected by available cultural beliefs and traditions, in ways that may be hard for parents to directly articulate. I opted for the term "parenting approaches" to avoid assumptions of deliberateness and calculability among a broader audience.

95. See Armstrong and Hamilton (2013) for more on college pathways.

Chapter One

1. As McCall (1992) quotes of Bourdieu (1984, 106): "There are as many ways of realizing femininity as there are classes and class fractions, and the division of labour between the sexes takes quite different forms, both in practices and in representations, in the different social classes."

2. For classic examples, see Goldthorpe (1980); Wright (1997).

3. This is a Bourdieusian (1977, 1984) approach to social class. It is built around the concept of habitus—taken-for-granted dispositions and ways of relating learned first through the experiences and activities of family life. Also see Lareau ([2003], 2011); Swidler (1986, 2001).

4. Hout (2012). Only recently have scholars have recognized the importance of considering mothers' class indicators alongside those of fathers; see Beller (2009).

5. During the initial years of the study, tuition, fees, and room and board came to more than $23,000 for out-of-state students and $12,000 for in-state students. By 2015 the disparity between the two rates had doubled.

6. See Lamont's (1992) work on the American upper-middle class.

7. See Armstrong and Hamilton (2013); Hamilton (2014) on the consolidation of privilege. Also see the assortative mating literature, e.g., Schwartz and Mare (2005); Sweeney (2002); Sweeney and Cancian (2004).

8. Aries (1965); Kett (1977); Zelizer (1985).

9. These assumptions were inaccurate. As Armstrong and Hamilton (2013) and Armstrong, Hamilton, and Sweeney (2006) document, college life routinely and predictably produces sexual assault, alcohol and drug abuse, and other hazards.

10. Horowitz (1987); Karabel (2005).

11. Bailey (1989); Waller (1937).

12. Horowitz (1987).

13. Armstrong and Hamilton (2013); Becker (1991); Hamilton (2014).

14. Coontz (1992).

15. Horowitz (1987).

16. Armstrong and Hamilton (2013) focus on women's own mobility narratives.

17. Hamilton (2014).
18. England (2010).
19. Settersten (2012); Settersten and Ray (2010).
20. Furstenberg et al. (2004).
21. Radford (2013); Rosenbaum, Deil-Amen, and Person (2006).
22. Silva (2013).
23. See Roksa and Potter (2011) and Streib (2013) on the intergenerational trans-mission of parenting styles with regards to younger youth.
24. Harding (2007) discusses the cultural diversity of disadvantaged urban neigh-borhoods and the ways it impedes the desired actions of youth. However, in this case, contact with diverse cultures is built over the course of a lifetime. Parents may be more readily positioned to utilize it as a resource.
25. Clark Kerr, former chancellor of the University of California, Berkeley, coined this term to describe public research universities, as these complex organizations at-tempt to serve a broad range of constituencies.
26. See Khan's (2011) description of the elite.
27. Heffernan (2015).
28. Stevens (2007).
29. See Delbanco (2012) and Nussbaum (2010) for an idealized notion of what col-lege can and should offer youth.
30. Vaisey (2009).
31. This is consistent with Bourdieu's (1977, 1984) notion of habitus.
32. Armstrong and Hamilton (2013).
33. Feiler (2014).
34. See Streib (2015).
35. See the "Methodological Appendix" for a discussion of the benefits of single versus joint interviews. Only three sets of parents opted for a joint interview.
36. This is consistent with research on the effects of divorce on children: marital conflict, rather than the act of divorce itself, is the central driver of many negative behavioral, emotional, and academic outcomes. See Amato, Loomis, and Booth (1995).
37. For more information on how divorce impacts intergenerational financial transfers, see Eggebeen (1992); Furstenberg, Hoffman, and Shrestha (1995); White (1992).
38. Divorced parents show lower levels of involvement with youth. See Hamilton, Cheng, and Powell (2007).

Chapter Two

1. Hays (1996).
2. Douglas and Michaels (2004, 6).
3. Hochschild (1989).
4. See Badinter (2010); Hays (1996); and Rizzo, Schiffrin, and Liss (2013) for more on how women internalize intensive parenting norms.
5. See Armstrong and Hamilton (2013) for more on "easy majors."
6. Alicia blamed her academic advisors for not providing information about when this class should be taken. Indeed, advisors are often the only source of guidance avail-

able to some students. In Alicia's case, however, she missed out on an opportunity to avoid the issue by ignoring her mother's advice.

7. Professional helicopters wanted their daughters to build the deep and rich ties that Chambliss and Takacs (2014) suggest are crucial for college success.

8. Funneling is a form of binge drinking in which a funnel device and tube are used to consume large amounts of alcohol in a rapid fashion. Gayle never revealed how she knew about funneling, but I suspected that she was following youth drinking culture as closely as she was as her daughter's post-college career prospects.

9. Gayle's concern is with date rape drugs that can be easily slipped into a drink. Setting a drink down increases the odds that this will happen without a woman's knowledge.

10. Rhonda's assessment was consistent with widely accepted sorority rankings. Jewish houses were not ranked as highly as other houses and reflected an anti-Semitism that was alive and well on MU's campus.

11. Armstrong and Hamilton (2013); Hamilton (2014).

12. Lareau ([2003], 2011).

Chapter Three

1. See Calarco (2011, 2014) for social class differences in help-seeking and problem-solving behaviors. Paramedics, from a range of class backgrounds, may have been offering their children an advantage in encouraging self-guided strategies, an issue I return to in the latter half of the book.

2. Croft et al. (2014) find that parents' gender roles at home predict girls' future occupational aspirations. In families that model a more egalitarian division of labor, daughters aspire to higher-paying careers.

3. Bourdieu (2004) offers the concept of "cleft habitus" to explain the disjointed experience of holding two habitus simultaneously. See Lee and Kramer (2013) and Lehmann (2014) for research on working-class students with this experience and Streib (2015) for the experiences of adults in cross-class marriages.

4. Roksa and Potter (2011); Streib (2013).

5. This life stage is currently associated with class privilege. See Osgood et al. (2004); Settersten and Ray (2010). However, as with childhood and adolescence, we would expect eventual trickle-down effects. See Aries (1965); Kett (1977); Zelizer (1985).

Chapter Four

1. Lareau ([2003], 2011).

2. See Hamilton (2013); Steelman and Powell (1989).

3. Schoeni and Ross (2005) find that young adults (ages eighteen to thirty-four) from families in the bottom half of the income distribution received three times less financial support from parents than those in the top half. College funding accounts for a large portion of the disparities. Also see Steelman and Powell (1991) and, for a review, Swartz (2009).

4. Pugh (2009).

5. See López (2003).

Chapter Five

1. This chapter can be read alongside chapter 5 ("Socialites, Wannabes, and Fit with the Party Pathway") of Armstrong and Hamilton's (2013) *Paying for the Party: How College Maintains Inequality*. Taking the parents' perspective offers a major departure with *Paying for the Party*. Based on what women said, it seemed like many parents were capable of offering, and happy to provide, this level of long-term support. However, parents struggled more than originally assumed, and none were pleased about the need for continued involvement and funding. Also see the "Methodological Appendix."

2. Fitting in socially came easiest for the wealthiest women, who had more resources and felt comfortable in elite social settings. Others had to work much harder, and it never felt natural. Armstrong and Hamilton (2013) refer to these two groups as socialites and wannabes, respectively.

3. Armstrong and Hamilton (2013); DeSantis (2007).

4. See Armstrong and Hamilton (2013) and Hamilton (2007, 2014) for more on normative femininity at MU and the term "blonde."

5. Hamilton (2013).

6. Herbert Simon (1955, 1957) first elaborated the concept of satisficing. Simon's theory of bounded rationality rejects the notion of fully utilitarian human actors. He recognizes that individuals often have limited information and conflicting desires. People tend to respond by satisficing—that is, meeting criteria for adequacy on multiple fronts, rather than maximizing their chances of securing a single outcome. In this case, students desire to stay in school and to enjoy their time at school. Satisficing, a calculated reduction in academic effort, allows them to achieve both goals.

7. Charles et al. (2009) rank college classes according to the ease of obtaining a high GPA. Arum and Roksa (2011) compare Collegiate Learning Assessment (CLA) scores across majors.

8. Armstrong and Hamilton (2013).

9. Five women were in communications of some sort. One was in human development (a modern-day equivalent of home economics). Two opted for less rigorous vocational fields—teaching and audiology. Abby was a psychology major. For her, however, this was far from a challenge.

10. Arum and Roksa (2014).

11. Arum and Roksa (2011); Charles et al. (2009).

12. Hamilton (2013); Steelman and Powell (1989).

13. See Kuh et al. (2005); Pascarella and Terenzini (2005); Tinto (1987, 1988).

14. Arum and Roksa (2014). These numbers exclude college graduates who were back in school full-time.

15. Lareau ([2003], 2011).

16. For examples, see Armstrong and Hamilton (2013); Bastedo (2009); Ro, Terenzini, and Yin (2013). As Pascarella and Terenzini (2005, 590) conclude, "Where students attended college had less impact than . . . [the] significant differences among individuals' experiences during college (within-college effects)."

17. Arum and Roksa (2014); Carnevale, Strohl, and Melton (2011); Roksa and Levey (2010).

18. For example, see Shierholz, Davis, and Kimball (2014) on the weak labor market prospects for the class of 2014.

19. According to 2010 Census data, the median age at first marriage for American women was 26.1; for men it was 28.2. Although class groups are beginning to converge, those with more education tend to marry later, on average, than others. See Manning, Brown, and Payne (2014).

Chapter Six

1. This chapter can be read alongside chapter 7 ("Achievers, Underachievers, and the Professional Pathway") of Armstrong and Hamilton's (2013) *Paying for the Party: How College Maintains Inequality*.

2. These two women, Brianna and Monica, are discussed at two separate points below.

3. Zelizer (1997).

Chapter Seven

1. This chapter can be read alongside chapter 6 ("Strivers, Creaming, and the Blocked Mobility Pathway") of Armstrong and Hamilton's (2013) *Paying for the Party: How College Maintains Inequality*.

2. Rosenbaum, Deil-Amen, and Person (2006).

3. Julie's parents, Rachel and Matt, were the only affluent parents to express openly anti-gay views. They hailed from a suburb known for its conservative Christian beliefs.

4. Prejudice may take a different form among affluent, educated whites. They may engage in symbolic forms of discrimination, framing their negative views toward other groups in ways that are indirect, subtle, and more consistent with the appearance of tolerance for diversity. See Hamilton (2007); and Schuman et al. (1988).

5. See Hamilton (2013).

6. Many of these women were still in school at the time of the last interview. I used their most recent GPA. Amy, who left MU early in the year, is not included.

7. Goldrick-Rab (2006).

8. Armstrong and Hamilton (2013).

9. See Musick, Brand, and Davis (2012).

10. See Silva (2013) for more on working-class distrust of postsecondary institutions.

11. Labaree (2010); Lareau ([2003], 2011); Lareau and Cox (2011); Pascarella et al. (2004); Radford (2013); Ryan (2010).

12. See Armstrong and Hamilton (2013) for more on what a functioning mobility pathway looks like.

Chapter Eight

1. See Lareau ([2003], 2011).

2. For example, in 1940 only about 14 percent of American youth continued schooling past high school. Most youth moved directly into full-time employment and family roles. See Arnett (2000).

3. See Lareau ([2003], 2011) for more on how elementary schools reward and embody more affluent parenting styles.

4. Gans (1962, xiii).

5. Horowitz (1987) provides a detailed history of American higher education. Also see Karabel's (2005) account of Harvard's, Princeton's, and Yale's efforts to continue excluding these groups in a changing higher education landscape.

6. See Lambert (2014); Morphew and Eckel (2009); and Newfield (2008) for commentary.

7. Desrochers and Kirschstein (2014); Ginsberg (2011). A number of these positions, however, were for non-instructional student services, not just business support.

8. SHEEO (2015).

9. Settersten and Ray (2010).

10. Coburn (2006); Cutright (2008).

11. Stevens (2007).

12. Rivera (2015).

13. Burd (2013).

14. On the concept of internal stratification, see Bastedo (2009) and Ro, Terenzini, and Yin (2013).

15. Armstrong and Hamilton (2013).

16. Reardon (2011).

17. See Kao and Thompson (2003) for a review.

18. Goldrick-Rab and Kendall (2014).

19. Bailey and Dynarski (2011).

20. Bailey and Dynarski (2011).

21. National Center for Education Statistics (2014). These numbers reflect first-time, full-time, BA degree–seeking students entering institutions in 2004. See Kao and Thompson (2003) and DesJardins, Ahlburg, and McCall (2006) for the mediating role of class.

22. Desrochers and Kirshstein (2013). The student services category can include spending on career and financial counseling, as well as intramural athletics, student centers, special programs, and student recruitment. It does not designate the targeted student populations.

23. Armstrong and Hamilton (2013) discuss "creaming programs," which cull the best and brightest of disadvantaged students—leaving the majority without assistance.

24. Stevens (2007).

25. For endowment data, see National Association of College and University Business Officers (2012). Habley (2004) reports that private schools devote twice the effort to advising as public schools.

26. Disadvantaged students often fail to meet criteria for admission at more prestigious schools, due to poor academic preparation. See Carnevale and Strohl (2010). Even the most talented of the less privileged attend elite schools at much lower rates than their affluent peers. See Radford (2013).

27. See Hout (1988). Recently, Torche (2011) replicated these findings with updated data—although the most recent waves of graduates are not included.

28. Shierholz, Davis, and Kimball (2014).

29. Carnevale, Strohl, and Melton (2011); Charles and Bradley (2002); Gerber and Cheung (2008); Roksa and Levey (2010); Schofer and Meyer (2005); Zhang (2005).

30. In Torche's (2011) supplemental PSID analyses, she finds a significant link between family origin and future earnings for women who graduate with a BA—but not men. One mechanism supporting class inequality among women may be the emphasis on traditional femininity, especially at schools like MU, as it is harder for middle- to low-income families to convert this into economic stability. See Gaddis (2015) for more on the extent to which race matters for students' abilities to translate *the same* degree into jobs of equal pay and prestige.

31. Mullen, Goyette, and Soares (2003) show a strong effect of class on students' entry into first-professional and doctoral programs. See Rivera (2015) for more on class background and securing elite jobs.

32. DiPrete and Buchmann (2013); England and Li (2006); Horowitz (1987).

33. Correll, Bernard, and Paik (2007); Reskin and Padavic (2002).

34. Connell (1995); Sweeney (2007).

35. Masculinities scholars often refer to the embodiment of these traits as "hegemonic masculinity," and it is understood to carry a wide array of benefits for the men who can successfully perform it. See Connell (1987, 1995).

36. Shulman and Bowen (2002).

37. Musick, Brand, and Davis (2012).

38. Buss et al. (2001).

39. See the assortative mating literature: Schwartz and Mare (2005); Sweeney (2002); Sweeney and Cancian (2004).

40. See DiPrete and Buchmann (2013) for a review of the limited literature on this topic; also see López (2003).

41. According to Buchmann and DiPrete (2006), the female advantage in college completion is largest in families with low-educated or absent fathers.

42. See Charles and Bradley (2009) and Hamilton (2014) for more on the difference between vertical gender inequities in higher education, which disadvantage men, and horizontal inequities, which disadvantage women.

43. See Fingerman et al. (2012) and Settersten and Ray (2010). Two edited MacArthur Foundation Series books on young adulthood—Osgood et al. (2005) and Settersten, Furstenberg, and Rumbaut (2005)—are useful references, although they do not focus on parents.

44. Kornrich and Furstenberg (2013).

45. McCloud and Dwyer (2011); Sullivan, Warren, and Westbrook (2000).

46. Evenson and Simon (2005); Nomaguchi and Milkie (2003).

47. Hays (1996); Rizzo, Schiffrin, and Liss (2013).

48. Lareau ([2003], 2011).

49. Schiffrin et al. (2014). Also see Padilla-Walker and Nelson (2012).

50. Hoffman (2015); Mistler, Reetz, Krylowicz, and Barr (2012).

51. The *New York Times* recently referred to youth in the communities surrounding elite schools like Stanford University as the "best, brightest—and saddest," after a rash of youth suicides. Wiseman (2015) connects these deaths to the increasing pressures to achieve, placed on youth—in part—by parents anxious to secure their children's futures. Lythcott-Haims (2015), a former dean at Stanford University, argues that over-

bearing parents caused students to struggle with depression and perform worse than they might have otherwise. Also see Deresiewicz (2014).

52. Several chapters in Danziger and Rouse (2007) address the increasing time that youth spend in the natal home, both in the United States and in other parts of the world.

53. See Johnson (2013).

54. Kluegel and Smith (1986).

55. The College Scorecard is the most recent effort. See US Department of Education (2015). The *U.S. News & World Report* website (which puts its most detailed information behind a pay wall) and a number of consumer based websites (e.g., unigo.com) have sprung up in the past ten to fifteen years.

56. Carey (2015); Kamenetz (2015).

57. Baum and Payea (2011).

58. College Board (2013b).

59. Darolia et al. (2014); Deming et al. (2014).

60. Rimer (2009).

61. Between 2010 and 2014, enrollment at for-profits declined significantly. However, during the 2014–2015 academic year, these declines slowed, in part because for-profit schools are becoming increasingly savvy at recruiting younger students. See the Hechinger Report (2015).

62. Rivard (2013). Some university leaders, however, are realizing that online education is not a financial silver bullet. Doing it well takes funds that cash-strapped institutions lack. For example, see Hiltzik (2014) for coverage of the University of California president Janet Napolitano's views on online education.

63. Espeland and Sauder (2007, 2009).

64. U.S. News & World Report (2014).

65. Bailey and Dynarski (2011).

66. U.S. News & World Report (2014).

67. See http://www.socialmobilityindex.org.

68. Karabel (2005); Stevens (2007).

69. Lifschitz, Sauder, and Stevens (2014).

70. Many schools ranked in the top ten of their categories—including Columbia University, Dartmouth College, Davidson College, Duke University, Harvard University, Pomona College, University of Chicago, and Williams College—refused to provide Pell Grant recipient graduation rates. See Morse and Tolis (2013). Perhaps to get around this issue, in 2014 *U.S. News & World Report* introduced a new "added value" measure, "graduation rate performance" (at 7.5 percent of the total score). It is intended to show "the effect of the college's programs and policies on the graduation rate of students after controlling for spending and student characteristics, such as test scores and the proportion receiving Pell Grants." See U.S. News & World Report (2014). However, this measure does a poor job of assessing how well disadvantaged students fare on campus.

71. In some countries, however, youth are sorted into educational pathways early on, making it difficult for some to reach higher levels of education or fill limited spots in public institutions. See Turner (1960) on sponsored versus contest mobility.

72. Aries (1965); Kett (1977); Zelizer (1985).

73. Arnett (2006); Labaree (2010).

74. One of the key differences between the two proposals is Obama's focus on community colleges, as opposed to any public sector school. Limiting the plan to community colleges may have unintended consequences for four-year schools, particularly near the middle to bottom of the prestige hierarchy (e.g., declining student enrollments and an increase in two-year transfer students needing remediation).

75. Mettler (2014).

76. College Board (2013b); Goldrick-Rab and Kendall (2014).

77. Vedder (2008).

78. Weissman (2013).

79. Baum and Payea (2011).

80. See http://www.safeandjust.org/schools-not-prisons.

81. Houle (2013).

82. Powell, Jordan, and Pizmony-Levy (2012) compare public opinion data regarding the locus of responsibility for college funding from 1980 (using the "High School and Beyond" survey) with a similarly constructed national sample in 2010. Also see Steelman and Powell (1991).

83. Powell (2016).

Methodological Appendix

1. I asked only the forty-six women who were actively participating in interviews at this point. Thirty-eight women agreed. Alyssa and Heather were the two low-income women mentioned above. Amy added one more family, for a total of forty-one.

References

Acocella, Joan. 2008. "The Child Trap: The Rise of Over-Parenting." *New Yorker*. http:// www.newyorker .com/arts/critics/books/2008/11/17/081117crbo_books_acocella.

Amato, Paul R., Laura R. Loomis, and Alan Booth. 1995. "Parental Divorce, Marital Conflict, and Offspring Well-Being during Early Adulthood." *Social Forces* 73: 895–915.

Aries, Philippe. 1965. *Centuries of Childhood: A Social History of Family Life*. New York: Vintage Books.

Armstrong, Elizabeth A., and Laura T. Hamilton. 2013. *Paying for the Party: How College Maintains Inequality*. Cambridge, MA: Harvard University Press.

Armstrong, Elizabeth A., Laura Hamilton, and Brian Sweeney. 2006. "Sexual Assault on Campus: A Multilevel, Integrative Approach to Party Rape." *Social Problems* 53: 483–99.

Arnett, Jeffrey Jensen. 2000. "Emerging Adulthood: A Theory of Development from the Late Teens through the Twenties." *American Psychologist* 55: 469–80.

———. 2004. *Emerging Adulthood: The Winding Road from the Late Teens through the Twenties*. New York: Oxford University Press.

———. 2006. "G. Stanley Hall's *Adolescence*: Brilliance and Nonsense." *History of Psychology* 9: 186–97.

Arum, Richard, and Josipa Roksa. 2011. *Academically Adrift: Limited Learning on College Campuses*. Chicago: University of Chicago Press.

———. 2014. *Aspiring Adults Adrift: Tentative Transitions of College Graduates*. Chicago: University of Chicago Press.

Badinter, Elisabeth. 2010. *The Conflict: How Overzealous Motherhood Undermines the Status of Women*. New York: Metropolitan Books.

Bailey, Beth L. 1989. *From Front Porch to Back Seat: Courtship in Twentieth-Century America*. Baltimore: Johns Hopkins University Press.

Bailey, Martha J., and Susan M. Dynarski. 2011. "Gains and Gaps: Changing Inequality in U.S. College Entry and Completion." *National Bureau of Economic Research Working Paper Series*.

Bastedo, Michael N. 2009. "Convergent Institutional Logics in Public Higher Education: State Policymaking and Governing Board Activism." *Review of Higher Education* 32: 209–34.

Bastedo, Michael N., and Patricia J. Gumport. 2003. "Access to What?: Mission Differentiation and Academic Stratification in U.S. Public Higher Education." *Higher Education* 46: 341–59.

Baum, Sandy, and Kathleen Payea. 2011. "Trends in For-Profit Postsecondary Education: Enrollment, Prices, Student Aid and Outcomes." *College Board Trends in Higher Education Series.*

Becker, Gary S. 1991. *A Treatise on the Family.* Cambridge, MA: Harvard University Press.

Beller, Emily. 2009. "Bringing Intergenerational Social Mobility Research into the Twenty-First Century: Why Mothers Matter." *American Sociological Review* 74: 507–28.

Berger, Joseph B., and Jeffrey F. Milem. 2000. "Organizational Behavior in Higher Education and Student Outcomes." In *Higher Education: Handbook of Theory and Research Vol. XV*, ed. John C. Smart, 268–338. New York: Springer.

Berman, Elizabeth P. 2012. *Creating the Market University: How Academic Science Became an Economic Engine.* Princeton, NJ: Princeton University Press.

Bettie, Julie. 2003. *Women without Class: Girls, Race, and Identity.* Berkeley: University of California Press.

Bickel, Robert D., and Peter F. Lake. 1999. *The Rights and Responsibilities of the Modern University: Who Assumes the Risks of College Life?* Durham, NC: Carolina Academic Press.

Binder, Amy J., and Kate Wood. 2012. *Becoming Right: How Campuses Shape Young Conservatives.* Princeton, NJ: Princeton University Press.

Blau, Peter, and Otis Dudley Duncan. 1967. *The American Occupational Structure.* New York: Wiley.

Bodovski, Katerina. 2010. "Parental Practices and Educational Achievement: Social Class, Race, and *Habitus*." *British Journal of Sociology of Education* 31: 139–56.

Bourdieu, Pierre. 1977. *Outline of a Theory of Practice.* Cambridge: Cambridge University Press.

———. 1984. *Distinction: A Social Critique of the Judgment of Taste.* Cambridge, MA: Harvard University Press.

———. 2004. *The Science of Science and Reflexivity.* Chicago: University of Chicago Press.

Brint, Steven G., and Jerome Karabel. 1989. *The Diverted Dream: Community Colleges and the Promise of Educational Opportunity in America, 1900–1985.* New York: Oxford University Press.

Bruni, Frank. 2015. "Today's Exhausted Superkids." *New York Times*, July 29. http://www.nytimes.com/2015/07/29/opinion/frank-bruni-todays-exhausted-superkids.html?_r=0.

Buchmann, Claudia, and Thomas A. DiPrete. 2006. "The Growing Female Advantage in College Completion: The Role of Family Background and Academic Achievement." *American Sociological Review* 71: 515–41.

Burawoy, Michael. 2009. *The Extended Case Method: Four Countries, Four Decades, Four Great Transformations, and One Theoretical Tradition.* Berkeley: University of California Press.

Burd, Stephen. 2013. "Undermining Pell: How Colleges Compete for Wealthy Students and Leave the Low-Income Behind." New American Foundation. http://newamerica.net/sites/newamerica.net/files/policydocs/Merit_Aid%20Final.pdf.

Buss David M., Todd K. Shackelford, Lee A. Kirkpatrick, and Randy J. Larsen. 2001.

"A Half Century of Mate Preferences: The Cultural Evolution of Values." *Journal of Marriage and Family* 63: 491–503.

Calarco, Jessica. 2011. "'I Need Help!': Social Class and Children's Help-Seeking in Elementary School." *American Sociological Review* 76: 862–82.

———. 2014. "Coached for the Classroom: Parents' Cultural Transmission and Children's Reproduction of Educational Inequalities." *American Sociological Review* 79: 1015–37.

Carey, Kevin. 2015. *The End of College: Creating the Future of Learning and the University of Everywhere*. New York: Riverhead Books.

Carnevale, Anthony P., and Jeff Strohl. 2010. "How Increasing College Access Is Increasing Inequality, and What to Do about It." In *Rewarding Strivers: Helping Low- Income Students Succeed in College*, ed. Richard D. Kahlenberg, 71–183. New York: Century Foundation Press.

Carnevale, Anthony P., Jeff Strohl, and Michelle Melton. 2011. "What's It Worth?: The Economic Values of College Majors." Washington, DC: George Washington Center for Education and the Workforce.

Chambliss, Daniel F., and Christopher G. Takacs. 2014. *How College Works*. Cambridge, MA: Harvard University Press.

Charles, Camille Z., Mary J. Fischer, Margarita A. Mooney, and Douglas S. Massey. 2009. *Taming the River: Negotiating the Academic, Financial, and Social Currents in Selective Colleges and Universities*. Princeton, NJ: Princeton University Press.

Charles, Camille Z., Vincent C. Roscigno, and Kimberly C. Torres. 2007. "Racial Inequality and College Attendance." *Social Science Research* 36: 329–52.

Charles, Maria, and Karen Bradley. 2002. "Equal but Separate?: A Cross-National Study of Sex Segregation in Higher Education." *American Sociological Review* 67: 573–99.

———. 2009. "Indulging Our Gendered Selves?: Sex Segregation by Field of Study in 44 Countries." *American Journal of Sociology* 114: 924–76.

Chen, Rong. 2012. "Institutional Characteristics and College Student Dropout Risks: A Multilevel Event History Analysis." *Research in Higher Education* 53: 487–505.

Choo, Hae Yeon, and Myra Marx Ferree. 2010. "Practicing Intersectionality in Sociological Research: A Critical Analysis of Inclusions, Interactions, and Institutions in the Study of Inequalities." *Sociological Theory* 28: 129–49.

Chua, Amy. 2011. *Battle Hymn of the Tiger Mother*. New York: Penguin.

Clarke, Averil. 2011. *Inequalities of Love: College-Educated Black Women and the Barriers to Romance and Family*. Ann Arbor: University of Michigan Press.

Coburn, Karen L. 2006. "Organizing a Ground Crew for Today's Helicopter Parents." *About Campus: Enriching the Student Learning Experience* 11: 9–16.

Coleman, James S. 1988. "Social Capital in the Creation of Human Capital." *American Journal of Sociology* 94: 95–120.

College Board. 2013a. "Trends in College Pricing: 2013." *College Board Trends in Higher Education Series*.

College Board. 2013b. "Trends in Student Aid: 2013." *College Board Trends in Higher Education Series*.

Conger, Dylan, and Mark C. Long. 2009. "Why Are Men Falling Behind?: Gender Gaps in College Performance and Persistence." *ANNALS of the American Academy of Political and Social Science* 627: 184–214.

Connell, R. W. 1987. *Gender and Power: Society, the Person, and Sexual Politics*. Stanford, CA: Stanford University Press.

———. 1995. *Masculinities*. Berkeley: University of California Press.

Coontz, Stephanie. 1992. *The Way We Never Were: American Families and the Nostalgia Trap*. New York: Basic Books.

Correll, Shelley, Stephan Bernard, and In Paik. 2007. "Getting a Job: Is There a Motherhood Penalty?" *American Journal of Sociology* 112: 1297–338.

Croft, Alyssa, Toni Schmader, Block, Katharina, and Andrew Scott Baron. 2014. "The Second Shift Reflected in the Second Generation: Do Parents' Gender Roles at Home Predict Children's Aspirations?" *Psychological Science* 7: 1418–28.

Crowder, Kyle D., and Steward E. Tolnay. 2000. "A New Marriage Squeeze for Black Women: the Role of Racial Intermarriage by Black Men." *Journal of Marriage and Family* 62: 792–807.

Cutright, Marc. 2008. "From Helicopter Parent to Valued Partner: Shaping the Parental Relationship for Student Success." *New Directions for Higher Education* 144: 39–48.

Danziger, Sheldon, and Cecilia E. Rouse, eds. 2007. *The Price of Independence: The Economics of Early Adulthood*. New York: Russell Sage.

Darolia, Rajeev, Cory Koedel, Paco Martorell, Katie Wilson, and Francisco Perez-Arce. 2014. "Do Employers Prefer Workers Who Attend For-Profit Colleges?: Evidence from a Field Experiment." National Center for Analysis of Longitudinal Data in Education Research, Working Paper.

Deil-Amen, Regina. 2015. "The 'Traditional' College Student: A Smaller and Smaller Minority and Its Implications for Diversity and Access Institutions." In *Remaking College: The Changing Ecology of Higher Education*, ed. Michael W. Kirst and Mitchell L. Stevens, 133–68. Stanford, CA: Stanford University Press.

Delbanco, Andrew. 2012. *College: What It Was, Is, and Should Be*. Princeton, NJ: Princeton University Press.

Dell'Antonia, K. J. 2013. "Helicopter Parents Make Children Miss Milestones." *New York Times*. http://parenting.blogs.nytimes.com/2013/01/25/helicopter-parents-make-children-miss-milestones/.

Deming, David J., Noam Yuchtman, Amira Abulafi, Claudia Goldin, and Lawrence F. Katz. 2014. "The Value of Postsecondary Credentials in the Labor Market: An Experimental Study." Working paper. http://scholar.harvard.edu/files/lkatz/files/resumeauditstudy_final_092114_dd.pdf.

Deresiewicz, William. 2014. *Excellent Sheep: The Miseducation of the American Elite and the Way to a Meaningful Life*. New York: Free Press.

DeSantis, Alan D. 2007. *Inside Greek U: Fraternities, Sororities, and the Pursuit of Pleasure, Power, and Prestige*. Lexington: University of Kentucky Press.

DesJardins, Stephen L., Dennis A. Ahlburg, and Brian P. McCall. 2006. "The Effects of Interrupted Enrollment on Graduation from College: Racial, Income, and Ability Differences." *Economics of Education Review* 25: 575–90.

Desrochers, Donna M., and Rita J. Kirshstein. 2013. "College Spending in a Turbulent Decade: Findings from the Delta Cost Project." Washington, DC: Delta Cost Project.

———. 2014. "Labor Intensive or Labor Expensive?: Changing Staffing and Compensation Patterns in Higher Education." Washington, DC: Delta Cost Project.

DiPrete, Thomas A., and Claudia Buchmann. 2013. *The Rise of Women: The Growing Gender Gap in Education and What It Means for American Schools*. New York: Russell Sage.

Doherty, Risa C. 2013. "The New Faces of College Admissions." *New York Times*. http://www.nytimes.com/2013/11/03/education/edlife/new-faces-of-college-admissions-parents.html?_r=1&.

Douglas, Susan, and Meredith Michaels. 2004. *The Mommy Myth: The Idealization of Motherhood and How It Has Undermined All Women*. New York: Free Press.

Downey, Douglas B. 1995. "When Bigger Is Not Better: Family Size, Parental Resources, and Children's Educational Performance." *American Sociological Review* 60: 746–61.

Druckerman, Pamela. 2012. *Bringing up Bébé: One American Mother Discovers the Wisdom of French Parenting*. New York: Penguin.

Dudley, Kathryn Marie. 1994. *The End of the Line: Lost Jobs, New Lives in Postindustrial America*. Chicago: University of Chicago Press.

Eccles, Jacquelynne S., Janis E. Jacobs, and Rena D. Harold. 1990. "Gender Role Stereotypes, Expectancy Effects, and Parents' Socialization of Gender Differences." *Journal of Social Issues* 46: 183–201.

Eggebeen, David J. 1992. "Family Structure and Intergenerational Exchanges." *Research on Aging* 14: 427–47.

England, Paula. 2010. "The Gender Revolution: Uneven and Stalled." *Gender & Society* 24: 149–66.

England, Paula, and Su Li. 2006. "Desegregation Stalled: The Changing Gender Composition of College Majors, 1971–2002." *Gender & Society* 20: 657–77.

English, Bella. 2013. "'Snowplow Parents' Overly Involved in College Students' Lives." *Boston Globe*, November 9.

Espeland, Wendy, and Michael Sauder. 2007. "Rankings and Reactivity: How Public Measures Recreate Social Worlds." *American Journal of Sociology* 113: 11–40.

———. 2009. "Rating the Rankings." *Contexts* 8: 16–21.

Etaugh, Clair, and Marsha B. Liss. 1992. "Home, School, and Playroom: Training Grounds for Adult Gender Roles." *Sex Roles* 26: 129–47.

Evenson, Ranae. J., and Robin W. Simon. 2005. "Clarifying the Relationship Between Parenthood and Depression." *Journal of Health and Social Behavior* 46: 341–58.

Feiler, Bruce. 2014. "This Weekend, College Is for Everyone." *New York Times*. http://www.nytimes.com/2014/11/02/fashion/college-family-weekend-isnt-just-for-parents-anymore.html?_r=0.

Fingerman, Karen L., Yen-Pi Cheng, Eric D. Wesselmann, Steven Zarit, Frank Furstenberg, and Kira S. Birditt. 2012. "Helicopter Parents and Landing Pad Kids: Intense Parental Support of Grown Children." *Journal of Marriage and Family* 74: 880–96.

Friedman, Hilary L. 2013. *Playing to Win: Raising Children in a Competitive Culture*. Berkeley: University of California Press.

Furstenberg, Frank F., Saul D. Hoffman, and Laura Shrestha. 1995. "The Effect of Divorce on Intergenerational Transfers: New Evidence." *Demography* 32: 319–33.

Furstenberg, Frank F., Sheela Kennedy, Vonnie C. McLoyd, Rubén G. Rumbaut, and Richard A. Settersten. 2004. "Growing Up Is Harder to Do." *Contexts* 3: 33–41.

Furstenberg, Frank F., Jr., Rubén G. Rumbaut, and Richard A. Settersten. 2005. "On the Frontier of Adulthood: Emerging Themes and New Directions." In *On the Frontier of*

Adulthood, ed. Richard A. Settersten, Frank F. Furstenberg Jr., and Rubén Rumbaut, 3–28, Chicago: University of Chicago Press.

Gaddis, Michael. 2015. "Discrimination in the Credential Society: An Audit Study of Race and College Selectivity in the Labor Market." *Social Forces* 93: 1451–79.

Gans, Herbert J. 1962. *The Urban Villagers: Group and Class in the Life of Italian-Americans*. New York: Free Press.

Geiger, Roger L. 2004. *Knowledge and Money: Research Universities and the Paradox of the Marketplace*. Stanford, CA: Stanford University Press.

Gerber, Theodore P., and Sin Yi Cheung. 2008. "Horizontal Stratification in Postsecondary Education: Forms, Explanations, and Implications." *Annual Review of Sociology* 34: 299–318.

Gibbs, Nancy. 2009. "The Growing Backlash against Overparenting." *Time Magazine*. http://www.time.com/time/magazine/article/0,9171,1940697,00.html.

Ginsberg, Benjamin. 2011. *The Fall of the Faculty: The Rise of the All-Administrative University and Why It Matters*. Oxford: Oxford University Press.

Giroux, Henry A. 2014. *Neoliberalism's War on Higher Education*. Chicago: Haymarket Books.

Goldin, Claudia, and Lawrence F. Katz. 2008. *The Race between Education and Technology*. Cambridge, MA: Harvard University Press.

Goldrick-Rab, Sara. 2006. "Following Their Every Move: An Investigation of Social-Class Differences in College Pathways." *Sociology of Education* 79: 61–79.

Goldrick-Rab, Sara, and Nancy Kendall. 2014. "Redefining College Affordability: Securing America's Future with a Free Two-Year College Option." Lumina Foundation.

Goldscheider, Frances K., Arland Thornton, and Li-Shou Yang. 2001. "Helping Out the Kids: Expectations about Parental Support in Young Adulthood." *Journal of Marriage and the Family* 63: 727–40.

Goldthorpe, John H. 1980. *Social Mobility and Class Structure in Modern Britain*. Oxford: Clarendon Press.

Grubb, W. Norton, and Marvin Lazerson. 2005. *The Education Gospel: The Economic Power of Schooling*. Cambridge, MA: Harvard University Press.

Habley, Wesley R. 2004. *The Status of Academic Advising: Findings from the ACT Sixth National Survey*. Manhattan, KS: National Academic Advising Association.

Hamilton, Laura. 2007. "Trading on Heterosexuality: College Women's Gender Strategies and Homophobia." *Gender & Society* 21: 145–72.

———. 2013. "More Is More or More Is Less?: Parental Financial Investments during College." *American Sociological Review* 78: 70–95.

———. 2014. "The Revised MRS: Gender Complementarity at College." *Gender & Society* 28: 236–64.

Hamilton, Laura, Simon Cheng, and Brian Powell. 2007. "Adoptive Parents, Adaptive Parents: Evaluating the Importance of Biological Ties for Parental Investment." *American Sociological Review* 72: 95–116.

Harding, David J. 2007. "Cultural Context, Sexual Behavior, and Romantic Relationships in Disadvantaged Neighborhoods." *American Sociological Review* 72: 341–64.

Hays, Sharon. 1996. *The Cultural Contradictions of Motherhood*. New Haven, CT: Yale University Press.

Hechinger Report. 2015. "Students Are Returning to For-Profit Colleges." *U.S. News*

& *World Report*. http://www.usnews.com/news/articles/2015/02/24/students-are
-returning-to-for-profit-colleges.

Heffernan, Lisa. 2015. "Our Push for 'Passion,' and Why it Harms Kids." *New York Times*.
http://parenting.blogs.nytimes.com/2015/04/08/our-push-for-passion-and-why
-it-harms-kids/?_r=0.

Henderson, Maureen J. 2013. "Why Entitled Millennials and Their Enabling Boomer
Parents Just Can't Quit Each Other." *Forbes Magazine*, January 7.

Hiltzik, Michael. 2014. "UC's Napolitano Throws Cold Water on the Online Education
Craze." *Los Angeles Times*. http://articles.latimes.com/2014/mar/26/business/la
-fi-mh-uc-prexy-napolitano-20140326.

Hochschild, Arlie, with Anne Machung. 1989. *The Second Shift: Working Families and the
Revolution at Home*. New York: Penguin.

Hoffman, Jan. 2015. "Anxious Students Strain College Mental Health Centers." *New
York Times*. http://well.blogs.nytimes.com/2015/05/27/anxious-students-strain
-college-mental-health-centers/.

Hoover, Eric, and Josh Keller. 2011. "The Cross-Country Recruitment Rush." *Chronicle
of Higher Education*. http://chronicle.com/article/The-Cross-Country-Recruitment
/129577/.

Horowitz, Helen Lefkowitz. 1987. *Campus Life: Undergraduate Cultures from the End of the
Eighteenth Century to the Present*. Chicago: University of Chicago Press.

Houle, Jason N. 2013. "Disparities in Debt: Parents' Socioeconomic Resources and
Young Adult Student Loan Debt." *Sociology of Education* 87: 53–69.

Hout, Michael. 1988. "More Universalism, Less Structural Mobility: The American
Occupational Structure in the 1980s." *American Journal of Sociology* 93: 1358–400.

———. 2012. "Social and Economic Returns to College Education in the United States."
Annual Review of Sociology: 379–400.

Jaquette, Ozan, and Bradley R. Curs. 2013. "The Effect of State Financial Support on
Non-Residential Enrollments for Public Universities." Paper presented at the 2013
Meetings of the Association for Education Finance and Policy.

Johnson, Monica K. 2013. "Parental Financial Assistance and Young Adults' Relationships with Parents and Well-Being." *Journal of Marriage and Family* 75: 713–33.

Kalleberg, Arne L. 2011. *Good Jobs, Bad Jobs: The Rise of Polarized and Precarious Employment Systems in the United States, 1970s to 2000s*. New York: Russell Sage Foundation.

Kamenetz, Anya. 2015. "DIY U: Higher Education Goes Hybrid." In *Remaking College:
The Changing Ecology of Higher Education*, ed. Michael W. Kirst and Mitchell L. Stevens, 39–60. Stanford, CA: Stanford University Press.

Kao, Grace, and Jennifer S. Thompson. 2003. "Racial and Ethnic Stratification in Educational Achievement and Attainment." *Annual Review of Sociology* 29: 417–42.

Karabel, Jerome. 2005. *The Chosen: The Hidden History of Admission and Exclusion at
Harvard, Yale, and Princeton*. New York: Houghton Mifflin.

Kett, Joseph. 1977. *Rites of Passage: Adolescence in America, 1790 to the Present*. New York:
Basic Books.

Khan, Shamus R. 2011. *Privilege: The Making of an Adolescent Elite at St. Paul's School*.
Princeton, NJ: Princeton University Press.

Kingston, Paul. 2000. *The Classless Society*. Stanford, CA: Stanford University Press.

Kluegel, James R., and Eliot R. Smith. 1986. *Beliefs about Inequality*. New York: Aldine De Gruyter.

Kohn, Melvin L. 1977. *Class and Conformity*. Chicago: University of Chicago Press.

Kornrich, Sabino, and Frank Furstenberg. 2013. "Investing in Children: Changes in Parental Spending on Children, 1972–2007." *Demography* 50: 1–23.

Kuh, George D., Jillian Kinzie, John H. Schuh, and Elizabeth J. Whitt. 2005. *Student Success in College: Creating Conditions That Matter*. San Francisco: Jossey-Bass.

Labaree, David F. 2010. *Someone Has to Fail: The Zero-Sum Game of Public Schooling*. Cambridge, MA: Harvard University Press.

Lake, Peter. 2013. *The Rights and Responsibilities of the Modern University: The Rise of the Facilitator University*, 2nd ed. Durham, NC: Carolina Academic Press.

Lambert, Matthew T. 2014. *Privatization and the Public Good: Public Universities in the Balance*. Cambridge, MA: Harvard University Press.

Lamont, Michèle. 1992. *Money, Morals, and Manners: The Culture of the French and American Upper-Middle Class*. Chicago: University of Chicago Press.

Lansley, Renée N. 2004. "College Women or College Girls?: Gender, Sexuality, and In Loco Parentis on Campus. PhD diss., Ohio State University.

Lareau, Annette. 2002. "Invisible Inequality: Social Class and Childrearing in Black Families and White Families." *American Sociological Review* 67: 747–76.

———. (2003) 2011. *Unequal Childhoods: Class, Race, and Family Life*. Berkeley: University of California Press.

Lareau, Annette, and Amanda Cox. 2011. "Social Class and the Transition to Adulthood: Differences in Parents' Interactions with Institutions." In *Social Class and Changing Families in an Unequal America*, ed. Maria J. Carlson and Paula England, 134–64. Stanford, CA: Stanford University Press.

Lee, Elizabeth M., and Rory Kramer. 2013. "Out with the Old, in with the New?: Habitus and Social Mobility at Selective Colleges." *Sociology of Education* 86: 18–35.

Lehmann, Wolfgang. 2014. "Habitus Transformation and Hidden Injuries: Successful Working-Class University Students." *Sociology of Education* 87: 1–15.

Leroux, Charles. 2008. "College Send Record Number of Rejections: Competition for Admission Soaring." *Chicago Tribune*. http://articles.chicagotribune.com/2008-04 -09/features/0804070360_1_applicants-rejection-letters-ivy-league-schools.

Levine, Arthur. 1980. *When Dreams and Heroes Died: A Portrait of Today's College Student*. San Francisco: Jossey-Bass.

Levine, Arthur, and Jeanette S. Cureton. 1998. *When Hope and Fear Collide: A Portrait of Today's College Student*. San Francisco: Jossey-Bass.

Lifschitz, Arik, Michael Sauder, and Mitchell L. Stevens. 2014. "Football as a Status System in U.S. Higher Education." *Sociology of Education* 87: 204–19.

Lombardi, Kate Stone. 2007. "High Anxiety of Getting into College." *New York Times*. http://www.nytimes.com/2007/04/08/nyregion/nyregionspecial2/08wecol.html.

López, Nancy. 2003. *Hopeful Girls, Troubled Boys: Race and Gender Disparity in Urban Education*. London: Routledge.

Loss, Christopher P. 2012. *Between Citizens and the State: The Politics of American Higher Education in the 20th Century*. Princeton, NJ: Princeton University.

Lucas, Samuel R. 1996. "Selective Attrition in a Newly Hostile Regime: The Case of 1980 Sophomores." *Social Forces* 75: 511–33.

Lythcott-Haims, Julie. 2015. *How to Raise an Adult: Break Free of the Overparenting Trap and Prepare Your Kid for Success*. New York: Henry Holt.

Maier, Kimberly S., Timothy G. Ford, and Barbara Schneider. 2008. In *The Way Class Works: Readings on School, Family, and the Economy*, ed. Lois Weis, 134–48. New York: Routledge.

Manning, Wendy D., Susan L. Brown, and Krista Payne. "Two Decades of Stability and Change in Age at First Union Formation." *Journal of Marriage and Family* 76: 247–60.

Marano, Hara Estroff. 2008. *A Nation of Wimps: The High Cost of Invasive Parenting*. New York: Broadway Books.

McCall, Leslie. 1992. "Does Gender Fit?: Bourdieu, Feminism, and Conceptions of Social Order." *Theory and Society* 21: 837–67.

McCloud, Laura, and Rachel E. Dwyer. 2011. "The Fragile American: Hardship and Financial Troubles in the 21st Century." *Sociological Quarterly* 52: 13–35.

McPherson, Michael S., and Morton O. Schapiro. 1998. *The Student Aid Game: Meeting Need and Rewarding Talent in American Higher Education*. Princeton, NJ: Princeton University Press.

Mettler, Suzanne. 2014. *Degrees of Inequality: How the Politics of Higher Education Sabotaged the American Dream*. New York: Basic Books.

Milkie, Melissa A., Kei M. Nomaguchi, and Kathleen E. Denny. 2015. "Does the Amount of Time Mothers Spend with Children or Adolescents Matter?" *Journal of Marriage and Family* 77: 355–72.

Mistler, Brian J., David R. Reetz, Brian Krylowicz, and Victor Barr. 2012. "The Association for University and College Counseling Center Directors Annual Survey." AUCCCD.

Morphew, Christopher C., and Peter D. Eckel. 2009. *Privatizing the Public University: Perspectives from Across the Academy*. Baltimore: Johns Hopkins University.

Morse, Robert, and Diane Tolis. 2013. "Measuring Colleges' Success Graduating Low-Income Students." *U.S. News & World Report*. http://www.usnews.com/education/blogs/college-rankings-blog/2013/10/17/measuring-colleges-success-graduating-low-income-students.

Mullen, Ann L., Kimberly A. Goyette, and Joseph A. Soares. 2003. "Who Goes to Graduate School?: Social and Academic Correlates of Educational Continuation after College." *Sociology of Education* 76: 143–69.

Musick, Kelly, Jennie E. Brand, and Dwight Davis. 2012. "Variation in the Relationship Between Education and Marriage: Marriage Market Mismatch?" *Journal of Marriage and Family* 74: 53–69.

National Association of College and University Business Officers. 2012. "Commonfund Study of Endowments."

National Center for Education Statistics (NCES). 2014. "Table 376: Percentage of First-Time Full-Time Bachelor's Degree-Seeking Students at 4-year Institutions Who Completed a Bachelor's Degree."

Newfield, Christopher. 2008. *Unmaking the Public University: The Forty-Year Assault on the Middle Class*. Reprint, Cambridge, MA: Harvard University Press.

Nikolopoulos, Stephanie. 2013. "Blame Parents for Millennials Acting Entitled: Helicopter Parents Have Trophy Kids Who End Up Boomerang Kids." http://stephanienikolopoulos.com/2013/06/12/blame-parents-for-millennials-acting-entitled-helicopter-parents-have-trophy-kids-who-end-up-boomerang-kids/.

Nomaguchi, Kei M., and Melissa A. Milkie. 2003. "Costs and Rewards of Children: The Effects of Becoming a Parent on Adults' Lives." *Journal of Marriage and Family* 65: 356–74.

Nussbaum, Martha C. 2010. *Not for Profit: Why Democracy Needs the Humanities*. Princeton, NJ: Princeton University Press.

O'Connor, Maureen. 2013. "Princeton Mom Sold a Self-Help Book." *New York Magazine*. http://nymag.com/thecut/2013/07/princeton-mom-sold-a-self-help-book.html.

Osgood, Wayne D., Michael E. Foster, Flanagan Constance, and Gretchen R. Ruth, eds. 2005. *On Your Own without a Net: The Transition to Adulthood for Vulnerable Populations*. Chicago: University of Chicago Press.

Osgood, Wayne, Gretchen Ruth, Jacquelynne Eccles, Janis Jacobs, and Bonnie Barber. 2004. "Six Paths to Adulthood: Fast Starters, Parents without Careers, Educated Partners, Educated Singles, Working Singles, and Slow Starters." In *On the Frontier of Adulthood: Theory, Research, and Public Policy*, ed. Richard A. Settersten, Frank F. Furstenberg, and Rubén G. Rumbaut, 320–55. Chicago: University of Chicago Press.

Ostrander, Susan. 1984. *Women of the Upper Class*. Philadelphia: Temple University.

Ozment, Katherine. 2011. "Welcome to the Age of Overparenting." *Boston Magazine*. http://www.bostonmagazine.com/2011/11/the-age-of-overparenting/.

Padilla-Walker, Laura M., and Larry J. Nelson. 2012. "Black Hawk Down? Establishing Helicopter Parenting as a Distinct Construct from Other Forms of Parental Control during Emerging Adulthood." *Journal Adolescence* 35: 1177–90.

Pascarella, Ernest T., Christopher T. Pierson, Gregory C. Wolniak, and Patrick T. Terenzini. 2004. "First-Generation College Students: Additional Evidence on College Experiences and Outcomes." *Journal of Higher Education* 75: 249–84.

Pascarella, Ernest T., and Patrick T. Terenzini. 2005. *How College Affects Students: A Third Decade of Research*. San Francisco: Jossey-Bass.

Patton, Susan. 2013. "Letter to the Editor: Advice for the Young Women of Princeton: The Daughters I Never Had." *Daily Princetonian*. http://dailyprincetonian.com/opinion/2013/03/letter-to-the-editor-advice-for-the-young-women-of-princeton-the-daughters-i-never-had/.

———. 2014. *Marry Smart: Advice for Finding THE ONE*. New York: Gallery Books.

Paulsen, Michael B., and Edward P. St. John. 2002. "Social Class and College Costs: Examining the Financial Nexus between College Choice and Persistence." *Journal of Higher Education* 73: 189–236.

Piketty, Thomas, and Emmanuel Saez. 2003. "Income Inequality in the United States, 1913–1998." *Quarterly Journal of Economics* 118: 1–39.

Postsecondary Education Opportunity. 2012. "Revenues and Expenditures of Public 4-Year Institutions by State, 1987 to 2010." *Postsecondary Education Opportunity*, no. 246 (December): 1–16.

Powell, Brian. 2016. "The Costs of Responsibility: How Americans View College Access and the Role of the Government, Families, and Youth in the Funding of Higher Education." Sociology Education Association Annual Conference, Asilomar, CA.

Powell, Brian, Kristin Jordan, and Oren Pizmony-Levy. 2012. "The Costs of Responsibility: Americans' Views on the Funding of College." Paper presented at the American Sociological Association Annual Meetings in Denver, CO.

Prescott, Brian T., and Peace Bransberger. 2008. *Knocking at the College Door: Projections of High School Graduates by State, Income, and Race/Ethnicity.* Boulder, CO: Western Interstate Commission for Higher Education.

Price, Derek V. 2004. *Borrowing Inequality: Race, Class, and Student Loans.* Boulder, CO: Lynne Rienner.

Pugh, Allison. 2009. *Longing and Belonging: Parents, Children, and Consumer Culture.* Berkeley: University of California.

Radford, Alexandria W. 2013. *Top Student, Top School?: How Social Class Shapes Where Valedictorians Go to College.* Chicago: University of Chicago Press.

Raley, Sara, and Suzanne Bianchi. 2006. "Sons, Daughters, and Family Processes: Does Gender of Children Matter?" *Annual Review of Sociology* 32: 401–21.

Reardon, Sean F. 2011. "The Widening Academic Achievement Gap between the Rich and the Poor: New Evidence and Possible Explanations." In *Whither Opportunity?: Rising Inequality, Schools, and Children's Life Chances,* ed. Greg J. Duncan and Richard J. Murnane, 91–116. New York: Russell Sage Foundation.

Reardon, Sean F., and Kendra Bischoff. 2011. "Income Inequality and Income Segregation." *American Journal of Sociology* 116: 1092–153.

Reskin, Barbara, and Irene Padavic. 2002. *Women and Men at Work,* 2nd ed. Thousand Oaks, CA: Pine Forge Press.

Ridgeway, Cecilia. 2011. *Framed by Gender: How Gender Inequality Persists in the Modern World.* New York: Oxford University Press.

Rimer, Sara. 2009. "At M.I.T., Large Lectures Are Going the Way of the Blackboard." *New York Times.* http://www.nytimes.com/2009/01/13/us/13physics.html ?pagewanted=all.

Rivard, Ry. 2013. "Udacity Project on 'Pause.'" *Inside Higher Ed.* https://www.inside highered.com/news/2013/07/18/citing-disappointing-student-outcomes-san-jose -state-pauses-work-udacity.

Rivera, Lauren A. 2015. *Pedigree: How Elite Students Get Elite Jobs.* Princeton, NJ: Princeton University Press.

Rizzo, Kathryn M., Holly H. Schiffrin, and Miriam Liss. 2013. "Insight into the Parenthood Paradox: Mental Health Outcomes of Intensive Mothering." *Journal of Children and Family Studies* 22: 614–20.

Ro, Hyun Kyoung, Patrick T. Terenzini, and Alexander C. Yin. 2013. "Between-College Effects on Students Reconsidered." *Research in Higher Education* 54: 253–82.

Robbins, Alexandra. 2006. *The Overachievers: The Secret Lives of Driven Kids.* New York: Hyperion.

Robinson, Keith, and Angel L. Harris. 2014. *The Broken Compass: Parental Involvement with Children's Education.* Cambridge, MA: Harvard University.

Roksa, Josipa, and Tania Levey. 2010. "What Can You Do with That Degree?: College Major and Occupational Status of College Graduates over Time." *Social Forces* 89: 389–415.

Roksa, Josipa, and Daniel Potter. 2011. "Parenting and Academic Achievement: Intergenerational Transmission of Educational Advantage." *Sociology of Education* 84: 299–321.

Rosenbaum, James E. 1997. "College-for-All: Do Students Understand What College Demands?" *Social Psychology of Education* 2: 55–80.

Rosenbaum, James E., Regina Deil-Amen, and Ann E. Person. 2006. *After Admission: From College Access to College Success*. New York: Russell Sage Foundation.

Rosenfeld, Michael J. 2007. *The Age of Independence: Interracial Unions, Same-Sex Unions, and the Changing American Family*. Cambridge, MA: Harvard University Press.

Rubin, Lillian B. 1976. *Worlds of Pain*. New York: Basic Books.

Ryan, James E. 2010. *Five Miles Away, a World Apart: One City, Two Schools, and the Story of Educational Opportunity in Modern America*. New York: Oxford University Press.

Schiffrin, Holly H., Miriam Liss, Haley Miles-McLean, Katherine A. Geary, Mindy J. Erchull, and Taryn Tashner. 2014. "Helping or Hovering?: The Effects of Helicopter Parenting on College Students' Well-Being." *Journal of Children and Family Studies* 23: 548–57.

Schoeni, Robert, and Karen E. Ross. 2005. "Material Assistance from Families during the Transition to Adulthood." In *On the Frontier of Adulthood: Theory, Research, and Public Policy*, ed. Richard A. Settersten, Frank F. Furstenberg, and Rubén G. Rumbaut, 396–416. Chicago: University of Chicago Press.

Schofer, Evan, and John W. Meyer. 2005. "The Worldwide Expansion of Higher Education in the Twentieth Century." *American Sociological Review* 70: 898–920.

Schuman, Howard, Charlotte Steeh, Lawrence D. Bobo, and Maria Krysan. 1988. *Racial Attitudes in America: Trends and Interpretations*. Cambridge, MA: Harvard University Press.

Schwartz, Christine R., and Robert D. Mare. 2005. "Trends in Educational Assortative Marriage from 1940 to 2003." *Demography* 42: 621–46.

Sennett, Richard. 1998. *The Corrosion of Character: The Personal Consequences of Work in the New Capitalism*. New York: Norton.

Settersten, Richard A. 2012. "The Contemporary Context of Young Adulthood in the USA: From Demography to Development, from Private Troubles to Public Issues." In *Early Adulthood in a Family Context*, ed. Alan Booth, Susan L. Brown, Nancy S. Landale, Wendy D. Manning, and Susan M. McHale, 3–26. New York: Springer.

Settersten, Richard A., Frank F. Furstenberg, and Rubén G. Rumbaut, eds. 2005. *On the Frontier of Adulthood: Theory, Research, and Public Policy*. Chicago: University of Chicago Press.

Settersten, Richard A., and Barbara E. Ray. 2010. *Not Quite Adults: Why 20-Somethings Are Choosing a Slower Path to Adulthood, and Why It's Good for Everyone*. New York: Bantam.

Sewell, William H., and Robert M. Hauser. 1976. "Causes and Consequences of Higher Education: Models of Status Attainment Process." In *Schooling and Achievement in American Society*, ed. W. H. Sewell, R. M. Hauser, and D. L. Featherman, 9–28. New York: Academic Press.

SHEEO (State Higher Education Executive Officers Association). 2015. "State Higher Education Finance: FY 2014." http://www.sheeo.org/sites/default/files/project-files /SHEF%20FY%202014–20150410.pdf.

Shierholz, Heidi, Alyssa Davis, and Will Kimball. 2014. "The Class of 2014: The Weak Economy Is Idling Too Many Young Graduates." *Economic Policy Institute* http:// www.epi.org/press/epi-report-class-2014-idled-weak-economy/.

Shoup, Rick, Robert M. Gonyea, and George D. Kuh. 2009. "Helicopter Parents: Examining the Impact of Highly Involved Parents on Student Engagement and Educational Outcomes." Paper presented at the 2009 Association for Institution Research Annual Forum.

Shulman, James L., and William G. Bowen. 2002. *The Game of Life: College Sports and Educational Values.* Princeton, NJ: Princeton University Press.

Silva, Jennifer. 2013. *Coming Up Short: Working-Class Adulthood in an Age of Uncertainty.* Oxford: Oxford University Press.

Simon, Herbert A. 1955. "A Behavioral Model of Rational Choice." *Quarterly Journal of Economics* 59: 99–118.

———. 1957. *Models of Man, Social and Rational: Mathematical Essays on Rational Human Behavior.* New York: Wiley.

Skenazy, Lenore. 2009. *Free-Range Kids: How to Raise Safe, Self-Reliant Children (without Going Nuts with Worry).* San Francisco: Jossey-Bass.

Smart, John. C., Kenneth A. Feldman, and Corrina A. Ethington. 2000. *Holland's Theory and the Study of College Students and Faculty.* Nashville, TN: Vanderbilt University Press.

Stacey, Judith, and Timothy J. Biblarz. 2001. "(How) Does the Sexual Orientation of Parents Matter?" *American Sociological Review* 66: 159–83.

Steelman, Lala Carr, and Brian Powell. 1989. "Acquiring Capital for College: The Constraints of Family Configuration." *American Sociological Review* 54: 844–55.

———. 1991. "Sponsoring the Next Generation: Parental Placement of Financial Responsibility for Higher Education." *American Journal of Sociology* 96: 1505–29.

Stevens, Mitchell L. 2007. *Creating a Class: College Admissions and the Education of Elites.* Cambridge, MA: Harvard University Press.

———. 2015. "Introduction: The Changing Ecology of U.S. Higher Education." In *Remaking College: The Changing Ecology of Higher Education*, ed. Michael W. Kirst and Mitchell L. Stevens, 1–18. Stanford, CA: Stanford University Press.

Stevens, Mitchell L., Elizabeth A. Armstrong, and Richard Arum. 2008. "Sieve, Incubator, Temple, Hub: Empirical and Theoretical Advances in the Sociology of Higher Education." *Annual Review of Sociology* 34: 127–51.

Strauss, Valerie. 2006. "Putting Parents in Their Place: Outside Class." *Washington Post*, March 21: A8.

Streib, Jessi. 2013. "Class Origin and College Graduates' Parenting Beliefs." *Sociological Quarterly* 54: 670–93.

———. 2015. *The Power of the Past: Class, Marriage, and Intimate Experiences with Inequality.* Oxford: Oxford University Press.

Stuber, Jenny M. 2011. *Inside the College Gates: How Class and Culture Matter in Higher Education.* Lanham, MD: Lexington Books.

Sullivan, Theresa A., Elizabeth Warren, and Jay Lawrence Westbrook. 2000. *The Fragile Middle Class: Americans in Debt.* New Haven, CT: Yale University Press.

Swartz, Teresa Toguchi. 2009. "Intergenerational Family Relations in Adulthood: Patterns, Variations, and Implications in the Contemporary United States." *Annual Review of Sociology* 35: 191–212.

Sweeney, Brian. 2007. "Dangerous and Out of Control?: College Men, Sexuality, and Subjective Experiences of Sexuality." PhD diss., Indiana University.

Sweeney, Megan M. 2002. "Two Decades of Family Change: The Shifting Economic Foundations of Marriage." *American Sociological Review* 67: 132–47.

Sweeney, Megan M., and Maria Cancian. 2004. "The Changing Importance of White Women's Economic Prospects for Assortative Mating." *Journal of Marriage and the Family* 66: 1015–28.

Swidler, Ann. 1986. "Culture in Action: Symbols and Strategies." *American Sociological Review* 51: 273–86.

———. 2001. *Talk of Love: How Culture Matters*. Chicago: University of Chicago Press.

Tatum, Beverly Daniel. 2003. *Why Are All the Black Kids Sitting Together in the Cafeteria?* New York: Basic Books.

Tinto, Vincent. 1987. *Leaving College: Rethinking the Causes and Cures of Student Attrition.* Chicago: University of Chicago Press.

———. 1988. "Stages of Student Departure: Reflections on the Longitudinal Character of Student Leaving. *Journal of Higher Education* 59: 438–55.

Tolman, Deborah, Meg I. Striepe, and Tricia Harmon. 2010. "Gender Matters: Constructing a Model of Adolescent Sexual Health. *Journal of Sex Research* 40: 4–12.

Torche, Florencia. 2011. "Is a College Degree Still the Great Equalizer?: Intergenerational Mobility Across Levels of Schooling in the United States." *American Journal of Sociology* 117: 763–807.

Turner, Ralph H. 1960. "Sponsored and Contest Mobility and the School System." *American Sociological Review* 25: 855–62.

University of Pittsburgh. 2014. "What FERPA Means for You and Your College Student." http://www.studentaffairs.pitt.edu/sites/default/files/PDFsandForms/Parents/FERPA.pdf.

U.S. Department of Education. 2015. "College Scorecard." https://collegescorecard.ed.gov.

U.S. Department of Labor. 2014. "College Enrollment and Work Activity of 2013 High School Graduates." http://www.bls.gov/news.release/hsgec.nr0.htm.

U.S. News & World Report. 2014. "How U.S. News Calculated the 2015 Best Colleges Rankings." http://www.usnews.com/education/best-colleges/articles/2014/09/08/how-us-news-calculated-the-2015-best-colleges-rankings?page=3.

Vaisey, Stephen. 2009. "Motivation and Justification: A Dual-Process Model of Culture in Action." *American Journal of Sociology* 114: 1675–715.

Vedder, Richard. 2008. "Federal Tax Policy Regarding Universities: Endowments and Beyond." Center for College Affordability and Productivity.

Vinson, Kathleen Elliott. 2012. "Hovering Too Close: The Ramifications of Helicopter Parenting in Higher Education." Working draft.

Waller, Willard. 1937. "The Rating and Dating Complex." *American Sociological Review* 2: 727–34.

Weis, Lois, Kristin Cipollone, and Heather Jenkins. 2014. *Class Warfare: Class, Race, and College Admissions in Top-Tier Secondary Schools.* Chicago: University of Chicago Press.

Weissman, Jordan. 2013. "How Colleges Are Selling Out the Poor to Court the Rich." *Atlantic Monthly*. May 12.

Western Interstate Commission for Higher Education. 2012. "Knocking at the College Door: Projections of High School Graduates." http://www.wiche.edu/info/publications/knocking-8th/knocking-8th.pdf.

White, Lynn. 1992. "The Effect of Parental Divorce and Remarriage on Parental Support for Adult Children." *Journal of Family Issues* 13: 234–50.

Wilkins, Amy C. 2008. *Wannabes, Goths, and Christians: The Boundaries of Sex, Style, and Status*. Chicago: University of Chicago Press.

Windolf, Paul. 1997. *Expansion and Structural Change: Higher Education in Germany, the United States, and Japan*. Boulder, CO: Westview.

Wiseman, Ben. 2015. "Best, Brightest—and Saddest?" *New York Times*. http://www.nytimes.com/2015/04/12/opinion/sunday/frank-bruni-best-brightest-and-saddest.html.

Wright, Erik Olin. 1997. *Class Counts*. Cambridge: Cambridge University Press.

Zelizer, Viviana A. 1985. *Pricing the Priceless Child: The Changing Social Value of Children*. Chicago: University of Chicago Press.

———. 1997. *The Social Meaning of Money: Pin Money, Paychecks, Poor Relief, and Other Currencies*. Princeton, NJ: Princeton University Press.

Zhang, Liang. 2005. "Do Measures of College Quality Matter?: The Effect of College Quality on Graduates' Earnings." *Review of Higher Education* 28: 571–96.

Zink, Janet, and Shannon Colavecchio-Van Sickler. 2006. "Persistent Parents Plague Colleges: Helicopter Parents' Second-Guess Grades and Stay in Constant Contact with Students." *St. Petersburg Times*. http://articles.orlandosentinel.com/2006-06-20/news/PARENTS20_1_helicopter-parents-boomer-parents-children.

Index

Note: Page numbers in italics refer to tables or figures.

academic achievement: financial support correlation to, 72, 92–93, 144, 145, 146; GPA for, 142, 145; paramedic success in, 144–46; professional helicopter success in promoting, 140, 142–44, 187–88

Academically Adrift (Arum and Roksa), 126, 127

academic counseling, 105–6, 150, 164–67

academic elites: career-building experience ideal of, 24–26, 39; cultivation of excellence ideal of, 36–37, 202–3

academic emergencies, 55–56, 147–48

academic focus. *See* professional helicopters; professional pathway

academic underperformance: failed classes, 62, 126; financial support correlation to, 122–24, 172–73; GPA, 123–24, 172–73; party scene derailment and, 122, 147–48, 153–54, 169–71, 185–86; pink helicopter upset about, 124–27; satisficing strategy, 122–24, 169–70, 190; working students and, 172–73

accountability: college outcomes, 8–9; professional helicopter support and, 72–73, 144

admissions competition, 5, 167, 180–81

adulthood: delayed, 158, 161, 201–2; early, 33, 110–11; experience ideal, 32–34, 39; hybridized experience ideal of, 35–36. *See also* young adulthood

appearance, as priority, 65–66, 121, 126

Armstrong, Elizabeth A., 10, 15–16, 175

Arum, Richard, 126, 127

autonomy. *See* independence

boomerang kids, 3, 134, 136, 150, 155, 203

boyfriends: abuse by, 178; breakups and distancing from, 67–68, 157–61, 179; problem, 67–68, 81–82, 116, 122, 178–80

Business School, MU, 53–54, 56, 82, 130, 143–44, 149–50, 195

bystander parenting: benefits and costs, 163; blame in, 165, 166, 171–74, 184–86; characteristics, 98–100, 99; college resources assumptions in, 100, 105–7, 162–67, 171–74, 175; college skepticism in, 32, 100, 184; college system as problem for, 185–86, 192–93; communication problems in, 104, 177–78, 179; delayed graduation in, 166–67, 176; detachment and overconfidence in, 98, 100–102, 104, 176–78; doubt in, 166; emergency non-response in, 101; financial support approach to, 99, 99–100, 105–6, 107–14, 171–74, 176–78; financial support post-college, 182–83; gender model in, 99, 115–16; graduate school false hopes in, 180–82; guidance inability in, 100–106, 162–67, 175; major selection assumptions in, 105–7, 164–67; outcome summary, 184–86; parent debt in, 107–10; party scene problems for, 122, 147–48, 169–71; post-college struggles from, 180–83; social class in, 99, 99–100;

bystander parenting (*continued*)
social experience assumptions in,
103, 106–7; student debt in, 109–10,
176–78; visions of college in, 39, 40.
See also supportive bystanders; total
bystanders

career-building: experience ideal, 24–26,
39; internships, 62–63, 86, 128–29;
paramedic involvement with, 77, 80–
81; passion and, 36, 148, 151–53; pink
helicopter concern for, 129–33, 138;
pink helicopter involvement with, 61–
63; social connections for, 54, 62–63;
vocational training as, 18, 32, 114–15,
153. *See also* professional helicopters;
professional pathway; work
city relocation, 133–37, 152–53, 156, 183
class. *See* majors; social class
college and university: academic counseling, 105–6, 150, 164–67; admissions competition, 5, 167; assistance
assumptions, 100, 105–7, 130, 162–67,
171–74, 175; assistance stratification,
195; assistance success, 149–50;
bystander problems with, 185–86,
192–93; completion, by income,
196–97; completion, delayed, 127–29,
146, 164, 166–67, 176, 190; completion, marriage gap after, 134–35, 139;
credential value, 138, 195, 205; family
relations with, 7–9, 187, 193–96; helicopter parenting in relation to, 5–6,
8–9, 194–95; historical changes in,
7–9, 193–96; market model, 8–9; non-
completion, 147–48, 153, 176; parent
dependence on, 7–9, 187, 193–96;
parent inexperience with, 100–106,
162–63; parent insider knowledge
of, 53–55, 149–50; pathway types in,
17–18; privatization in, 8–9, 187–209;
ranking changes, 205–7; state relations to, 7, 8; transfers, 146, 174–75;
tuition, 5, 8–9; visions, 24–44; 112
competition: college admissions, 5, 167;
college ranking changes and, 205–7;
graduate school admissions, 180–81;
intensive parenting, 50
complementarity, 29, 39, 40, 64–66
concerted cultivation, 12–13, 137, 201–2

counseling, 105–6, 150, 164–67
courses. *See* majors; major selection
Creating a Class (Stevens), 2
credential value, 138, 195, 205
cultivation: concerted, 12–13, 137, 201–2;
of excellence, 36–37, 202–3; of fun,
58–63, 120–22, 137; of independence,
35–36, 78–82, 83, 89–90, 153–54; of
success, 52–58, 142–44
culture: belief justification by, 38; hybridized class, 34–36, 87–91

debt: middle-class risk of, 209; parent,
69, 70, 87, 107–10, 135, 201; student,
109–10, 157, 176–78
decision-making skills, 79–81. *See also*
independence
degrees, value stratification of, 205. *See
also* majors; major selection
dependence: of college on parents, 7–9,
187, 193–96; delayed adulthood and,
158, 161, 201–2; gender equality and,
200; helicopter fostering of, 3, 119,
130–32, 201–2; on marriage for economic security, 29, 64–66, 116, 134;
of parent on student, 109–11, 114. *See
also* independence
depression, 136, 181, 201
disagreements: bystander blame and,
165, 166, 171–74, 184–86; gendered,
41–43; parental, on visions of college,
41–44, 112; personality clash with
paramedic parenting, 96–97, 148;
personality clash with pink helicopters, 28, 59
division of labor: gendered, 50–52; paramedic, 77, 93–95; pink helicopter, 49,
61; professional helicopter, 49, 50–52
divorced parents: bystander support
inconsistency of, 111–13; communication lack between, 96, 111–12;
demographic of, 24, 44; hybridized
class culture from, 89–90; parenting
approach change for, 89–90, 96;
visions of college disagreements of,
43–44, 112

economic security: adult experience
ideal of, 34; career-building ideal
for, 25; cultivation of independence

for, 83, 89; cultivation of success for, 52–58, 142–44; gendered parenting on, 14–15; marriage for, 29, 64–66, 116, 134; mobility experience ideal of, 30–32; recession without, 130–32, 138, 183; social class categorized by, 21–24, 23

education: opportunity gaps, 196–98; of parents by social class, 23; *See also* college and university; majors

emergencies: academic, 55–56, 147–48; bystander non-response to, 101; financial, 70–71, 108–10, 112–13, 173–74; health, 47, 92, 147–48; paramedic response to, 91–93, 147–48; pink helicopter response to, 47, 61; professional helicopter response to, 47; social, 47, 61, 92–93

emotions: depression, 136, 181, 201; detachment and overconfidence, 98, 100–102, 104, 176–78; doubt, 166; happiness, 140; isolation, 92, 93, 172; stress, 3, 92, 173, 201–3

employment. *See* work

excellence, cultivation of, 36–37, 202–3

extracurricular activities: isolation resolved by, 92; for professional pathway, 56, 149, 194; sports, 28, 47, 122

family-college relations, 7–9, 187, 193–96

Family Education Rights and Privacy Act (FERPA), 7

family structure: divorced, 24, 43–44, 89–90, 96, 111–13; social class categories by, 23; widowed, 30, 41

fathers: education and occupation of, by social class, 23; emotional support from, 93–95; in helicopter household, 50–52; mothers' parenting disagreements with, 41–43; in paramedic household, 93–95

femininity: appearance and, 65–66, 121, 126; classed, 14–15; normative, 64–66, 115–16, 198–99

FERPA. *See* Family Education Rights and Privacy Act

financial aid. *See* loans; scholarships and grants

financial emergencies, 70–71, 108–10, 112–13, 173–74

financial support: academic achievement correlation to, 72, 92–93, 144, 145, 146; academic underperformance correlation to, 122–24, 172–73; bursts, 111–13, 156–57; bystander approach to, 99, 99–100, 105–6, 107–14, 171–74, 176–78; bystander post-college, 182–83; cross-class parents, 42–43; for delayed graduation, 127–29; ending, 72–73, 112–13, 135–36, 155–57, 173–74, 189; for graduate school, 154–55; long-term, 127–29, 154–57, 182–83, 200–203; middle-class challenges with, 73–75, 191; motivation from, 72, 92–93, 146; moving to city, 133–37, 183; as obligation of college, 164, 171–74; as obligation of government, 207–9; as obligation of parent, 49, 68–73, 99, 107–8, 209; as obligation of student, 109–11, 114, 155–57; as obligation shared, 84–87, 108, 109; paramedic approach to, 77, 84–87; paramedic post-college, 155–57; parental debt for, 69, 70, 87, 107–9, 135; of parent by student, 109–11, 114; pink helicopter approach to, 49, 69–71, 75; pink helicopter class challenges with, 75; pink helicopter extended college, 127–29; pink helicopter post-college, 133–37, 138–39; professional helicopter approach to, 18, 49, 71–73, 144; professional helicopter post-college, 154–55; single mothers without, 98–99; smart money, 156–57; by the state, 7, 208–9; success indicator by level of, 189; tuition increase and, 5, 8–9; visions of college comparisons by, 39; windfall child-rearing, 113. *See also* loans; scholarships and grants

first-generation college students, 88, 152, 186, 197

food: resources, 174; service work, 98, 151, 182

fun, cultivation of, 58–63, 120–22, 137. *See also* party scene

Furstenberg, Frank, 32–33

gender: bystander model of, 99, 115–16; classed femininity and, 14–15;

gender (*continued*)
  complementarity, 29, 39, 40, 64–66,
    199; division of labor by, 50–52;
    equality, 14, 35, 82–83, 199–200;
    normative femininity and, 64–66,
    115–16, 198–99; normative mascu-
    linity and, 199; paramedic model of,
    77, 82–84; parenting biases by, 14–15;
    pink helicopter model of, 49, 64–66,
    200; privatization biased by, 198–
    200; professional helicopter model
    of, 49, 50–52, 66–68, 200; research
    demographics, 11; visions of college
    comparisons by, 39, 41–43
grade point average (GPA): of academic
    achievers, 142, 145; of academic
    underperformers, 123–24, 172–73; of
    bystander students, 172–73; employer
    expectations of, 130; falling, 56,
    102–3, 147, 150–51, 170–71; financial
    support correlation to, 122–24, 172–
    73; graduate school rejection and,
    180–81, 182; holistic approach to, 145;
    as success indicator, 189; worst, 172
graduate school, 140, 148, 198; bystander
    false hopes for, 180–82; financial sup-
    port for, 154–55; rejection, 180–81
graduation: delayed, 127–29, 146, 164,
    166–67, 176, 190; marriage gap after,
    134–35, 139; not reaching, 147–48, 153,
    176; statistics by income, 196–97; as
    success indicator, 189
grants. *See* scholarships and grants

Hamilton, Laura T.: research and back-
    ground of, 9–10; works of, 15–16, 175
health: emergencies, 47, 92, 147–48;
    helicoptering impact on, 201–2
helicopter parenting: adulthood delayed
    in, 158, 161, 201–2; benefits and costs
    of, 3–4, 120; causes of, 4–6, 194–95;
    characteristics of, 3, 48–49, 49, 194;
    college move-in day responses, 1–2;
    for cultivation of fun, 58–63, 120–
    22, 137; for cultivation of success,
    52–58, 142–44; demographics of, 48;
    dependence fostered by, 3, 119, 130–
    32, 201–2; division of labor in, 50–52;
    emergency responses, 47, 61; fathers
    and, 50–52; gender model in, 49,

50–52, 63–68, 200; health impacted
    by, 201–2; middle-class challenges
    with, 73–75, 150–51, 191; as mother's
    job, 50–52; paramedic comparisons
    to, 78–79, 140–42, 141, 202; resources,
    49, 73–75; social classes in, 49, 73–75;
    social connections in, 54, 61, 62–63,
    128–29, 131–33; type comparisons,
    39, 40, 48–49, 49; vision of college
    in, 39, 40. *See also* pink helicopter
    parenting; professional helicopter
    parenting
homemakers, 14, 23, 29, 115
homophobia, 59–60, 168
hybridized: class culture, 34–36, 87–91;
    experience ideal, 34–36, 39

ideals. *See* marriage ideals; visions of
    college
income: graduation statistics by, 196–97;
    inequality, 5, 193, 196–98; 193; social
    class categories by, 23. *See also* social
    class
independence: cultivation of, 35–36,
    78–82, 83, 89–90, 153–54; hybridized
    experience ideal of, 35–36; passion
    discovery in, 148, 151–53; personality
    clash with, 95–97, 148; relationships
    ended or delayed for, 67–68, 157–61;
    research assumption of, 6; risks, 141,
    146–48; as success indicator, 189
in-state residency, 5, 23, 212
intensive parenting, 50. *See also* helicop-
    ter parenting
internships, 62–63, 86, 128–29
intervention. *See* emergencies; helicop-
    ter parenting
isolation, 92, 93, 172

jobs. *See* career-building; work

labor. *See* division of labor; work
Lareau, Annette, 12–13, 202
loans: bystander assumptions about,
    105, 172, 174; finding, 91, 113–14;
    parent debt from, 69, 87, 107–10, 135;
    socialist subsidization of, 207–9;
    student debt, 109–10, 157, 176–78
lower-middle class: adult experience
    ideal of, 33–34; characteristics of, 23,

24; exploitation of, 203–5; hybridized, 90–91; mobility experience
ideal of, 30–32; privatization harmful
to, 195, 196–98

majors: accounting, 82, 152–53; business-
lite, 53–54; dentistry, 53–55, 102–3,
143, 181; double, 150–51, 190; easy,
126–27, 129, *189*; health care, 115, 153;
interior design, 166–67; marketing,
54; media and communications, 49,
53–54, 62, 126–27, 130, 132, 155, 166,
175; MU Business School, 53–54, 56,
82, 130, 143–44, 149–50, 195; science,
148, 180–81; sports communications,
62, 126, 127, 132, 155, 166, 175; teaching, 25, 114, 127, 166, 177; vocational
training and, 18, 32, 114–15, 153
major selection: bystander assumptions
about, 105–7, 164–67; bystander guidance inabilities, 100–106, 162–67, 175;
credential value and, 138, 195, 205;
paramedic approach to, 80–81, 145;
pink helicopter approach to, 61–62,
74, 126–27; professional helicopter
approach to, 53–56, 143–44; switching, 148, 165–67, 180–81; work different from, 98, 151–53, 181–82
market: approach, 8–9; disruption and
innovation, 203–5. *See also* privatization
marriage ideals: bystander, 116, 178–80;
economic security, 29, 64–66, 116,
134; gap in, 134–35, 139; independence and delay of, 67–68, 157–61;
Mrs. degree, 29, 65, 199; paramedic,
81–82, 83–84, 153; peer, 39, 40, 67–68,
83, 159–60; pink helicopter, 49, 64–
66, 134; pragmatic, 39, 40; professional helicopter, 49, 66–68, 157–59;
social class differences in, 14–15, 199.
See also Mrs. degree (MRS)
masculinity norms, 199
middle class: characteristics of, 21, 23,
24; debt risk of, 209; femininity
defined by, 15; financial support
challenges of, 73–75, 191; helicopters,
73–75, 191; mobility experience ideal
of, 30–32; parenting and outcomes
by, 12–13; socialist solutions for, 209

Midwest University (MU): Business
School, 53–54, 56, 82, 130, 143–44,
149–50, 195; demographics, 10–11,
32, 137; drawbacks of, 11, 18, 36–37,
53, 185–86; family ties to, 32; focus
of, 17–18, 28, 53–54, 137; homophobic
conflict at, 59–60, 168; leaving, 146–
47, 153, 174–76; national ranking of,
130, 138; parenting approach best for,
187–91; parenting approach worst
for, 192–93; religious conflict at,
59–60, 168
mobility: downward, 191, 193; experience ideal of, 30–32, *39*; hybridized
class culture and, 87–89; party scene
derailment from, 185–86
mobility pathway: 18, 185–86
money. *See* economic security; financial
support
mothers: education, occupation, and
class comparison of, 23; father parenting disagreements with, 41–43;
helicoptering as job for, 50–52
Mrs. degree (MRS), 11, 29, 65–66, 83, 199
MU. *See* Midwest University

natural growth, 12, 13, 99
networking. *See* social connections

occupations, of parents by social class,
23. *See also* career-building; majors;
work
out-of-state residency, 5, *23*, 212
outsourcing. *See* privatization

paramedic parenting: academic achievement outcomes, 144–46; benefits and
costs of, *141*; career-building involvement, 77, 80–81; characteristics of,
76–78, *77*; college non-completion,
147–48, 153; communication, 78–79,
160; division of labor, 77, 93–95;
emergency responses, 91–93, 147–48;
emotional support, 144–46, 153–54;
by fathers, 93–95; financial support approach, 77, 84–87; financial support post-college, 155–57;
gender model, 77, 82–84; helicopter
comparisons to, 78–79, 140–42, *141*,
202; hybridized experience ideal of,

paramedic parenting (*continued*)
34–36, *39*; independence cultivation,
35–36, 78–82, 83, 89–90, 153–54;
major selection approach, 80–81,
145; marriage ideals, 81–82, 83–84,
153; outcome success, 140, 144–46,
153–54, 191–92; party scene approach,
79–80, 147; personality clash with
daughters, 96–97, 148; risks of, 141,
146–48; social classes in, 77, 77–78,
87–91; visions of college, *39*, 40
parenting approach: classed, 12–13;
defining, 16–17; gendered, 14–15,
190–91; outcomes, 15–19, *17*, 187–93,
189; success trifecta, 188; visions
into practice and, 37–41, *39*; windfall
child-rearing, 113. *See also* parents;
paramedic parenting; pink helicopter
parenting; professional helicopter
parenting; supportive bystander parenting; total bystander parenting
parents: education and occupation by
social class, *23*; research demographics of, 7–9; visions of college, 24–37
party pathway: 17, 41, 53, 66, 120, 125–26,
144, 170
party scene: bystander problems with,
122, 147–48, 169–71; derailment,
122, 147–48, 153–54, 169–71, 185–86;
gendered parenting differences in
approaches to, 43; media portrayal of,
29, 137; minimization of, 57–58, 144,
145; paramedic approach to, 79–80,
147; pink helicopter support for,
58–63, 120–22, 137; pink helicopter
underestimation of, 125–26; professional helicopter concern for, 56–58,
66–67; risks, 56, 122, 147–48, 169–71;
safety in, 27, 43, 57–58; social experience ideal and, 26–30, 39
passion: as hobbies, 166; independent dis-
covery of, 148, 151–53; pre-college, 36
Paying for the Party (Hamilton and Armstrong), 15–16, 175
peers: marriage to, *39*, 40, 67–68, 83, 159–
60; party safety and, 58; professional
helicopter involvement with, 58
personality: clash with paramedic
parenting, 96–97, 148; clash with
pink helicopters, 28, 59; learned de-

pendence, 3, 119, 130–32; roommate
challenges with, 59
pink-collar jobs, 15, 24, 166
pink helicopter parenting: academic
underperformance outcomes, 122–
27, 190; approach characteristics,
48–49, *49*; benefits and costs of, 120;
career-building concern, 61–63,
129–33, 138; dependency outcomes,
3, 119, 130–32; division of labor, 49,
61; emergency responses, 47, 61;
financial support approach, 49, 69–
71; financial support post-college,
133–37, 138–39; fun cultivation,
58–63, 120–22, 137; gender model,
49, 64–66, 200; graduation delay
outcome, 127–29; homophobia,
59–60; major selection approach,
61–62, 74, 126–27; marriage ideals, 49,
64–66, 134; middle-class challenges,
75, 191; naïveté of, 75, 124–27, 137–39;
outcome summary, 190–91; party
scene underestimation, 125–26;
social experience ideal of, 26–30, *39*;
sorority importance for, 60–61, 121–
22; visions of college , *39*, 40
poor. *See* lower-middle class; working
class
post-college support: bystander, 182–83;
forced by privatization, 200–203;
living at home for, 3, 134, 136, 150,
155, 203; paramedic, 155–57; pink
helicopter, 133–37, 138–39; professional helicopter, 154–55; as success
indicator, *189*. *See also* graduate
school; success; work
privatization: best parenting approach
for, 187–91; costs, 196–203; gender bias, 198–200; market-based
solutions to, 203–5; post-college
financial support forced by, 200–203;
racial bias of, 11, 121, 197; social class
bias, 195, 196–98; 205–7; socialist
approaches to, 207–9; status-based
solutions, 205–7; trend toward,
8–9, 187, 193–96; worst parenting
approach for, 192–93
professional helicopter parenting:
academic achievement outcomes,
140, 142–44, 187–88; accountability

approach, 72–73, 144; approach characteristics, 48–49, *49*; benefits and costs of, *141*, 195; career-building experience ideal of, 24–26, *39*; communication style, 55–56, 58; defining, 48; division of labor for, *49*, 50–52; emergency response, 47; financial support approach, 18, *49*, 71–73, 144; financial support post-college, 154–55; gender model, *49*, 50–52, 66–68, 200; insider knowledge, 53–55, 149–50; major selection approach, 53–56, 143–44; marriage ideals of, *49*, 66–68, 157–59; middle-class challenges, 73–75, 150–51, 191; outcome failures, 150–51, 153, 191; outcome successes, 140, 142–44, 187–88; paramedic similarities to, 78–79, 140–42, *141*, 202; social experience and partying views, 56–58, 66–67; visions of college, *39*, 40
professional pathway: 17–18, 53, 143–46, 149–50, 169, 186, 190

racial bias and inequality, 11, 121, 197
recession, 130–32, 138, 183
relations, college-family, 7–9, 187, 193–96. *See also* boyfriends; marriage ideals
religious conflicts, 59–60, 168
relocation, for work, 133–37, 152–53, 156, 183
remediation, 165
resources: academic counseling, 105–6, 150, 164–67; bystander, *99*; college assistance assumptions, 100, 105–7, 130, 162–67, 171–74, 175; college assistance success, 149–50; essential, 136–37; food, 174; helicopter, *49*, 73–75; internal stratification of, 195; paramedic, *77*. *See also* social connections
risks: bystander parenting, *163*; middle-class debt, 209; paramedic and independence, *141*, 146–48; party scene, 56, 122, 147–48, 169–71; professional helicopter minimization of, 146
Roksa, Josipa, 126, 127

safety: gendered parenting differences in, 43; hybridized experience ideal and, 35–36; party, 27, 43, 57–58; peer, 58; social experience ideal and, 27
satisficing, 122–24, 169–70, 190
scholarships and grants: assumptions and confusion surrounding, 105–6, 113–14, 171–74; challenge of finding, 55, 91, 113–14; historical changes in, 7–9; professional helicopters on, 55, 72; rejection, 112, 171; social class bias for, 195; socialist approach to, 207–9
sexual orientation: homophobia, 59–60, 168; research demographics, 11
single parents, 44, 98–99
social class: of bystanders, *99*, 99–100; career-building ideal and, 25; category characteristics, 21–24, *23*; crossing, 40, 42–43, 122, 147–48; of helicopters, *49*, 73–75; hybridized, 34–36, 87–91; marriage ideals by, 14–15, 199; of paramedics, *77*, 77–78, 87–91; parent education and occupation by, *23*; parenting by, 12–13; party scene derailment of, 122, 147–48; privatization biased by, 195, 196–98; research selection of, 10–11; visions of college by, *39*
social connections: of bystanders, 182; career-building, 54, 62–63; demand for higher, 59, 61; of helicopters, 54, 61, 62–63, 128–29, 131–33; for work, 128–29, 131–33, 152, 182
social emergencies, 47, 61, 92–93
social experience: academic underperformance associated with, 122–27; bystander assumptions about, 103, 106; failed, 121–22, 133–34; graduation delayed for, 127–29; ideal, 26–30, *39*; isolation from, 92, 93, 172; pink helicopter cultivation of fun for, 58–63, 120–22, 137; pink helicopter misunderstanding of, 121–22, 125–26; professional helicopter recognition of, 56–58
socialism, 207–9
social mobility. *See* mobility
sororities: fear of, 60; pink helicopter importance of, 60–61, 121–22; professional helicopter view of, 56–57, 66–67; supportive bystander assumptions about, 103, 106–7, 170. *See also* party scene; social experience

state: college relations to, 7, 8; funding, 7, 208–9; residency comparisons, 5, 23, 212

Stevens, Mitchell, 2, 194

stress, 3, 92, 173, 201–3

students: academic achiever, 72, 92–93, 140, 142–46, 187–88; academic underperformance strategy, 122–24, 169–70, 190; college relations to, 7–8; debt of, 109–10, 157, 176–78; entitlement of, 3, 85; financial support as obligation of, 109–11, 114, 155–57; financial support as obligation shared with, 84–87, 108, 109; financial support of parents by, 109–11, 114; first-generation, 88, 152, 186, 197; remedial, 165; research demographics of, 9–11; talent and strengths identification for, 53–54, 145, 151–53; transfer, 146, 174–76; working, 74, 85–86, 108, 110–11, 172–73

success: college and university assistance, 149–50; cultivation of, 52–58, 142–44; indicators, 189; paramedic parenting outcome of, 140, 144–46, 153–54, 191–92; parenting approach comparison of, 187–93, 189; parenting trifecta for, 188; professional helicopter outcome of, 140, 142–44, 187–88

supportive bystander parenting: characteristics of, 99, 99–100; college resource assumptions of, 106–7, 162–67, 173–74, 175; earlier involvement, 101–2; financial support approach, 99, 99, 107–9; guidance limitations, 102–3, 162–67, 175; mobility experience ideal of, 30–32, 39; overconfidence, 98, 100–102, 104, 176–78; sorority assumptions, 103, 106–7, 170; visions of college, 39, 40

time management, 102–3, 110–11, 145

total bystander parenting: adulthood experience ideal of, 32–34, 39; characteristics of, 99, 100; college noncompletion outcomes, 176; college resource assumptions of, 105–6, 162–67, 171–73; detachment and overconfidence, 98, 100–102, 104; financial

non-support approach, 99, 100, 105, 109–14; guidance limitations, 100–101, 104–6, 162–67, 175; student employment as a result of, 110–11, 172–73; visions of college, 39, 40

transfer students, 146, 174–76

tuition: increase in, 5; privatization and, 8–9, 193–94. *See also* financial support; loans; scholarships and grants

unemployment, 131, 136

Unequal Childhoods (Lareau), 12–13

university. *See* college and university

upper class: characteristics of, 21, 23, 194; disruptive innovation benefits for, 205; employer search for markers of, 194; privatization bias for, 196–98; working-class mobility into, 87–89; working students, 85–86

upper-middle class: career-building experience ideal of, 25–26; characteristics of, 21, 23; market disruption innovation for, 205; privatization bias for, 196–98

U.S. News & World Report, 205–6, 207

visions of college: adult experience, 32–34, 39; career-building experience, 24–26, 39; cultivation of excellence, 36–37, 202–3; disagreements on, 41–44, 112; divorce disagreements around, 43–44, 112; gendered parenting differences in, 41–43; hybridized experience, 34–36, 39; mobility experience, 30–32, 39; not represented, 36–37; practice consistence with, 37–40, 39; practice inconsistence with, 40–41; social experience, 26–30, 39

vocational training, 18, 32, 114–15, 153

widowed parents, 30, 41

windfall child-rearing, 113

women: appearance of, 65–66, 121, 126; classed femininity of, 15; equality of, 14, 35, 82–83, 199–200; as homemakers, 14, 23, 29, 115; normative femininity of, 64–66, 115–16, 198–99; research demographics on, 11

work: food service, 98, 151, 182; graduation delayed instead of, 127–29;

internships, 62–63, 86, 128–29; looking for, 129–33; major selection different from, 98, 151–53, 181–82; media and communications, 62–63, 127, 132, 155, 166; moving for, 133–37, 152–53, 156; overqualified, 98, 151, 181–82; passion for, 148, 151–53, 166; pink-collar, 15, 24, 166; placement, 130, 149–50, 194; poor prospects for, 133–37, 180–83; social connections for, 128–29, 131–33, 152, 182; statistics, 131–32; students at, 74, 85–86, 108, 110–11, 172–73; as success indicator, 189; unemployment, 131, 136; value of, 85; vocational, 18, 32, 114–15, 153; wage-premium, 5. *See also* career-building

working class: adult experience ideal of, 33–34; boyfriend problems in, 178–80; characteristics of, 23, 24; college resources assumptions of, 100, 105–7, 162–67, 171–74, 175; college skepticism of, 32, 100, 184; exploitation of, 203–5; fatherly emotional support in, 94–95; femininity, 15; financial support as shared obligation, 87; financial support assumptions of, 105–6, 113–14, 171–74; middle-class solutions for, 193; mobility into upper class, 87–89; parent debt in, 107–10; parenting and outcomes by, 12–13; post-college struggles of, 180–83; privatization bias against, 195, 196–98; student debt in, 109–10, 157, 176–78

young adulthood: as best time of life, 27; life stage recognition of, 7; research assumptions on, 6; unsettled period, 13